Whistling Girl

A Memoir
by
Ann Marcus

Published By
Mulholland Pacific
Publishing
Los Angeles, California

Whistling Girl

Author: Ann Marcus
Copy Editor: Caroline Criss

Published By:
Mulholland Pacific Publishing
P.O. Box 1193
Studio City, CA. 91614
(818) 755-0101 • Fax: (818) 755-0102
Orders: (800) 347-2736
E-mail: probity@earthlink.net
Web Site: http://www.probitynet.com/mp

Manufactured in the United States Of America

Copyright © 1998 by Ann Marcus All rights reserved. No part of this book may be reproduced or transmitted in whole or part in any form or by any means, electronic, mechanical or digital, without written permission from the publisher, except for inclusion of brief quotations in a book review or media interview.

10 9 8 7 6 5 4 3 2 1

ISBN: 1-880867-00-1

Library of Congress Catalog Card Number:
97-92654

*For Ellis
and our children and their children
and for
Tracy and Ray*

Contents

Preface 11

1. Yes, Gertrude, There Is A There, There 13

2. My Kind Of Town, Little Falls Was 16

3. Interlude In Teaneck 26

4. "Oh Western, Brave Western".. 29

5. The Graduate 40

6. To *Life*, To Life, L'CHAYIM! 49

7. I Can't Go Home Again, Either 62

8. *Life* Goes On 69

9. Beginnings And Endings 88

10. For Better, For Worse, In Sickness and In Health 97

11. Westward Ho! 111

12. I'm Ready For My Close-up, Mr. De Mille, Are You? 122

13. Miracle On Camellia Avenue 131

14. Broadway Unbound 140

15. Tune In Tomorrow 150

16. The Truth About Mary Hartman's Waxy Yellow Buildup 163

17. What's The Worst Thing That Can Happen To You? 176

18. Back To The Future 184

19. "The Life And Times Of Eddie Roberts"-- And Others 196

20. All My Children—Not The Soap.................201

21. Home Again 212

22. The Best Of Times . . .The Worst Of Times 222

23. On The Banks Of The River Jordan.................233

24. Life With Its Joys And Its Sorrows 244

25. Ellis 261

26. And Five Plus Three Is Eleven 269

27. Chock Full O' Knots 278

28. Life In The Slow Lane 287

29. Ray Gets Married. . . And Other Excellent Adventures 291

30. Is Anatomy Destiny?.................298

31. Together Again 302

32. Epilogue: "What's It All About, Alfie?".................307

About The Author 309

*"Whistling girls and crowing hens
often come to very bad ends."*
(Miss Helen Mack, 3rd grade teacher, Little Falls, NY circa 1930)

"Not necessarily."
(Ms. Ann Marcus, Sherman Oaks, CA circa 1998)

Preface

When I turned thirty—sometime in the Fifties—I wrote a nostalgic piece called "Remembrance Of Things In The Not So Distant Past." A kind of summing up if you will. Not that I contemplated a Sylvia Plath-type tragedy; I simply felt that contemporary life was moving so frantically, I wanted to catalogue what I remembered as a kid.

In the fast paced days of the Eisenhower administration (when Betty Furness was pitching refrigerators on TV), I harkened back to the Atwater Kent crystal radio set we had in our parlor that leaked acid on the rug, and to the Hoover vacuum with a blimp-like bag that inflated with a whoosh.

By the time I reached thirty, iceboxes were a thing of the past. Attics and cellars were disappearing along with great hiding places and homemade root beer. I had a feeling that the "good old days" were slipping away, and it was going to be downhill from then on. I was thirty, and I think I was jumping the gun.

The other day I was driving with Ollie, my not-quite golden retriever, and half-listening to Linda Wertheimer on National Public Radio's *All Things Considered*. She was interviewing members of a Black church on how they felt now that the GOP had captured Congress and were attacking affirmative action, and welfare, and taxes, and all those Republican buzzwords.

The interviewees covered the age spectrum, and all had articulate comments about how bad things are concerning opportunities for minorities, race relations, and inner city violence. All of them, that is, except for the lone senior citizen who hadn't said anything until Linda urged him to comment. He said simply, "I'm an optimist." He certainly was aware of all the problems—hell, he'd lived through them, but he still felt a sense of hope. He felt that people were working on the problems, and that maybe some of them could be solved.

His comment made my day. I thought perhaps there's something to be said about reaching senior citizenship beyond Social Security, Medicare, and getting into movies at reduced prices. Maybe our failing eyesight softens things; our hearing loss cuts out mean-spirited cacophony, and our selective memory focuses on things worth remembering—things that help us deal with and overcome some of life's recurring problems.

My God, I think I'm turning into an optimist myself!

Chapter 1

Yes, Gertrude, There Is A There, There

I grew up in Little Falls, a small town in upstate New York. There's only about half of it left now, not even an exit on the Thruway. But when I was born it was a Sinclair Lewis-type town with a Main Street, a large farm machinery factory, a bicycle works, and it was the home of Junket.

I've never eaten Junket. Besides the name, it wiggled and looked nasty. I'm not even sure it's still on the market. I know for sure that the farm machinery and bicycle factories are gone, along with half of Main Street and all the shops including (long, long ago) my father's men's clothing store ("Good Goods at Lowest Prices Always").

I'm not sure if the lift lock is gone. Little Falls was on the Erie Canal (we locals called it the Barge Canal). Since there were waterfalls on the Erie, the barges that plied the canal had to be lifted from the bottom of the falls to the top. So the boat would enter a "lock," the gates would close, water would be pumped in to lift the boat up, the gates would open, and the barge would go on its merry way. Little Falls was famous for its lift lock. Well, maybe not as famous as Paris for the Eiffel Tower, or New York City for the World Trade Center, but we always took visitors to see the lift lock—purported to be the second highest lift lock in the world! Come to think of it, I never knew where the highest lift lock was.

We thought it was pretty neat. I say "we" because I was the youngest of three children—my sister Blanche (who only kept that name until she escaped to Broadway and then Hollywood), and my brother, Ray (who's still Ray). I was born Dorothy Ann, but I never liked "Dorothy," in spite of "*The Wizard of Oz*", and lopped it off later in life.

And now I have to apologize to my beautiful sister, Tracy (the name thrust upon her by a PR man who didn't think "Blanche" would cut it in the movies). Tracy has been bugging my brother Ray (a writer) and me (also a writer) for decades to write a Rashoman-like novel or screenplay about our childhood in Little Falls. She has it all worked out in her director's mind. She even has the title: "The Second Highest Lift Lock in the World."

But I'm no fool. I know who'd have the best material. Tracy. Or, if you like, Blanche. She's the gorgeous sister—the one with the white, white skin and the blue, blue eyes and the flaming red hair. The one who emerged like a chrysalis into a full-blown beauty with tons of boyfriends. She had Colgate College men pursuing her when she was still in high school! She was a cheerleader, star of all the school plays, and the scandal of the town when her formal portrait in her senior prom gown showed cleavage AND her panty line.

How would I come off in this three-way memoir? I was brown haired and plain. A tomboy. A good sport. A friend to all, and a sister to every other Girl Scout. Forget it. Tracy never cracked a textbook, yet she aced all her classes; brother Ray was brilliant, and won a scholarship to Cornell. I was the "black sheep of the family," according to Miss Munson, the high school Latin teacher. I still remember the day Mother took me aside to say, in effect, "Look, you may not be as quick and flashy as your brother and sister, but remember, slow and steady wins the race."

So forget it, Tracy. Write your own "Coming-of-Age in Little Falls" memoir; I'm just going to touch on it lightly here.

I loved being a kid in Little Falls.

My brother and I were best buddies. We played with a wonderful group of kids we called "The Backyard Gang." We acted out all the Saturday matinee serials and movies: the chariot race in *Ben Hur*, and all the Ken Maynard, Tom Mix, Hoot Gibson cowboy and Indian movies (my favorites). Me, a dyed-in-the-wool liberal from

Yes, Gertrude, There Is A There, There

my first vote for Roosevelt's fourth term to the present day, yet I loved shooting Native Americans with my six-shooter cap pistol. Our gang created Eskimo villages by freezing blocks of ice and making igloos, improvised circuses, skated, skied, went sledding in winter, swam, played ball, went camping in the summer. No Chuck E. Cheeses, no Disneyland, no expensive birthday parties with Astrojumps and surprise visits from Barney and the Mighty Morphin Power Rangers. It all seems quite wonderful now. But certain days stick in my mind. Especially one clear, cold winter's day.

I was sledding on my Flexible Flyer down the hills in Eastern Park, less than half a block from our house. It got later and later and all the kids, even brother Ray, went home; but I continued to trudge up the snowy hill and ride down again. The park lights finally came on and, as I finished one last ride, I lay on my sled and watched the snow gently falling—filtered through the light from the street lamp—and I knew that this was a moment I'd always remember. Life was good. When I went home the Little Falls *Evening Times* would be there, and I could read "Alley Oop" and "Freckles and His Friends." The house would be warm, and supper would almost be ready. Dad would be home from the store, and maybe he'd be in a good mood, not depressed the way he often was those days. Maybe he'd brought a surprise from Maltby's, the dingy hole-in-the-wall that carried odds and ends including some inexpensive toys. I had a great sense of well being. It was an epiphany.

And that's the way I remember my childhood and Little Falls.

And that's why, in 1945 when I was a rookie reporter on *Life* magazine, I persuaded the editors to use Little Falls as their model of a small town at war for a photographic essay, "Life on the Home Front." They assigned me to accompany famed photographer Alfred Eisenstadt.

Seven years before, when I was fifteen (after my father died and my mother remarried), I had left Little Falls and moved to suburban New Jersey. I guess it was that wonderful sense of there, there in Little Falls that made me want to show it off, to share it with *Life's* huge readership—that made me want to go home again.

15

Chapter 2

My Kind Of Town, Little Falls Was

I was crazy about Uncle Wiggly Long Ears when I was a child. He was that rabbit gentleman who had a pal named Nurse Jane Fuzzy Wuzzy. Nurse? Wiggly wasn't sick; he wasn't even married with children, so what was he doing with Fuzzy Wuzzy? Okay, it was a more innocent time. Maybe she took care of his nieces and nephews. What delighted me was the promise at the end of each chapter to tell another adventure, but only if something outrageous didn't happen first—like, for instance, if the cup didn't sneeze, causing the dish to fall out of the cupboard—miraculously escaping injury and running off with the fork, who had fallen madly in love with her.

I'm afraid the literary pattern was set. So, I can't tell you about Eisenstadt and Little Falls and my Thomas Wolfeian adventure back home until I tell you more about my background, including one or two outrageous things.

****

My mother, Ida Orenge, was born in Syracuse, New York. Her mother, Rachel, had emigrated from Lithuania and became the second or maybe third wife of Joseph Orenge, a macho kind of guy who had stopped off in England long enough to marry, and sire a child or two, before making his way to the USA alone.

I never got to know Grandmother Rachel. She died before I

My Kind Of Town, Little Falls Was

was born. I remember her framed picture on Mother's dresser. She looked plump, and old-fashioned, and kind of sad. With good reason I learned later, since Grandfather Joseph was a bad apple. Mother didn't like him. Even my mild-mannered father kicked him out of the house and refused to let him visit. Fortunately, I only have a dim memory of him; he died when I was very young.

Joe reportedly ran for socialist mayor of Jersey City once, but I think it's just a family myth. Even if he did, I'm sure he got creamed. What isn't a myth is that he was a rotten provider, and the family was dirt poor. As the oldest of six, Mother had to leave school in the sixth grade to help support them. But what an education she gained in those six years! I still remember her reciting some of the poetry she learned in school: Emerson, Whitman, Wordsworth, Longfellow ". . . This is the forest primeval; The murmuring pines and the hemlocks . . ."

Mother never stopped learning. I remember the pleasure and pride she felt preparing papers to read at the Delphian Society which the upper-crust, college-educated Little Falls ladies asked her to join, never guessing she didn't even have a high school diploma.

Mother rode herd on her brothers and sisters, seeing to it that at least some of them continued their educations. My dashing Uncle Ed Orenge was a World War I pilot and a college graduate, the first in his family. Mother's youngest sister, my Aunt Nettie, studied French, became an assistant to a French importer in New York, and was earning an unheard of $25,000 a year when she left her job to get married in the '20s!

Mother was strikingly good looking—long, silky brown hair gathered in a bun at her neck, classic features, a Gibson-Girl figure. No wonder she attracted a handsome beau from a wealthy New York German-Jewish family when she went to the Jersey shore on vacation. He asked to take her out when they got back to the city, but when he showed up at the railroad flat in Hoboken and met her immigrant mother he disappeared after their first date.

She was twenty-nine when she met Father, way past time when women married. I'm pretty sure it wasn't a passionate love match.

Whistling Girl

Dad was good looking, a gentle man with wavy, reddish hair and blue eyes; but given to moods, and bouts of depression.

Dad came to this country from Russia when he was six. His family settled in Utica, New York, twenty-two miles west of Little Falls, a huge metropolis of 50,000! He had lots of siblings—maybe eight. I'm not quite sure since some of them died in infancy.

Some of my most cherished memories of Dad were the times he'd gather us all in one bed, and tell us about his adventures with his older brother Moe while peddling farm tools, household goods, and jewelry from a horse and buggy to the farmers.

During the week they were gone, they would sleep in fields or in a friendly farmer's barn. Then, on the weekend, they'd make it back to Utica where Uncle Moe would decide he'd had enough of the peddler business and would sell the horse and buggy to my father. Dad would groom the horse and stock the buggy with supplies. But by Monday morning, Uncle Moe would decide he'd made a mistake, give Dad his money back, and become his partner again.

This happened two or three times before Dad got wise to the con. He had spent the weekend scrubbing down the horse, buying and loading supplies while dapper Uncle Moe went off dancing and romancing.

I guess that's why several years later, when Dad was a partner with Moe and another brother in Goldstone Brothers (a large clothing store in Utica), he decided to strike out on his own in the much smaller town of Little Falls.

And that's where he brought his bride, my mother Ida Orenge, who must have had a lot of adjusting to do. There was no theater, no opera, no Ethical Culture lectures, and very few Jewish people in this socially segregated small town.

If Mother felt alienated or lonely or unhappy, I never knew it as a child. To me she was radiant; full of fun, energy, and a zest for life. If her best friends were limited to the wives of the other Jewish merchants, that was fine with her. She became their natural leader, organizing spirited bridge games or exciting excursions in our big Buick touring car. On these outings she'd gather up her friends, and

My Kind Of Town, Little Falls Was

take off for far away places like Saratoga Springs or Canajohari just for lunch. There was always a wonderful adventure to tell us about later, like the time she was driving down the Fairfield gorge and accidentally put her foot on the clutch instead of the brake. The car went careening down the hill doing sixty, the ladies shrieking for their lives, but somehow Mother got them back in one piece.

One summer day Mother piled Ray, a neighbor kid named Eddie, and me in the Buick, and drove to a cow pasture halfway between Little Falls and Herkimer. A couple of World War I pilots in rickety, open cockpit biplanes had flown in and were selling rides for five dollars a person. The next thing I knew, Mother had bought rides for Ray and Eddie, and then allowed the pilot to hoist me into the forward cockpit at no extra charge. I was terrified, but didn't utter a word. I wasn't going to let Ray and Eddie—and especially Mother—think I was a sissy.

I've read so many reminiscences, memoirs, autobiographies—and fiction, too, written by my ethnic colleagues about their Jewish mothers who were on top of them like tents. Who nudged, cajoled, threatened, and smothered them. Not my mother. She was proud when we accomplished things, disappointed when we didn't, but not for long. Mostly, she was a role model before anyone had thought up that term—a shining example of making the best of things. She was certainly Jewish and proud of it, but acted more like a native New Englander—a little repressed, I guess. Not able to show her emotions easily. Not always there when I needed her, but that only made me appreciate her more when she <u>was</u> there. (Have I picked up some of her sunny traits? I hope so.)

My problem with Mother was that I could never quite . . . get at her. Connect. Tell her how I felt. Hear how she felt. There were always too many things left unsaid. Maybe I just wanted more attention. Maybe I wanted to be a spoiled brat instead of a good sport.

****

My father's bouts with depression got more severe in the early '30s. I have a feeling he could have been treated successfully with some form of Prozac or other contemporary chemical medication, but of course miracle drugs weren't available then. In fact, no one thought of consulting a psychiatrist in those days—even though Papa Freud was flourishing in Vienna at the time.

Dad lost a considerable amount of money in the Wall Street Crash of 1929, and his business was way off, but that wasn't the only reason he was slipping away. It was a combination of things that dragged him down. He felt responsible for the death of his favorite sister in childbirth since he'd introduced her to her husband; he was oversensitive to tragedies he'd read in the papers (like the Lindbergh baby kidnapping), and would obsess over them; and—God knows what else.

I knew something was terribly wrong the last week of January 1933, when my aunts and uncles from Utica camped out at our house practically every day. One night that week, Mother motioned for me to follow her into the kitchen. When I did, she told me I should tell Daddy how much I loved him. I found that very strange.

"Why?" I asked. "Why should I do that? Doesn't he know that?"

"Yes he does, dear," she said. "But sometimes it's necessary to tell people things they already know. To remind them. Do it for me, and give him a hug before you go up to bed."

So I did. He was sitting in the green Queen Anne chair and I dutifully climbed into his lap. He didn't really look at me, and his breath was bad, but I told him I loved him and I hugged him. He patted me absent-mindedly, and I climbed down. After that, Ray and I went up to bed.

It must have been two hours later when I was wrenched awake by the most awful sound I've ever heard. It took a moment before I recognized that it was Mother crying out.

"Myron . . . My-ron!!" came her unearthly scream. "What have you done!?"

I lay in bed, rigid, terrorized. And then I heard people scrambling up the stairs. I didn't want to know what had happened. I didn't want to see. I ran into Ray's bedroom and got in bed with him. He must have felt the same way because I don't remember him leaving the room.

Father had said he was going up to bed, but instead went into the bathroom and cut his throat with his straight razor. Without a sound. Then he went back to his bed to die. But he didn't die. He was still alive when they took him to the hospital. Ray and I somehow managed to fall asleep again after the ambulance took him away. When we woke up early the next morning, Elsie Nast, Mother's best friend, was sitting at the foot of the bed. Dad had died during the night.

Our sister Blanche, who was a freshman at the University of Michigan, came home for the funeral. The first thing she did when she got to the house was to approach Dad, laid out in his coffin in the living room, and put her hand on his chest. I guess she wanted to make sure his heart wasn't still beating.

We literally lived next door to death on Burrell Street. Our closest neighbor, Cal Newitt, was the local funeral director. He lived with his charming young wife and baby on the second floor of his establishment. The working quarters (embalming lab, storehouse, and casket display room), bordered our non-fenced-in backyard. We used to play hide-and-seek in and among the large crates in which the coffins were shipped. Mr. Newitt had a spooky old handyman—skinny, not-all-there Mr. Van Slyke, who once gave me a handful of chewing tobacco claiming it was chocolate sprills (the kind we used to sprinkle on ice cream cones).

My brother and sister and I were used to seeing the large Packard hearse, and we were always aware when they were "working" on someone. They didn't always close the door to the embalming room; and I remember peeking in every once in awhile, and seeing a body lying on a metal table with apparatus hanging over it and fluids draining from it. Things I wish I hadn't seen.

As a result, I developed a distinct distaste for death. I was aware of my own mortality sooner than most kids. Maybe that's why I've been able to fend it off several times, and probably that's why I push it away as much as I can when it happens to people I love. I know it's there. I know it's inevitable, but I'll deal with it later.

Tracy, on the other hand, has never gotten over her extreme

anxiety—okay, panic—when it comes to death. She's still searching for a way to deal with it. When she was a kid, she'd wake up in the middle of the night with mysterious attacks that would scare the hell out of Mom and Dad—not to mention Ray and me. She'd scarcely be able to breathe, her heart would pound, her body would shake, and she'd be totally freaked out. While Mother tried to calm her and Dad called Dr. Santry, Ray and I would slip out of the house in our pajamas and walk around and around the block praying, "please God, don't let Blanche die... please God, don't let Blanche die." It must have worked because she didn't.

Our prayers were more or less improvised, because our religion was, too. We were Jews, outsiders, in a completely Christian community. There were the Loomis Street Catholics (mostly working class), the upper crust Episcopalians, and then (in descending order of clout), the Presbyterians, Methodists, Congregationalists, Baptists, Lutherans, several lesser Protestant sects, and us.

I remember my childhood as a blissful time, but I'm aware of the psychological tricks we play on ourselves to deny or hide the things we don't want to remember. Sure there were incidents—stupid, dumb, bigoted incidents that I won't or can't forget.

One of my earliest memories is being whisked inside by Mother as a bunch of men in white sheets marched down our street. It was 1925 and it was the KKK, and since there weren't any black people in Little Falls, they were parading around in those goofy outfits to show how much they hated Catholics—and us.

There were, of course, the usual taunts hurled at us by a few kids. They said I killed their Lord. Me. Dottie Ann Goldstone. Yeah, right. Mother gave us a special retort to that one: "Your Lord was a Jew, nyah, nyah." (Actually the "nyah, nyah" was mine). Christmas carols in school were a little dicey. I sort of hummed through the "Chri-ist the Lord" part. Other than that, things were pretty much okay religion-wise. The Backyard Gang was totally loyal. Fred Teall, Jane and George Norris, Eddie Shauman, Margaret Duddleston (love that name), Billy Wing, Andy Little—they didn't seem to notice we were different. Nor did my classmates—tubby, wonderful, witty Bud Dale, Cathy Viola (whose

My Kind Of Town, Little Falls Was

father was a reputed bootlegger!), Toady Rahme, Fred Wilcox. Neither did my Girl Scout friends: Louise Chapel (Chappie) Tanzer (whose dentist father was mayor), or Jane Rasch, or Jean Hamilton. (How come I remember them so vividly, when I have trouble remembering the names of people I met last week?)

But identifying as a Jew was a problem in Little Falls. To begin with, we didn't have our own place of worship. On the High Holy Days (Rosh Hashana, Yom Kippur), Dad would get his tallis, yarmulka, and prayer book (kept in a blue velvet bag embroidered with the Star of David), and go off to the Hippodrome Movie Theater which the Jewish families rented for the occasion. The Hippodrome was the second movie house in town, barely able to compete with the more upscale Rialto. Dad and his friends would hire an Orthodox rabbi for the services, usually an ancient fellow with a tobacco-stained beard, who would drone on and on in Hebrew, not a word of which any of us Jewish kids understood. So we'd run around the balcony and play games, and hope that God wouldn't be mad at us.

Mother, who wasn't very religious or observant, finally decided we needed some Jewish orientation, so she organized a Sunday School, renting space from the Women's Christian Association. Only I fell through the cracks. I was too young for one class, and too old for the other. So I spent my time coloring biblical pictures of Moses parting the waves and such.

Mostly I remember waking up on Sundays to the mournful sounds of old Mr. Reardon pushing his wheelbarrow and calling out . . . "Sun-day pay-purrs!" This, of course, meant the *New York Herald Tribune* and the rotogravure section and the funny papers (we didn't call them "comics"). My favorites were "Lester dePester" and "Mr. and Mrs. Bybriggs." It wasn't until years later that I realized the strip was actually called "Mr. and Mrs." and that it was written by Briggs.

After we bought the paper, it was off to Sunday school and then to the Greeks on Main Street for half a pint of heavy whipping cream. Then home for a high calorie, red meat dinner of roast beef, mashed potatoes and Mother's scrumptious chocolate roll with

23

whipped cream.

Things changed, of course, after Dad died. Tracy (Blanche) transferred to Cornell to be closer to home; Mother took over the store, depending a lot on Dad's super assistant and salesman, Paul Kruger. Ray, at thirteen, became the man of the house. I was eleven and busy burying my feelings about the loss of my father. I can't remember a thing about his funeral or burial. All I remember is acting sad when people came to pay their respects, even though I wasn't allowing myself to feel anything. And I remember a day about a month later when I came home from school and saw Mother pick up the phone and call Dad at the store to find out when he was coming home. Her anguish when she realized what she'd done will always be with me.

Funny about siblings. Where I suppress things, Tracy lets go completely. To this day if she accidentally bumps into something she lets out an ear-splitting scream; whereas, under similar circumstances, I sharply and silently draw in my breath. I've stored up a lot of screaming that way which I only let out every long once in awhile. Such as the time, years later, but long before the dawn of the New Age, when I had been lured into a weird type of group therapy, part psychodrama and part plain psycho. At any rate, there I was in a private session one day, lying on a Barcalounger in a dark room wondering what I was doing there; when all of a sudden this unearthly howl worked its way up from the soles of my feet out through my mouth, without my realizing I had made the noise. What followed was a torrent of rage and grief—not that my father had died, but the way he had died—leaving me, deserting me. How could he have done that to me!? I hated him. I loved him. I wanted him. I needed him. I never went back to that therapist.

****

Several years rolled by without too much trauma. Mother was a darn good businesswoman. The store was doing well. We moved from our brick house on Burrell Street to the upper floor of an old Victorian wooden house on Gansvoort Street, owned by Judge

Schall and his dotty wife.

Ray was caught by old Mrs. Schall sunbathing, naked, on the roof with Ursula Hunt.

I was caught at a Girl Scout dance necking with Johnny Mulford by mean Miss Barbour, the Girl Scout leader.

Tracy dropped out of Cornell in her sophomore year to pursue an acting career in New York.

In 1936 Ray went off to Cornell on scholarship. I finally had Mother all to myself. But not for long. The year before she had gone to Rochester to visit friends and met Abe, a recent widower from New Jersey. He was tall and hardy with a remarkable resemblance to Jim Farley, Roosevelt's Postmaster General. They got married in the fall of '36, shortly after Ray left home.

And shortly after that, we moved away from my beloved Little Falls to one of the fastest growing and most nondescript suburbs in the country

There was definitely no there, there in Teaneck.

Chapter 3

Interlude In Teaneck

I hated Teaneck. I never liked our fake Tudor house on Winthrop Road, and I didn't much like my stepfather Abe Rapfogel. He loved to tease. I'd come down to the breakfast nook (I didn't much like that, either), when Abe and Mother and my two younger stepsisters were already halfway through their corn flakes and Abe would cheerily call out, "Good morning, Speedy."

Teaneck, or more specifically West Englewood, was not my kind of town. It was pre-mall, but post-character. Our house was on a pleasant suburban street, but it wasn't in a real neighborhood. I couldn't get on my bike and go anywhere. No Main Street, no parks, no place like O'Rourke and Hurley's drugstore. O'Rourke and Hurley's. Just saying the name conjures up pungent medicinal smells mingling with the aroma of strong coffee and hot fudge sauce. There was no place like that in Teaneck where friends could meet. There weren't many friends, for that matter.

Of course there were my two younger stepsisters, Geraldine and Ruth. Jerry, who was eight when our families merged, spent her time playing school in the "rec" room (the plywood-paneled cellar). She was a nice enough little kid, but I was fifteen. And then there was Ruth, only a year younger than me, but extremely shy and introverted, and not interested in the things I was. Besides, she had recently lost her mother, and that had to be even tougher than losing a father.

So, again, Mother took me aside to tell me that she knew I'd understand that she had to pay a lot of attention to Ruth and Jerry because they so desperately needed a mother. Sure I understood. Of course I was desperately needy, too, but I was a good sport. Still.

I missed my friends 250 miles away in Little Falls. I missed my brother Ray, who was further away at Cornell. I missed Tracy, who made things even worse by swooping in on us from her madcap theatrical life in New York to visit and experiment on the right makeup for me so that I'd snare a boyfriend at Teaneck High.

I hated Teaneck High. It was vast. Huge. There were two thousand students. So many families were moving into the community that no one paid any attention to new kids like me—except for blimpy, four-eyed Donald Voss, who delighted in dropping hand-drawn swastikas on my desk. I sincerely hope something bad happened to him.

Things got better. Somewhat. By the second year I was writing a column for the high school paper called "Ends 'N Odds." It almost got picked up by the *Hackensack Bergen Evening Record* after I wrote about a training school for Santa Clauses. But when they found out it was pure fantasy, they weren't interested.

There were other highlights, though. I finally got the high school editor to ask me out a couple of times. And I was cast in a school play in a racy, sexy part (probably due to Tracy's make over), in which I had a memorable line. When someone referred to me as a young lady in the play, I responded "I may be young, but I'm no lady!" I liked that.

Also, I was somewhat famous—or infamous—because of a class trip to the New York World's Fair in 1939. We were gathered at the entrance in front of a statue of Mercury—the god of commerce, travel and thievery. The god with the helmet with those wings on it. The one on the run who's carrying some kind of gadget in one hand close to his genitals. I looked up at him and without thinking said, "Gosh, he looks like he's carrying a nutcracker." Instant fame—at least with the boys in the class.

The best times were when Ray came home on vacation from Cornell. Ray has always had a great sense of adventure. He never

Whistling Girl

plans things—just takes off, and unique and wonderful things happen. I love that about him, although it has driven the women in his life bananas.

One time, we went to New York, and on a whim he stopped at a pier on the Hudson River where the German liner, the Bremen, was docked. This was in '38 or '39 when Hitler was either on the brink of invading Poland, or already had. We were keenly aware of what was going on, especially of Hitler's extreme anti-Semitism. But we were curious, too, and since the ship was open to the public, we went aboard for a tour.

It's a wonder we got off alive. We goose-stepped all over that ship improvising badly accented gibberish, and trying to imitate Hitler in the newsreels we had seen. I shudder to think of what could have happened: TWO TEENAGERS KILLED IN FREAK ACCIDENT WHILE TOURING DOCKED GERMAN LINER!

One Christmas vacation, Ray drove home in an old '32 Ford he had bought for fifty dollars and named Fernabelle. When it was time for him to go back to college, it snowed so hard he had to leave the car and take the train. So Fernabelle fell into my hands. What a sense of power and freedom! I could escape. Not that I did, but I could! How great to drive to school—late as usual, but not out of breath! The other day I was driving on Pacific Coast Highway in Malibu with the top down on my fourteen-year-old convertible when I suddenly saw her again. Fernabelle Ford! Gloriously restored and proudly displaying an antique auto license plate. Of course, she wasn't *my* Fernabelle. Mine had never looked that good, but she was the same make and model. So I drove parallel to her and beeped my horn. She "ca-hoogahed" back at me—two antiques giving each other a symbolic high five.

I graduated from Teaneck High with few regrets in 1939, and left for college in the fall with great anticipation.

Chapter 4

"Oh Western, Brave Western..."

Instead of following Tracy and Ray to Cornell, I went to Western College for Women in Oxford, Ohio. No, not Ohio Wesleyan, not Western Reserve. Western College. Everyone who's ever gone there, including I'm sure, our celebrity alumna Donna Shalala, gets a little defensive about it: "...you've never heard of it; it's very small; it's a sister college (stepsister) of Mount Holyoke; I enrolled because my mother (sister, aunt, favorite teacher) went there...."

I went there because I hadn't sent in applications to the snobby Eastern women's colleges—or Cornell—on time. Maybe my stepfather Abe was right; I was a procrastinator. While I was fretting about the situation and wondering what to do, Ray came home for spring vacation and went to the library to research other possibilities. He found a Western College brochure that looked promising. The college was old, small, liberal arts, far from Teaneck, and willing to accept applications well into May.

I was only going to go for a year and then transfer, but I stayed all four years, having the time of my life. It was beautiful physically, relaxed socially, and challenging scholastically. It reminded me of Little Falls.

I remember taking off for orientation week from Penn Station with seven other freshmen from the New York area. We were a mixed bunch, roughly divided between New Yorkers—those who I thought were sophisticated mainly because they smoked—and the rest of us suburbanites. I chose to identify with the sophisticates, and went off to the smoker with them. Among the "others" was Martha McKee, who became my lifelong friend.

At that first meeting in the station, I thought Martha (accompanied by her pale, bespectacled boyfriend), was impossibly square. It was stifling that September day, but we were all wearing one of our new collegiate outfits, ranging from skirts and sweaters to woolen dresses in fall colors. Martha was wearing a blue and green plaid dress with a white collar, white gloves, and a felt hat. No one else wore a hat—or gloves, and I don't think she was ever that chic again. Her complete indifference to the fashion world was only one of the things I loved about Martha. A few years ago we went back to Western for an important reunion and appeared in a condensed version of Sondheim's Follies. At the time I was Supervising Producer of the prime time serial, *Knots Landing,* and very busy. So I asked the show's wardrobe department to find me something appropriate to wear. They came up with a gorgeous beaded gown slit up the side, which Linda Grey had worn in *Dallas.* Martha, busy editing books, wore an ancient evening gown she bought for five dollars at a garage sale in her Forest Hills neighborhood.

On that grueling sixteen-hour train ride to Cincinnati, we new freshmen tried to impress each other with how much we knew about literature and the arts. We started out discussing a few of our favorite things, and ended up shouting the names of all the literary and cultural icons we could think of: "John Dos Passos!" "Yes!" would come the enthusiastic acknowledgment. "Theodore Dreiser, Katharine Cornell, Faulkner, Martha Graham, Dorothy Parker, Hemingway, F. Scott Fitzgerald!" Actually, I don't think we were familiar with half of them. But what difference did it make? We were on our way to learning everything there was to know in the universe!

Poor old Western went down the tubes in the '70s. It was one of the oldest women's colleges in the country, having been founded in 1853, but it simply couldn't stay afloat financially. It finally sank after a short and unsuccessful fling at co-education, and was taken over by neighboring Miami University, which maintains it as a

"Oh Western, Brave Western..."

tutorial college under its jurisdiction. But the lovely campus is still there, and the venerable old buildings; plus a diehard group of alumnae who gather now and again to sing the old songs and tell the old stories.

Some of my favorite memories are of the dramatic productions at Western; especially the plays of Shakespeare presented at the beautiful Ernst Nature Theater. This was an outdoor theater carved into a hillside, the seats gently terraced in a lovely setting—an Elizabethan two-tiered stage accommodating all the alarums and trumpetings. It was a place of magic and romance—with intriguing origins.

The man who donated the theater, Senator Ernst of Ohio, was rumored to have had a tragic love affair with Gertrude Leonard, the professor of drama who presided over the premises for decades. She was still directing plays when I was there, with her quavering voice, her thin white hair, strong bifocals, and even stronger opinions about the theater. Even in 1939 she was old fashioned, the antithesis of "method" acting.

Miss Leonard hardly encouraged us to create inner lives for our characters. It was more a question of rhythm and line readings. I'll never forget Elinor Bratten as the sheriff in Susan Glaspel's *Trifles*. Elinor was tall and therefore drafted to play men's roles. She was a nice person, but an awful actress who rushed her lines, so Miss Leonard had her count during rehearsals: "For all their worries . . . (One, two, three) " . . . what . . . (four, five) " . . . would we do . . . (six, seven) " . . . without the ladies?!" What was astonishing is, it worked! We did some terrific productions: *As You Like It, A Midsummer Night's Dream, Much Ado About Nothing*.

Martha McKee and I were always competing for the leads. I played Beatrice in *Much Ado. . .* , but she got the part of Rosamund in *As You Like It*. I was the knight in *The Knight of the Burning Pestle*, but she played Terry, the Katharine Hepburn role, in *Stage Door*. I was stuck with tragic Kay, who leaps to her death in the second act. But I got to come back in the third act as Mr. Gretzle, the Hollywood producer.

One of the most startling productions we did was *The Corridors of the Soul,* a wildly experimental Russian drama by Nicholas Evreinov. Miss Leonard wouldn't have anything to do with such trash, so Martha and I produced, directed, and acted in it. Martha even designed the scenery—the most ingenious part of all since the action took place inside a man's chest. The main prop was his heart. When his inamorata (me) threw him (Martha) over, his heart broke, spewing blood all over the stage. Good thing it only ran for one performance. While she was helping to build the set, Martha fell in love with the school carpenter, John Bockover, but it was unrequited, I think, except for long, mooney looks and sighs, and a lot of time spent in the carpentry shop.

Probably the most fun we had, theatrically, was writing and producing the class musical, *Orange Is My Mother's Hen House,* (Martha's title). I dreamed up an enormous hoax to fuel interest in the production. We planted stories in the campus paper about the friction among cast members during rehearsals, the temper tantrums, and the rampant jealousies. A week before the show was to open; we broke the story that our leading actress, Peg Posz, walked out—quit! More stories appeared speculating about whether the production would be cancelled.

Of course it wasn't. The curtain rose opening night on a castle in Transylvania (it was a play about vampires). A few minutes into the act, Peg stormed into the theater, demanding her role back, shouting that she had been forced out by that jealous bitch, Betty Crawford, her understudy!

Pandemonium broke out; the curtains were jerked closed. The class president nervously appeared onstage, apologized, and asked her classmates to rally round, vowing that the show <u>would</u> go on! And it did—not the vampire vehicle, but a satirical revue. We were a smash.

Aside from theater, Martha and I re-energized the literary quarterly, *The Western Oxford,* renaming it *Scope* (not at all as refreshing as its later day namesake, the mouthwash). We filled it with long, depressing essays and meandering free verse. Not surprisingly, it didn't last long. So, while Martha got involved in student government, I turned my attention to editing the paper, *The Western*

Round-Up. I changed the format, added several features, and insisted on writing dreary editorials about Big Issues. Instead of commenting on the noise in the dorms, or restrictive curfews, or the dress code, I wrote lofty pieces on The Labor Movement, Population Problems, Free Speech. Actually, I was desperately trying to impress the head of the Sociology department who didn't think I was a serious student.

It didn't work. Professor Mueller never took me seriously. Worst of all, readership was falling off. I knew I had to do something or the paper would be heading for its last Round-Up.

I asked Martha to write a provocative letter to the editor. I didn't care what it was about as long as it would shock the campus community into reading the paper.

Ever up to a challenge, Martha wrote a stunning letter probing the value of religion, and questioning the very existence of God! I ran it on the front page, headlined in big, bold type above the masthead.

The results were beyond my wildest dreams. The campus went nuts. The *Round-Up* was inundated with replies from the president, deans, faculty, students, and alumnae. I even think John Bockover sent a letter! Speakers were recruited; seminars, prayer meetings, candlelight processions were held. I loved every minute of it. So did Martha whose soul was saved. Two years after graduation she married a Congregational minister.

* * * * * * * *

Unlike Forrest Gump's mother, I don't think life's like a box of chocolates; it's more like a glass of water. You know, the glass is either half full or half empty. I seem to see it as half full which is good, I guess, unless I stare at it too long. Then I may be looking through the glass—darkly. Was everything that great in Little Falls? No. Was college just one laugh-studded episode after the other? Hardly.

For one thing, there was the episode in Mr. Carother's European History class. I've always loved history, and I was doing well in that freshman class. I liked Mr. Carothers, too. He was young and bright—and kind of cute. But one day, he started talking about the discrimination against the Jews in Germany: the yellow band with the Star of David they had to wear, being forced to give up their seats on public transportation, humiliated by so many other restrictions, but not yet rounded-up and gassed. And this man—this teacher—wondered aloud to the class if these actions were really all that bad. You see, he explained, he had spent time in New York. He had ridden on the subways, and maybe there were reasons.

My heart stopped. I couldn't believe it. I still can't believe it. And I didn't say anything. He looked at me and knew how badly he had wounded me, and I even think he was embarrassed, BUT I DIDN'T SAY ANYTHING! How could that have happened? Why didn't I tell the idiot off? Throw my books at him on my way out of the classroom? These are things I've done a thousand times in my mind since then. He never apologized, but he never said anything like that again. I ignored him for the rest of the term. He gave me an "A."

Fortunately, there weren't other incidents like that at Western. The college tried very hard to be as ecumenical as possible. I remember a Sunday service at Kumhler Chapel celebrated by a priest, a minister, and a rabbi. When the three of them tried to cram into the pulpit it was pretty funny—but very healing.

I majored in Sociology, which I loved because it was about people and how they live; the effects of race, religion, culture, environment. It was about problems and what causes them. It even had some answers. The head of the department was Clara Helen Mueller, who was an inspiration. Frosty, arrogant, humorless—but what a teacher. She left me with a lifelong passion for learning about other peoples, other cultures, ideas, politics. She had iron-grey hair, a hawk-like nose, wore steel-rimmed glasses, and had a grasp of her subject matter that was dazzling. There she was, this treasure of knowledge, hidden away at tiny Western—the chauvinism of the times keeping her from teaching at one of the more prestigious universities. It was a boon for us lucky few at Western. Even though she thought I majored in extra curricular activities, I'll

"Oh Western, Brave Western..."

always be grateful for what I learned in her classes.

One Thanksgiving, our roommate Charlotte Auten invited Martha and me to her home in Cass City, Michigan. Charlotte's family was very hospitable, although I felt as if I was on display. I don't think they'd ever seen a Jew up close and personal. I remember taking great care with my diction and manners because I was representing the entire race. That kind of experience happened a lot in America's heartland. Jews were a curiosity in small Midwestern towns—exotic, different. Boo!

* * * * * * * *

The word "fiasco" generally comes to mind when I think of dating at Western. There were two Jewish fraternities at Miami: one for rich kids, and one for the others. I was never the sweetheart of ZBT (I think that was the rich one), and only so-so popular with the boys of Phi Ep. Not that I was restricted to dating only Jewish boys. There were lots of attempts to fix freshmen up with blind dates, and both campuses arranged mixers. But I never found anyone at college to whom I could really give my heart. That didn't keep me from getting pinned, though. I didn't want to miss anything, so I dated one of the fraternity brothers long enough to get pinned, made the gossip column, and broke up with him shortly after.

It wasn't that I didn't try to find that certain someone. One night Judy Bosson and I accepted blind dates with two very tall, very horny basketball players who picked us up in a car—which was a little strange since everyone walked to town. The reason soon became apparent when they parked near some woods, and started pawing us and breathing heavily. Judy, who was a marathon talker not quite five feet tall, didn't let her date get to first base. She kept up a rapid fire, one-way conversation that totally deflated his id. Disgusted, he drove us to The Huddle where we jitterbugged (coming up to their navels) the night away. With curfew beckoning, we insisted on piling classmates and their dates in the car with us on the ride back to the dorm.

There was always safe, dull Milton Wenger. He was studying

Library Science and loved books, which somewhat compensated for his sweaty palms. He was a presentable escort for various occasions and the inevitable proms, although I've had an aversion to gardenias ever since pinning on his last overpowering corsage.

In 1940, the Navy came to the rescue when a training program for radio corpsmen was established on Miami's campus. I dated several of them, but they kept getting shipped out after completing the course.

The Sunday Pearl Harbor was bombed, I was at the movies in town. It was a dismal, rainy, cold December day and I had been putting off a Sociology paper. I was planning to get at it as soon as I got back to the dorm. When I arrived at Peabody Hall, it was so quiet—no music coming from the rooms, no horsing around—I knew something was wrong. People were standing around in groups, not saying very much. No one knew quite how to react, what to do. We all had family members or boyfriends in the service. We didn't know what to expect. There were no instant television pictures of the devastation, no hasty but reassuring interviews with government or military leaders. Nothing except the radio and sketchy accounts of what had happened.

I didn't want to think about my brother who had been drafted several months before. I went to the library to work on my paper, knowing Miss Mueller wouldn't let the mere outbreak of World War II excuse an overdue assignment. But I couldn't concentrate. My thoughts kept going back to the last time the family had been together. Mother had rented a big two-story cottage on Twin Lakes in the Pocano Mountains of Pennsylvania for the entire summer. Tracy could only come for a short stay because she was doing summer stock at a theater on Long Island. But Ray and I were there all summer along with our stepsisters, Abe (who came up on weekends), Mother, and a parade of school friends and relatives.

I had felt there was something special about that vacation — that I had to cram as much fun as I could into each day—as though I knew things weren't ever going to be the same. Europe was being torn apart, Japan was crushing China; but most of us refused to think about it.

In the Poconos, we were having a rollicking good time: lots of swimming, hiking, canoeing, berry picking, hilarious word games after dinner, and midnight dips.

It should have been a perfect summer because I love doing all those things, but somehow it wasn't. I began to store things in my memory: sunsets, insects buzzing lazily in the fuchsia that bordered the porch, the special sad sound doves made in the early evening, Mother playing bridge with her usual aplomb—looking tan and healthy and happy.

One night, Ray was pumping water—a daily chore so that we'd have running water in the house. I joined him under the porch. We could hear Glen Miller's "Moonlight Serenade" on the radio. (What is there about popular music that can so evoke a time and place?) I wanted to talk to him, to tell him how unreal I felt things were, and how scared I was. I knew he'd be drafted soon, and it wouldn't be long before the country would be drawn into the war, and I was afraid I'd lose him. He was only two years older, but he had taken on an almost father-like role.

I didn't have to tell him how I was feeling. He seemed to know. We've always been in sync like that. I asked if he was afraid. He said he wasn't afraid of being killed, only of being horribly wounded—of losing a limb or being blinded. I didn't know what to say. I couldn't bear to think about it. I urged him to finish and join the rest of us upstairs.

We played charades that night, and we were particularly brilliant—and silly.

Back in the Alumnae Hall Library on the night of that infamous attack, I knew I wasn't going to write my Sociology paper, no matter what Miss Mueller thought. I headed back for the dorm, and found that Judy Bosson's mother had sent her usual goodies along with Judy's clean laundry. I sat around her room with my friends munching crackers and cheese and homemade cookies, and talked about nothing at all.

A year later, Ray had gone through basic training, been promoted to warrant officer, and was stationed briefly at Patterson Field near Dayton, Ohio. He came to visit at Western one weekend, lugging a portable record player and a stack of records for my roommates and me. We insisted he stay in our dormitory, in the haunted room of our late founder, Helen Peabody. That first night ghostly singing coming from the corridor awakened him. He opened the door a crack, and saw what looked like an ethereal parade of angels—young women in robes, holding lighted candles. He thought they were after him (he's always been a devil with women), but they were merely undergraduates serenading their Big Sisters.

My senior year at Western, Ray went to Officer Candidate's School and joined the Eighth Air Force in England. Life went on rather unspectacularly that last year in college, in spite of the war. If anything, campus life was even more bucolic, since the administration imported sheep to crop the grass to save gasolene and manpower. We also grew vegetables in Victory Gardens. I know this for a fact because there's a picture of me with a hoe over my shoulder. (I wish there were a picture of me with a broom in my hands since Martha and Charlotte claimed that I never helped clean the suite of rooms we shared. They even said I asked where we kept the dustpan the last week before graduation!)

There was one rather amazing incident that concerned an older man and me. By older I mean he must have been close to thirty. His name was Will, and he was a good friend of my brother-in-law. He was a PR man, an East Coast rep for one of the Hollywood studios, and he had his eye on me, although I wasn't aware of it. At any rate, he went to extreme lengths to get me away for a weekend.

He was doing publicity for *The Male Animal*, the James Thurber movie. Part of Will's elaborate publicity campaign was a contest to elect a "male animal" from the Ohio State student body where Thurber had been an undergraduate. As a magnanimous gesture, I thought, he suggested I run a contest at Western to elect a "female animal" who would have an all expense-paid trip to Columbus, join in the premiere, and meet the press. And incidentally, I'd get to go, too.

Not only did I run the campaign through the *Western Round-Up*, but I got permission from the dean for Peg Posz (who won the contest), and me to fly off to Columbus with Will. Dean C.B. (for Clutch Bosom), was a little wary until I assured her that Will was an old family friend—like an Uncle to me.

Except that Uncle Will didn't act like an old family friend. After depositing Peg in her room at the hotel, he took me to my room. Only my room was his room. I finally got it. And I acted so shocked and hurt that I scared him out of his wits. Funny thing is, I wasn't scared as much as incredulous that he would think I'd be interested in him. He was middle-aged, thirty! The truly embarrassing thing is, I did sleep in the same bed with him, although nothing carnal happened. Except I gave him permission to put his hand on my breast after he assured me that was all he wanted. And that's the way I fell asleep. I woke up with my virginity intact—but not my dignity. I felt a number of things, mostly confusion. First of all, I wasn't nearly as sophisticated as I thought I was. Secondly, there I was about to graduate, and I had this nagging suspicion that I'd never find anyone whom I could really love.

Mother came out to Western for graduation weekend—her first and only visit. She had been busy with the family, and was still managing the clothing store in Little Falls, making frequent trips there. I loved showing her off. And I loved showing off for her. We reprised the Tree Day play, *Much Ado About Nothing*, and she was really impressed. One night when we were dressing for dinner, she asked me to feel something in her breast. It was a small lump, that I didn't think was much of anything. She didn't, either, but she promised to look into it.

I left Western not knowing what the future would hold, but excited about it anyway. I loved the theater, but I was also fascinated with words. Martha and Charlotte went to Chicago and got jobs with the Red Cross. I went to New York determined to be a journalist. What? Me compete with Tracy? Not on your life!

Chapter 5

The Graduate

It was June 1943. The world was falling apart. Our forces were locked in a fierce battle with Rommel in North Africa; in the Pacific, the Marines and the Navy were fighting island-to-island. England was being pummeled daily by German bombers. Unspeakable things were happening in the Warsaw ghetto. In Russia, the Germans had reached Stalingrad. In spite of all this, I felt exhilarated to be alive at such an exciting time—and back in New York.

I wasn't exactly in New York. I was back in Teaneck until I could afford a place of my own. But, I had this great sense of anticipation. I knew I wouldn't be stuck there long.

Ray was in England, an intelligence officer in the Eighth Air Force, dodging V-2s and writing fascinating letters home. Mother took great delight in reading them aloud at Friday night services in the Teaneck Reform Temple.

Tracy had just been in a short-lived disaster on Broadway called "Behind Red Lights," in which she played a prostitute. She was married to Jerry, a lanky, Gary Cooper-like attorney, who had given up his law practice to write for radio. They lived in a duplex on 58th Street between First Avenue and very chic Sutton Place. Things were a little tight financially, but friends were always dropping in and using their phone—so they had a pay phone installed in their hallway which I thought was madly exotic.

Mother was in the process of selling the clothing store in Little

Falls to Paul Kruger, the manager who had started as a kid with my father. She was in good spirits, active in the community and with her friends, and didn't mention the lump in her breast—which I soon forgot about. My stepsisters were in school, Geraldine in high school, Ruth studying dietetics. Abe was still Abe in his Abe sort of way—teasing me about being late, and a little suspicious of how I might influence his daughters now that I was a college graduate. That was because I drank a little and smoked a little, and when I had a date in the city I didn't always make it back to Teaneck. I explained to both Mother and Abe that I had an open invitation from Tracy and her husband to sleep on their couch on those occasions, but I'm not sure he believed me.

One of my dates was John McKee, Martha's older brother, who had graduated from Harvard the year before. He was working as a copy boy on the *New York Daily News* while waiting to be drafted. It wasn't a serious relationship. It was hard to be serious about a guy who was in love with whomever he was with—at the moment. I realized this when he visited me at Western the spring before graduation and I found him in the gazebo making out with Charlotte Auten, our other roommate. On the other hand, he might have come out to see Charlotte—who could have seen the two of us necking in back of Mary Lyon Hall. So why was I still going out with him? Mostly because he was there.

I think I was trying to make more of the relationship than was there, engaging in frustrating sexual encounters where everything happened except the Real Thing. After one of these dates, I'd arrive at Tracy's duplex drained and confused, and wondering if I'd ever really fall in love. Tracy was very comforting. We were becoming much better friends.

When John enlisted less than a month after I graduated, it solved a problem for both of us. He tried to get his job for me, but the City Editor didn't go for the idea of a girl copy boy.

I really wanted that job. I think I'd always wanted to be a newspaperwoman. Why else hadn't I identified with the usual Hollywood stars when I was growing up? I never wanted to be Claudette Colbert or Greta Garbo or Carole Lombard; my favorites were Glenda Farrell and Claire Trevor. You didn't see Glenda and Claire playing Russian empresses or poor little rich girls. They played sob sisters—tough, smart reporters in trench coats who duked it out with Lee Tracy and James Cagney and made it first with the front-page story.

I <u>had</u> to get that job, so I brought in reinforcements. Tracy knew Douglas Watt, the drama critic on *The News*, and she could be persuasive. Doug went to bat for me and the City Editor caved in. I got a job on the staff of the largest metropolitan daily in the country. I was the only copy boy in New York with a D-cup! My salary was fifteen dollars a week. Even in those days it was below the poverty level. I had to continue living in Teaneck and commute. Even so, I was gloriously happy.

The Daily News was located on Forty-Second Street near Third Avenue, which still had the elevated roaring over it. I'd arrive every afternoon at four (the graveyard shift) and leave at midnight. I'd ride the A-Train up to 168th Street, take a bus across the George Washington Bridge back to Teaneck, and walk about a mile home. Not as grueling as Abe Lincoln trudging miles through the snow to get to school, but it was dark and I was twenty-one, five feet two and a half inches, 102 pounds, and alone. Yet I never felt afraid. Things have definitely changed.

Newspapers have changed, too, but not the essentials. *The Daily News* was as sensational a tabloid then as it is now. Captain Patterson, who published the paper, would appear in the newsroom in his trademark shirt sleeves, suspenders, and white sneakers and demand more gore. While reporters covered the major crimes, fires, mayhem and gore, I, along with my fellow copy boys, kept busy sharpening pencils, going down to the greasy spoon for coffee, carrying clips from the morgue to the rewrite men, and running copy from the city desk to the press room. It turned out I was no Glenda Farrell or Claire Trevor. I was just the kid who answered the bellow ". . BOY!"

But I was learning about newspapers, and so were my colleagues who sat on the bench with me. We all wanted to be writers—journalists, novelists, playwrights, even poets. There were several four-Fs (not qualified for military service), a skinny young guy who told dirty stories and was thinking about entering a seminary, a couple of guys waiting to be called into the service, and Tom Halloran, who latched onto me immediately. It wasn't that he was attracted to me—he simply needed someone to read his endless stream-of-consciousness saga that the others had given up on long before I was hired. Actually Tom's ouevre wasn't bad. It needed to be cut—at least 80 percent of it—and the rest, edited. But try telling that to a budding novelist unless you're Maxwell Perkins!

Soon after my arrival, a few more girls were hired as "boys." We all posed in the den of the lecherous photographers with me in the center holding a large calendar with the date, August 22, 1943. I was 22 on the 22nd.

The Night City Editor, George Kelly, was a tough old bird right out of Ben Hecht and Charles McArthur's "Front Page." He was large, gray, with a pot belly and fierce blue eyes that could bore into you like lasers. True to his movie prototype, he had a heart of gold. I'm pretty sure he liked me. He ran my tail off. But in between my mundane tasks, he taught me a lot: how to write a compelling lead, how to condense the facts into a compact, simple style, and how to drink bourbon at Costello's bar on Third Avenue—although he was never anything except fatherly toward me.

When he thought I was ready, he sent me out on a couple of stories. The first one was a jumper—a woman who had leaped off the Empire State Building. By the time I got there she was in a canvas body bag, thank God. Not very much was known about her. It didn't even make the paper. After that there was a bank heist which rated a couple of lines on a back page. Then he did a really nice thing—he sent me out on a feature story and gave me a byline. Two Irish brothers hadn't seen each other in seventeen years. One brother was from the States, the other from Ireland. They met on a battlefield in Italy, and sent pictures of their meeting to their sister who lived in Brooklyn. I interviewed the sister in January, and the editor held the story for two months and ran it on the eve of St. Patrick's Day.

Meanwhile, two things happened that changed my life.

Whistling Girl

Mother hadn't done anything about the lump in her breast, but soon after I got the job on *The News*, she told Tracy about it. Tracy immediately set up an appointment with her gynecologist, and the three of us went together. His diagnosis was devastating. He didn't tell Mother that afternoon, but he did tell Tracy and me that from what he had observed, Mother had a cancerous growth that he was almost sure had metastasized. She would have to have immediate surgery.

To this day I keep wondering what would have happened if there had been as much information and publicity about the early detection of cancer then as there is now. <u>If only</u> I had known how insidious that damn lump was when she first showed it to me. <u>If only</u> she had recognized what it was when she first noticed it. Would she have lived another twenty years, traveled, grown old, known my children? Fruitless speculation.

This time, unlike the shock and surprise of my father's death, I knew in advance that Mother was going to die. I couldn't deny it, push it aside, ignore it. It was a double dose of reality. When Dad died, I blocked off my feelings and transferred them to Mother. I was always worried that something would happen to her, was always conscious of my time with her, was always trying to find a way to—I don't know—get to some inner truth, discover her essence. It was always impossible.

I tried every way I could to push the inevitable away, but this time it refused to disappear. It lodged in my stomach, in my throat, in my heart. It was the first conscious thought I had on waking up, the last when I fell asleep.

Oh, I functioned. I managed to forget it for whole chunks of time. But then it would return, on its own timetable, and descend like a heavy curtain of despair.

I didn't think I could survive, but it was Mother who made it possible. She was a fighter. She gave me hope against all odds. If anyone could beat it, she would. And she had an incredible sense of humor, even finding funny stories to tell about her hospital stays. She had a running battle with the frosty English nurse at Doctors' Hospital after one of her surgeries. Miss Easton, it seems, was annoyed because Mother had called for the bedpan a number of times during the night. As Mother told it Miss Easton finally said, "What is it, Mrs. R, nerves?" "No," said Mother adopting a clipped British accent, "it is not nerves; it is habit!"

At this same hospital stay, she wrote cheery letters to Ray in the Eighth Air Force in England, never telling him about her illness. She wouldn't allow any of us to tell him about it either. Instead, she described the beautiful view from the window of an apartment overlooking the East River, which she enjoyed while "visiting a friend."

Between radiation treatments there were times when she seemed her old self. Then she and her younger friends—she always attracted younger people—would carry on their high-spirited activities: charity work, the Sisterhood, forays into New York, dinners with other couples. Also, she was close to her siblings after the move from Little Falls, and always enjoyed visiting them.

When Mother was feeling well (or at least claimed she was), I could breathe again—always aware that these were gifts from a dwindling supply. Sometimes Mother and I would take walks before I set off for my job in New York. We'd go up our street, Winthrop Road, until we reached the section where the houses got bigger and the landscapes more elaborate. Mother would point out the beauty, totally enjoying it. But I didn't want to talk about trees and flowers and gardening. I wanted to talk about all the things she knew that I didn't, all the wise things she could teach me that I was going to lose forever. Yet I still couldn't reach that core, and since I couldn't unlock her secrets, I agreed that the landscaping was beautiful; and that, yes, we'd better get back because I'd be late for work. Whatever I did those last three years of Mother's life, her illness was always with me, suppressed at times, overwhelming at others.

I don't believe there's a Benevolent Someone watching over us, but I'm surpassingly grateful that a couple of months after Mother's first operation I met Ellis. I have Tracy to thank for that.

Tracy ran into Sgt. Ellis Marcus in front of the Russian Tea Room on 57th Street, and invited him to a party at her duplex. He was in the Signal Corps Motion Picture unit in Astoria, Long Island. She had studied with his brother, Marc Daniels, who was with *This Is the Army* in Italy, and had taught at the American Academy of Dramatic Arts. Ellis had been a student there and an assistant stage manager before he was drafted.

    I went to the same party, dreading it. I know. I know. I said Tracy and I were friends and we were, but I still felt self-conscious and awkward around her wildly sophisticated theater friends. So I arrived with an attitude. I did an exaggerated Ina Claire—a sort of satire on theater patois: "Dahling!" I gushed to my sister when I found her with a group that included Ellis, "How too, too delightful to see you! Kiss, kiss. . . ." or something equally inane. Tracy refused to notice how silly I sounded, and urged me to tell the group about my fascinating job on the paper. (Fascinating? I was a copy boy. But Tracy always has a way of enhancing whatever I do.) Embarrassed, I muttered something and slunk off to find a large piece of furniture to hide behind.

    I wound up sitting on the floor of the deserted study in front of the tiny fireplace, when someone came in and sat next to me. It was Ellis.

    "Are you always that affected?" He asked. I glanced at him. He was sort of short, with G.I. wire-rimmed glasses covering blue eyes, ruddy skin, good teeth, and a strong build. I took an immediate dislike to him. Didn't he know I was kidding? Did he really think I talked like that? On the other hand, why did I care what he thought? Why do I <u>always</u> care what people think? Damn.

    He wanted to know if I was an actress. Absurd. Me? An actress!? (I loved acting. Why did I think his question was so outlandish?) I took a breath, and tried to regain some semblance of composure.

    "No," I told him, "I'm not an actress. I'm a copy boy for the *New York Daily News*, and that was a stupid act I put on back there. I always act dopey around my sister's friends because they make me nervous." He nodded. He told me he had an older brother whose friends made him nervous, too.

    It was getting warmer in the study in front of the tiny fireplace with its tiny, specially cut logs. We started to talk. He was funny, smart, easygoing, and something was happening between us. Did I mention his thick, wavy brown hair? I said he could call me.

The next day, I was down in the bowels of the press room with last minute copy. The presses were rolling and the noise was ferocious, when a call came through for me. It was Ellis.

He took me to dinner at a storefront on Third Avenue with sawdust on the floor and oilpaper on the tables. There weren't many diners, but I recognized two of them:Jean Gabin and Marlene Dietrich. An auspicious beginning, I thought. Not only that, but I ate my first lobster. Not only that, but I looked more closely at Ellis and decided that he was a cross between John Garfield and Marlon Brando, with a touch of Robert Walker. I knew that night he was someone special.

His friends, his wonderfully vibrant, literate, irreverent Army buddies, called me "Flash." They were screenwriters or wannabes—some of them from Hollywood, all of them attached to the Army Signal Corps, turning out training films. We had good times together: seeing plays, going to movies, eating, drinking, riding double-decker busses down Fifth Avenue (deliberately calling every other building the "Flat Iron Building" to confuse the tourists). We celebrated New Year's Eve in Times Square, met for blissfully stolen moments in Tracy's duplex, spent weekends in the country at the parents of one of his army buddies. There was good talk, good food, and good fun. I was able to open up to him about Mother, and he was warm and supportive, solid as a rock.

I was falling in love. It was strange to be so happy and so sad at the same time.

Mother seemed relieved when she met Ellis and saw how close we had become in such a short time. She must have been worried about me. Now she could see that I'd have someone to love, to share with, to depend on. And Ellis was all of that. I had met him in late December 1943, got engaged in March, and planned to get married in June. I'm not sure I wanted to rush things so, but I felt pressured because of Mother's illness. I wanted her at our wedding. I needed her there, and I couldn't take any chances that she wouldn't make it.

Ellis and I would have been happy with a simple ceremony, but Mother was determined to launch our marriage with a grand affair, so she and her best friend, Ceil Fields, spent weeks planning the event.

A couple of months before the wedding, I had taken my one byline across town to the headquarters of *Life Magazine*, where I calmly presented it as my "last" byline as though it were one of many. I also blithely invented a year of newspaper experience on the *Cincinnati Star Times* preceding my job on *The News*. It was an out-and-out lie. I'd never written a word for the *Star Times*. In those days (before fax machines and computers), you could get away with stretching the truth a little. I salved my conscience knowing in my heart that Claire Trevor would have done the very same thing.

It got me an interview with Bernice Schrifte, the chief of research on the editorial staff. Somehow, I convinced her that I was just the kind of experienced journalist *Life* needed, and I was hired. She asked what I was earning at *The News,* and I told her (lying through my teeth), that I made forty dollars a week. She nodded and said that the starting salary at *Life* was forty-five dollars. Would that be all right with me? I managed, demurely, to agree to the terms.

Ellis and I celebrated at Lum's Garden, our favorite Chinese restaurant on West 45th, where a seven-course dinner cost eighty-five cents. It was my treat.

After that, we strolled up Broadway to 59th Street and had Brandy Alexanders in a cocktail lounge overlooking Central Park. It was one of those nights when I almost forgot about Mother.

Chapter 6

To LIFE, To Life, L'CHAYIM!

Most of the researchers at *Life* were recruited from the same snobby seven sister colleges that had rejected me when I had applied four years earlier. The recruits joined the staff as trainees for a year or two before becoming full-fledged researcher/reporters. Since I had joined the staff only six months out of Western College as a "seasoned professional," I couldn't help feeling a little smug—even though I'd done it by telling a few white lies. It did make me a little nervous, especially since the head of research ran a very tight ship.

Bernice Schrifte was small and feisty, with short red hair and a somewhat beaky nose, which might have added to my feeling that she was watching me like a hawk. Schriftie, the name everyone called her except to her face, ruled by intimidation.

"Miss Goldstone!" she called in her deep throaty voice after I'd been there about a month. I had tried to glide past her without being seen. Caught like an errant schoolgirl, I entered her office. She didn't invite me to sit down or tell me she'd be with me in a minute. Instead, she continued working on something I inferred was extremely important, and then (when she was good and ready), she looked up from her desk.

"Your copy was late yesterday."

"Only a few minutes," I said as pleasantly as possible.

"Late is late!"

I tried looking earnest. "Yes, but isn't it better to be a few minutes late and get the material right, than on time and wrong?"

She stared at me much longer than necessary. "See that you get your copy in on time—and right."

Actually, we got along fine. The trick was to let her win, but not to act intimidated. If you were a wimp she'd really make your life miserable.

Schriftie assigned me to the photo lab first so that I'd become familiar with the primary reason *Life* was the most popular magazine in the country—the pictures. Instead of working at the Time-Life Building in Rockefeller Center, I reported to the foul-smelling lab across the street—where the pictures that came in from staff photographers around the world were processed. My job was to sort them out in sequence, caption them from the sketchy material that was sent with them, and send them across the street to the editorial offices.

One of the most famous wartime photographers, Margaret Bourke-White, was working for *Life* as a correspondent with General ""Vinegar"" Joe Stilwell in the Far East when I was hired. The photo technicians loved to belittle the talents of the star photographers, and they took special delight in trashing Bourke-White's work. They complained it was out of focus, poorly lighted, or not properly framed. No matter how daring and remarkable she was—hanging out of fighter planes during aerial combat, capturing the heroism and misery on the battlefield—according to the guys who processed her film, they were responsible for her success. To put it in their words: they saved her ass.

After a couple of weeks of inhaling chemicals and labeling pictures, I finally made it across the street to the editorial offices on the 31st floor at 9 Rockefeller Plaza.

I was assigned to the National Affairs department at about the time Roosevelt announced his candidacy for a fourth term, dumped Henry Wallace, and chose Harry Truman, as his running mate. I was sent out to Lamar, Missouri, to cover Truman's notification ceremony, and I was scared to death. I had next to no experience, and I was about to interview the Democratic candidate for vice-president of the United States! The ceremony was the kickoff of

Truman's official campaign, and the Democrats were looking for down-home votes by holding an old-fashioned church supper in the town where Truman was born.

Before I left for St. Louis, Myron Emanuel, a veteran researcher, took me out to lunch.

"Since you're new I thought you might be able to use a little advice," he said over club sandwiches at Schrafft's around the corner on Fifth Avenue. "There are a few really important things you ought to know before you leave for Missouri."

I was extremely grateful, and a little worried. Was my terror showing? Did he know what a tenderfoot I was?

"We're all in this together," he said, "and we're counting on you to keep up your end; make it work. Do you follow me?"

Of course I did. Who said news people were cynical? What spirit. It was an honor to be on a staff that had such integrity.

"I'm anxious for any pointers you can give me," I told him. I explained that I hadn't really covered politics when I was on *The News*. (True enough, I ran copy and sharpened pencils . . .)

"I'm talking about your expense account," he said a little impatiently. "You can't tell them what you actually spend. You have to . . . play with the figures a little. Be imaginative. If you come up with a per diem that's way below the usual, the standard, it'll look . . . you know . . . strange. Understand?"

I certainly did. They gave me a hundred dollars in cash for the trip. I counted and recounted the money. I'd never seen that much cash at one time.

I took an overnight train to St. Louis, slept in a Pullman berth for the first time, and met up with Jerry Cooke, the *Life* photographer who was going to Lamar with me.

What a trip. It was early summer—and hot. I had a bad case of hay fever, and we drove through miles and miles of Missouri farmland where the ragweed was as high as an elephant's eye. I don't think I've ever sneezed that much. My nose ran constantly. I finally tied Jerry's large handkerchief around my face and just let it drip.

Jerry Cooke was a character. He had taken an all-American name, but he was actually a Polish refugee who had learned English by listening to radio jingles. So, while I sneezed and dripped, he sang about Piel's Light Beer of Broadway fame, and drove like a madman in the rented convertible, with the top down, all the way from St. Louis to Lamar.

We reached Lamar in plenty of time to set up for the church supper. Jerry was in great spirits. I was a limp rag with swollen eyes and a red nose, but determined that my first real assignment would be memorable.

But what is memorable about a church supper? Certainly not the menu: creamed chicken, biscuits, and strawberry shortcake. The entertainment? The church choir sang and Truman made a dull, flat speech in his pleasant but dull, flat no-nonsense style. The other guests? They were a group of mostly portly, comfortable, middle-aged, longtime friends of the Trumans. The men (like Harry) dressed in seersucker suits, and the women (like Bess) were in wrinkled linen pastels or flowered silk dresses.

The only memorable incident (and only memorable for me), occurred after dinner when Harry and Bess were leaving and I ran after them to ask the candidate a redundant question or two. Jerry took my picture with the future "the buck-stops-here" President." It wasn't used in the story that ran in *Life*, but I kept it for posterity. Only I'll never be able to show it to my grandchildren, because somewhere along life's travels, I lost it.

When I got back from Missouri, I went to work for Roger Butterfield, the political editor. He was writing a close-up of Thomas E. Dewey, the Republican candidate running against Roosevelt in the 1944 election. I know this sounds immodest, but I think I uncovered something that caused Dewey to lose the election.

But I'm getting ahead of myself again. On a weekend during the first month on my new job, Ellis and I flew down to Pittsburgh for a Passover Seder, presided over by his father, Harry, whom I loved immediately. "I'm glad you met me," he said with a hug when we arrived at the three-story brick house in Squirrel Hill. His mother, Amelia, a third-generation American, took a little longer to get to know, but the wait was worth it. She was affectionate and devoted to her family. I was given the third floor guest room. Ellis was in his old room on the second floor.

The Marcuses had a large, extended family including an active "cousins' club." Ellis' sister, Miriam, was an enthusiastic booster of the club. She had married Carl Cherin, a Harvard law graduate who had clerked for Supreme Court Justice Frankfurter, when she was a senior at Wellesley. She was now back home working with her Dad, a kitchen cabinet representative, while Carl was in the Army in the Far East.

Ellis' older brother, Marc Daniels, was still in Italy, but no longer touring with *This Is the Army*. He was in the real war, having transferred to an artillery battalion. Marc, who was born Daniel Marcus, had reversed his name when he went into show business. People don't often change their names now, but they did back then.

The Seder that Passover was everything a religious celebration should be—warm, loving, joyous—even spiritually renewing. And fun. Harry kept repeating the blessing for wine, and we had to drink each time he did. We were all pretty wasted by the end of the meal.

When Harry and Amelia came to Teaneck a few weeks later to meet Mother and Abe, there was instant rapport. Mother not only felt that I was in good hands with Ellis, but that I would also have a solid family backing us up.

The wedding was approaching and had grown to elaborate proportions. Where Ellis and I had wanted a simple affair, Mother, with the help of her friend Ceil, had arranged for the ceremony to take place in the Basildon Room of the Waldorf Astoria. Afterwards the hundred or so guests would be treated to hot and cold *hor d'oeuvres*, luncheon, and dancing.

Decades later, I paid an eerie visit to the Basildon Room. I had come in from the West Coast for a story conference and found myself near the Waldorf, so I wandered inside. Sure enough, the room was still there—only it was being renovated. It was deserted except for a few naked work lights casting ghostly shadows on the once brocaded walls. Did I hear distant voices and music, or was my overworked imagination trying to recreate that day, June 11, 1944?

Whistling Girl

The wedding pictures show me looking somewhat strained in my white silk suit that Tracy, my matron of honor, helped me pick out instead of a traditional wedding gown. I think I was trying to be patriotic and not use rationed material that could have been used for parachutes, although later I wished I hadn't been so altruistic. In those same pictures, Ellis looks about sixteen—a very handsome sixteen—in his tailor-made, enlisted man's uniform.

The night before the wedding, when I was trying to get to sleep in Teaneck, I had a moment of sheer terror. "My God," I thought, "this is for life. Why am I rushing things? Is it too late to call it off? Am I really in love? How do I really know? Shouldn't I think about this a little more? It's 'til death do us part. Help!"

But there I was the next day, in the bride's dressing room, waiting with thumping heart as the syncopated, jazzy strains of "Here Comes the Bride" could be heard at someone else's wedding in the ballroom next door. Thank goodness Mother had arranged for a simple organ to accompany me down the aisle on the arm of my stepfather Abe.

All my Goldstone aunts and uncles and cousins (who weren't stationed overseas), were there, as were Mother's Orenge siblings and kin. Ellis' extended family, his army buddies, a few of my new friends from *Life*, and old ones from school were there, too. I missed Martha, who was stuck in Chicago but sent her parents as surrogates.

Ellis smashed the glass under his foot. Everyone shouted *"L'Chayim!"* and the serious eating and drinking began. During the toasts, Uncle Moe (the same Uncle Moe who had bought back into Dad's horse and buggy peddling business so many years before), was feeling no pain as he raised his glass. He didn't really offer a toast—it was more a musical salute. To the tune of the preschool song, "If you're happy and you know it, clap your hands..." Uncle Moe sang, "How do you do, Miss Bride, how do you do? How do you do, Miss Bride, how do you do? How do you do, how do you do etc., etc., etc., how do you do, Miss Bride, how do you do?" You had to have been there.

Ellis had made secret reservations at the Hotel Pierre before we left on our honeymoon. When we got there we were met at the door to our room by the house detective.

"Sgt. Marcus?" he asked suspiciously.

Ellis nodded.

"Can I see some ID?" the well-dressed but burly gentleman asked.

"What's going on?" Ellis demanded.

The detective stood his ground. "I'm sorry, sir, but I got to make sure you are who you say you are."

Ellis began to smile. He seemed to understand, although I certainly didn't. "There's someone in our room, right?"

"There was," said the house dick, "a whole bunch of them, but I cleared them out."

Ellis showed him his ID, tipped him and told me what must have happened. One of his army buddies (it turned out to be Sgt. Jerry Thomas), had raced over to the Pierre ahead of us. Jerry and his girl friend had signed the register as Sgt. Ellis Marcus and bride, gone up to the room with his pals, and had been waiting to jump out of closets at the appropriate moment and surprise us. The only lingering evidence was a note still floating in the toilet: "Kilroy was here."

Our honeymoon hideaway couldn't have been more appropriately named. Schroon Manor. It was on beautiful Schroon Lake in the Adirondacks. Ellis' friend, Capt. Julian Blaustein, had arranged for his mother, who owned the small hotel, to open up two weeks early just for us. No one was there except Mrs. Silbert and her husband. It was cold, but that only made our major recreation at Schroon Manor more enjoyable.

We had our first argument when I got up on the gunnels of the canoe and began jouncing the way I used to at Girl Scout camp. Ellis got mad because, he claimed, he was afraid I'd tip the canoe over and hurt myself in the frigid water. I claimed he was only concerned about the expensive camera equipment he had borrowed from his brother Marc's first wife, Meg Mundy (who happened to be beautiful, classy, and cold—as well as one of the most sought after models in New York).

It was fun making up over a romantic dinner in Schroon Manor's deserted dining room, except that Mrs. Silbert kept coming over to nudge us to "eat . . . eat."

We moved to 65th street just off Central Park West when we got back. Our first home. It was in an old brownstone with polished brass bannisters that had been converted into several apartments. Ours was one large furnished room with a fake fireplace, a lumpy bed, and a tiny kitchen. Idyllic. It was almost as though we were living in normal times. Ellis went to work every morning at the Signal Corps Film Center in Astoria, Long Island. I took the bus or walked to the Time/Life building. Heaven.

A month or so before the wedding, Ellis had put in for OCS (Officer Candidate School), and a few weeks after our honeymoon, his application was approved. He was ordered to Fort Monmouth, in southern New Jersey. At the beginning of the war they called the second lieutenants that made it through OCS 90-day wonders. I guess they hadn't turned out so wonderful, because by the time Ellis went to OCS to become an officer and a gentleman, the training had lengthened to 120 days.

So off he went, and in one of his first harried letters to me he wrote:

> *Dearest Pooh,*
> *I have just completed a test in Organization I. There is half a period left and the instructor said we could study something if we wanted. I've decided to study you. Let me see—Height, 5'2; weight, 104 lbs.—light as a summer breeze in one's lap or in one's arms; hair, nut brown, soft, with golden high-lights and graceful, sweeping curls; complexion, light olive, soft, quiet and very warm; eyes, brown, clear, bright, variable according to the emotion; throat . . .*

I've got to stop his letter here, not because it gets steamier (it does) but because he described my eyes as . . . BROWN! We were married six weeks and he didn't know my eyes are BLUE! (Poor guy, I teased him about that for years).

While Ell was at OCS, I was working on the 1944 presidential election, gathering colorful background material for a *Life* closeup on the GOP candidate, Thomas E. Dewey. Dewey had made a name for himself as a young, crime-busting Manhattan D.A. and had gone on to become Governor of New York. FDR, looking tired and ill, was running for his fourth term against this much younger challenger, but one of the popular political axioms at the time was: "Don't change horses in midstream."

I guess it's about time I explain that boastful cliffhanger I mentioned about being responsible for Dewey's defeat. Here's how it happened:

I interviewed as many of his friends, colleagues, advisers, teachers, and former neighbors as I could, directing the memos to Roger Butterfield, who was writing a long political profile on Dewey. The idea was to find as much colorful background material as I could—not just the dull facts and figures. One of my first interviewees was Dewey's voice teacher, Percy Rector Stephens, who said Dewey ". . . had a good voice and used it well, but he sang too intelligently. He didn't have the singer's temperament, not enough impulse." Deems Taylor, the composer and critic, told me that if Stephens had given Dewey an "unreserved green light, he would have given up law."

But that's not what defeated Dewey.

I talked to Mr. and Mrs. Dewey's former neighbors at 1148 Fifth Ave., all of whom had nothing but the nicest things to say about them. Even the doorman, William (Call me Billy) Phelan said Mr. Dewey was a square shooter. "You can't say too much about the Governor that he won't back up himself," said Billy, who went on to say, "Mr. Dewey is far-fetched in everything he does. Know what I mean? He sees things in the future." That information didn't lose the election for Dewey, either.

I interviewed John Foster Dulles, who was Dewey's foreign affairs adviser. I was feeling quite important to be discussing such significant matters with such a prestigious gentleman, until he answered the phone and explained to the caller, "I can't talk to you now because I'm being interviewed by a little girl from *Life*."

I didn't squeal on Dulles, but even if I had, it wouldn't have affected the outcome of the election. The electorate had never heard of P.C. in those days.

Not even the story I got from Dewey's paperboy, Marvin, cost him many votes. When Dewey was Manhattan's D.A., he bought his periodicals and whatnots from a stationery store where Marvin worked. One Christmas Eve, the Deweys were decorating their tree and ran out of tinsel, so Marvin trudged over and delivered some extra. Dewey answered the door.

"Are you the boy who delivers the papers?" he asked.

"Yes," said Marvin, who was 17.

"Do you deliver the papers every day?" asked the D.A.

"Yes, sir," said Marvin.

"Well," said Dewey, "if you're the boy who delivers the papers, I have something for you." He turned and went back into the apartment for a moment. When he returned, he handed Marvin something. It was a dime.

Okay, so the candidate was tight. Not a bad attribute for a presidential nominee. That certainly didn't lose him the election.

It was what happened when I went to Albany, the capitol of New York, to interview Dewey face-to-face. He was affable, straight forward, and didn't hesitate to answer the questions I asked about his taste in literature (history, detective stories), music (chamber music and opera), food (lots of fresh fruits and vegetables), and other hard-edged questions. Actually, I was treading water—trying to uncover something colorful, something special, something out of the ordinary. Up to that point my report was going to read like an obituary. The Governor was sitting in his office and the *Life* photographer, George Skelton, was taking pictures as we parried. Then the Governor was summoned out of the room for a moment and—THE BIG DISCOVERY WAS MADE. HE HAD BEEN SITTING ON TWO TELEPHONE BOOKS SO THAT HE'D LOOK TALLER!

I scooped the world with that information—which was not only used in the *Life* closeup, but was picked up by every daily and popular periodical of the time. And if you don't think that had something to do with his defeat, then just remember what that picture of Governor Dukakis in his Snoopy helmet, riding around in that tank did to him in 1988!

Meanwhile, Ell was progressing through his officer training course in the Signal Corps. I tried to get down to Fort Monmouth on those weekends he had time off, but it wasn't easy. The New Jersey Central managed to scare up some rolling stock that must have been left over from the Civil War. It was old, uncomfortable, and took hours to get there with frequent stops to rest. Actually, the train stopped to let more important troop trains and the like whizz by.

There was no air conditioning and the windows hadn't been opened since 1921—except once. That was the day I was *en route* wearing my brand-new, tomato-colored, linen suit. I smiled when a gentleman tried to open the window next to me, knowing it wouldn't budge, but he somehow managed to pry it open and I was covered from head to waist in a rain of soot.

Fortunately, I met a young woman in the lavatory who helped me try to repair the damage. Her name was Muriel Goldman and she was on her way to visit her OCS husband, too. When the train wheezed into the station, both our husbands were in their crisp khakis to meet us. We got off wilted, hot, and in my case, with remnants of soot on my once smashing suit.

Stanley Goldman, poet, art connoisseur and scholar, was in the same battalion company as Ellis, and he and Muriel became lifelong friends—in spite of the fact that Stanley washed out of OCS and spent the rest of the war in the Aleutians writing for an Army newspaper with Dashiel Hammett.

Ellis, true to his mensch-like self, became the company commander. He had that terrific capacity for doing things well—whether it was getting a perfect score on the math SAT, soldiering, carving a turkey, fixing stopped up drains, or assembling complicated do-it-yourself whatevers.

I couldn't wait for him to finish OCS in October. When he did, we were sure he'd be reassigned to the training film studio in Astoria, Queens. But they didn't invent that word, SNAFU, during World War II for nothing. After he became a second lieutenant, we had two beautiful weeks together before he got his orders to report to a replacement depot on the West Coast. We both thought he was going to end up in an invasion of Japan. It was much too scary to talk about. Instead, we crammed as much as we could into the rest of his two-week leave.

The day he left, I slipped a mushy note into the pocket of his pajamas before he packed them. We all saw him off at Grand Central:Tracy and her husband Jerry, Marc's wife Meg, and a bunch of our buddies. They don't make train stations like Grand Central anymore. If you were going to say goodbye to your soldier husband, whom you thought was off to join an invasion of Japan, there was no better Grand Opera setting than that vast, marbled, high-domed, bustling, busy place to do it in. We had had our private moments alone, now there was only time for one last hug before he ran for the train. Then the train was moving out, and I turned blindly to fall into someone's arms for comfort. I thought they were Tracy's, but they were Meg's and they were comforting, and I was glad she was there.

In the following weeks and months before he was permanently assigned, Ellis ended up in Hawaii in charge of an Army newsreel team. I went back to my job on *Life*, grateful to be kept busy and distracted.

One of the pleasant distractions was the arrival of a new researcher/reporter, Marietta Peabody Fitzgerald. Marietta must have been close to thirty when she came aboard, quite a bit older than most of us. She was a classic beauty. Exquisite. Blonde, tall, and with a Boston Brahmin pedigree that was awesome. Was it her father or brother who was Governor of Massachusetts? Was it her grandfather or great-grandfather who founded Groton? All I know is that she was luminous—and that most of her peers on staff resented the hell out of her. Rumors circulated that she got her job through pull. There were whispers that she wasn't very bright, and lots of other mean spirited gossip. I thought she was terrific. I was delighted when she was assigned to the National Affairs Department—with me.

One of the tedious tasks we researchers had was to place dots over every word of text to be published attesting to the validity of the facts—which were supposed to be checked out from unimpeachable sources such as the *New York Times, The Congressional Record*, etc. Marietta didn't bother with these intermediary research tools. She went to the source. If she were checking a story on President Roosevelt, she'd call the White House and talk to her pal FDR, Jr., who acted as aide to his father.

"Darling," she'd say, "did your Dad tell Senator Taft to bug off about his meeting with Stalin?"

I loved it. And I loved Marietta. She was sharper than a serpent's tooth. You don't become Adlai Stevenson's good friend or Ambassador to the United Nations unless you are.

This icon of the socially elite loved telling bawdy stories. I remember a typical one about the royals of England. Seems Marietta was on friendly terms with them, and visited now and then. One time, as the guests were about to leave, Prince Philip made farting noises as they bowed out of the royal presence.

It was about two months after Ellis shipped out that I got a plum assignment. It was a chance to star my old hometown, Little Falls, in a riveting essay in the pages of *Life Magazine*. I was more than ready.

Chapter 7

I Can't Go Home Again, Either

Life
Time & Life Building
Rockefeller Center
New York 20, N.Y.
March 4, 1945

Darling,
Monday morning and back to work with my eyes shut tight, and a fierce desire to tell you how passionately in love with you I am . .
. . I have opened my Mark Cross folder full of your pictures, and you are staring at me—smiling, laughing, and in one you are look- ing wet and naked and sexy. How I would love to climb in that bath- tub with you!
But on to more Life-like things. I've got a WONDERFUL ASSIGNMENT! The editors want to show how the war has affected a typical small American town. I was flattered that Schrifte picked me to do the research. It will be a long picture essay, and I imme- diately told them I knew just the town.
"Yeah?" said John Field, the waspy Newsfront editor. "What town?" So I said Little Falls, New York, my old hometown where I was born and raised. They had decided on Dunkirk, N.Y., which is near Buffalo, but they are still open to suggestion. So probably later today we will decide which town we want to do and I'm keeping my fingers crossed.

I Can't Go Home Again, Either

The story is really a sociological study of how the institutions that make up a small town—family, church, schools, work, social intercourse—how they are affected by the war. You know I majored in sociology so don't laugh at me.

I stayed over with Tracy and met Mother and Abe after her x-ray treatment Saturday morning. She's so brave and upbeat and even though I know she felt awful, she insisted we all have lunch. I went back to Jersey with them and spent the weekend reading For Whom the Bell Tolls, and walking in the sun with Mom.

Tracy, Jerry and a bunch of other people came over late Sunday afternoon. We played Categories, and Mother came in second after Jerry (but he probably cheated). We really needed you for a couple of good, cheery routines. Oh well, Pooh Blossom, there'll come a day. And until it does, please know that I'm yours, yours ——- forever.

P.

* * * * * * * *

March 9, 1945

Darling, darling . . .
I rushed out of the station and couldn't wait til I got back from Little Falls because I knew there would be some letters from you. I peeped in the mailbox and I could only see one very thin-looking envelope, but when I finally opened the box, 2 v-mails and 3 air-mails popped out at me. I was like a kid who's trying to eat his cake and save it, too. I read them very slowly and savored every word.

Little Falls was some experience to say the least. You can imagine the circumstances. I left when I had started my sophomore year at high school. But our family was more or less an institution in the town. Both Tracy and Ray had gone through high school there, and our store had been there over 25 years. The town is just small enough (11,000) so that everyone knows everyone else.

I burst on the town like a veritable bombshell! MY GOD, IT'S LITTLE DOTTIE GOLDSTONE! AND SHE'S GOING TO DO A

Whistling Girl

STORY ON THE TOWN FOR <u>LIFE</u>! I felt funny after the editor decided to send me up there because I didn't think people would take me seriously. But everyone thought I was most grown up, and why not? After all, I'm married now.

I planned to stay at the WCA where I had gone to Brownie and Girl Scout meetings and where Mother had started a Sunday School, but the Blumbergs (Arnold was Mother's attorney), insisted I stay with them. Thank God, because the Snyder Hotel is really dreary.

The people in Little Falls were wonderful although they embarrassed me a little. I wish they wouldn't think the magazine is so terrific, or that I've somehow changed, become sophisticated or different. It made me uneasy to have some of the girls I knew in school act shy in my presence. But they weren't the only ones, even people of terrifying authority like the high school principal were slightly—just slightly—in awe.

But it was terrific fun. I talked to everyone—the Mayor, the secretary of the Greater Little Falls Assoc., the banker, the grocer, the mill owners, the high school teachers, school supervisor, young girls, mothers, veterans' adviser, head of the draft board, police and fire chiefs—EVERYBODY. I walked the length and breath of the town filling my notebook and trying not to feel like the female version of Thomas Wolfe.

Now the big question is, "Will <u>Life</u> do the story?" Tomorrow I have to go into the office and convince them that it would be worthwhile.

It's supposed to be a study of how the war affects a typical small town. And yet, Little Falls seems as remote from the war as the moon, at least on the surface. It's not a war boomtown, although some of its industry has converted to war work. It isn't rich, although everyone seems to have more money than before, and business is good. There isn't a large army camp nearby, so you rarely see soldiers on the street except local boys home on furlough. But underneath the business-as-usual atmosphere there's a great loneliness, almost a bereftness. It is so noticeable that all the finest young men are gone. The young girls dance in the Corner

Tavern together and drink beer and laugh. There have been several casualties for a town of its size, and these are felt by the whole town because everyone knew the boys. People seem to be holding their breath, waiting for the time when they can go back to the way things were.

It's so strange for them to have relatives in exotic places all over the world. Given their druthers, I don't think many Little Falls people would go very far from home. They might go to Albany or New York, but those places are considered foreign, and mostly they "stay in their own backyards." They're a little suspicious of other people and other places, and yet their sons and daughters, brothers and husbands are all over the world. Will it change them? And if it does, in what way?

Well the story has lots of possibilities but when I try to translate that into picture ideas, I feel at a loss.

I wish you were here for several obvious reasons, but besides those, you could help me focus on the project. That's because you have a wonderful sense of organization and objectivity.

Maybe a good night's sleep will clear my brain. I've been riding the rails for a long time, so I'll say good night you wonderful pooh blossom. If I could only be with you.

P.

* * * * * * * *

March 12, 1945

Darling . . .

Just came from a story conference with Alfred Eisenstaedt, photographer; John Field, editor; and Bill Churchill, picture editor, and we sewed up the Little Falls story. My God, they are really going to do the story up brown. They were talking in terms of 10-page spreads, full-page pictures, even cover possibilities! I tried to act as nonchalant as possible, but under the circumstances, I felt just like the Little Falls hick I am.

So now I'm cleaning things up, and tomorrow Alfred and I will *leave for L.F. on the 9:20 train—and damn it, I've made a vow to be on time.*

Alfred is one of the best photographers, but he's a prima donna. He's a small, brown, long-nosed gent who speaks with an accent, and is very artistic.

I'll probably be in L.F. for over a week, and the hardest part is that I won't be getting any mail from you. I'll write to you as often as I can, but you'll understand if the letters are brief. Here are a few things to remember:

1. *I love you.*
2. *You are the only and fairest pooh blossom of them all.*
3. *My postwar life is one big you.*
4. *You make me want to have babies.*
5. *When you come home we will spend 4 weeks in bed.*
6. *No other man has 1 billionth of your charm and personality and sex appeal.*
7. *I am mad for you.*
8. *You are my valentine, my dream boy, my pin-up boy, my man-of-the-year.*

All my love to you, dearest of the people I love,
Pooh

* * * * * * * *

March 13, 1945

Darling,
Here I am back in Little Falls with Alfred Eisenstaedt and red carpets and brass bands!

The Blumbergs, who are very good friends of Mother, have insisted that I stay with them at their home and of course it's much more comfortable than the dreary local hotel. Besides, it keeps me from the clutches of Alfred.

The Mayor has given us the town's police car with a driver, and this afternoon we drove around town getting locations for pictures.

Gee, are we ever causing excitement here! Everyone wants to get in the picture. I certainly hope the story runs. If it doesn't, they'll run me outa town the next time I show up.

Because this is the first day on the job, I don't have much to tell you except that I love you. And I want you.

I hope you've started your assignment, honey, because I know how awful it is to sit around with nothing to do. Try thinking about the wonderful time we're going to have when you come home.

Goodnight, lamb

* * * * * * * *

April 2, 1945

My Most Beloved Pooh,

Again I spent the weekend in Teaneck because I want to be with Mother as much as possible. She tries so hard to act as though everything's going to be all right, yet we both know it really isn't. But it's our secret. We talk about everything except what's really on our minds.

Well, onto much less profound things. Things like Life magazine and how it works. I think I'm beginning to understand a little more about it. You wouldn't believe the amount of petty intrigue and downright skullduggery that goes on. I know perfectly well that 9 out of 10 stories that get assigned never see the light of day, but my contention is that decisions should be made on an adult basis.

Take my Little Falls story. I worked from morning until night for three weeks to do that story. I did it for John Field, who is editor of Newsfront and who is also trying to take over Roger Butterfield's job in National Affairs. When I finally got back and the pictures were printed, they looked very good to me. So the next step as far as I'm concerned is to show them to the managing editor, who, of course, knew the story was being shot. But this wasn't done.

John Field (the jerk who's bucking for a better job), knows I've been assigned to the Washington bureau for a month. When I asked him why he wouldn't show the pictures to Longwell, the managing editor, while I was still here so I could explain them, he gave me a *really dumb answer. He said he wasn't on very good terms with Longwell because he had been "pushing" too many stories. So we had better wait for the right "psychological moment." Now if he could enter Longwell's office when he was discussing the photographic essay for the next week, and if there were any doubts about the essay already planned, and if John were able to say at the right time, "how about running the Little Falls story," and if that struck a spark in Longwell's ear—THEN we could show the pictures.*

And Ellis, I'm not kidding, that's actually the way Field (that ass kisser), explained it to me. What I want to know is how the hell does the magazine get out every week? Don't you think this sounds like a high school magazine? And yet if I went to Longwell myself, I would be out of place and it wouldn't do any good because he would protect John.

So phooey, it might be used and it might not, but I'm not going to worry.

All I care about is Mother feeling better, Ray being able to get home to see her, and you, You, YOU!

I love you,
Pooh

(The photographic essay of "Little Falls, A Small Town at War," never ran in the magazine.)

Chapter 8

Life Goes On

Life
Washington Editorial Offices
815-15th Street N.W.
Washington, D.C.
April 13, 1945

Dearest Ellis,
Everyone will remember how he heard the news about Roosevelt yesterday, just like everyone will remember Dec. 7. I had left the office early to do some errands, and when I got into a cab about 6:05 the driver said, "I guess we don't have a president." I actually gasped - afraid of what he meant. But the radio was on, and it was all too true.

I feel a personal loss, and a kind of selfish hurt because if anyone could prevent another war, he could. And you and I have a big stake in the future because we're going to raise a family. I'm so uneasy now. Truman doesn't come up to Roosevelt in stature or statesmanship at all. Everyone who knows him here thinks he's a hell of a swell guy, but he just isn't up to what the times demand. And isn't it peculiar how circumstances have made him President?

I knew what to expect when I got back to the office. Whenever there's a catastrophe that's when I hate newspaper people most. Maybe the movies are to blame. They glamorize the profession so they give journalists overblown egos. And now newspaper people imitate the movies.

The feeling in the office was one of bravado: "Let's carry on, gang, there's a tough night's work ahead of us." Maybe I'm a hyp - ocrite because I certainly love this job, but I didn't like the way my colleagues, with their studied cynicism, relished this awful tragedy.

I was immediately dispatched to the White House where Truman was about to be sworn in by Chief Justice Stone. Throngs of people were milling about opposite the White House, and the place was surrounded by M.P.'s, Secret Service and police. I walked through the West Gate after assuring the guards that I was with Life. *George Skadding, the photographer, was already there.*

I got to the press room and found literally hundreds of reporters, photographers, movie men, press secretaries, cops, etc., pushing and shoving and perspiring. So, of course, I pushed and shoved my way as far as I could. They didn't allow any reporters in the Cabinet Room where Truman was sworn in except representa - tives of the three news services. But Skadding got in. I could just catch a glimpse of what was going on, and it all happened so fast. It was over in about five minutes.

The lucky ones up in front would shout things back like: "Mrs. Truman and Margaret just came in." "Admiral Leahy and Gen. Marshall are there." And then someone screamed out "7:09!" Immediately there was a mad scramble to the Press Room and tele - phones.

Well, I don't work for a daily, and I was there to get color stuff, so I pushed into the Cabinet Room as the members of the Cabinet exited. I caught a glimpse of Biddle, Stimson, Joe Martin, and I exchanged a long, painful look with Frances Perkins. George took a couple of shots of the small Bible that Truman held during the ceremony. It had been taken from Roosevelt's desk.

I phoned in the stuff I had seen and overheard, and we hung around waiting for something to happen. Hassett, Roosevelt's sec - retary, called a press conference every once in awhile, and every - one crawled over everyone else getting into his office even though nothing important was announced. George and I also went outside to catch the crowds hanging around in LaFayette Square—stand - ing silently and staring for the most part. I tried to overhear some -

thing quotable, but everyone was saying pretty much what everyone else was saying. Except for one damn army officer who made me mad. He was strolling down the street by the park, and he said, "He was in there too long, anyhow."

I checked with the office again, and Purcell sent me over to Truman's apartment building. Nothing there but a lot of Secret Service men who wouldn't let me near the apartment. Tom McAvoy, another Life fotog, was there and I got him to take a couple of shots of the one window that was aglow, Truman's. Then we went to St. John's Church where the President used to go, but there were just a few people there and we didn't want to disturb them.

We went back to the office. It was after midnight and I was tired. Staff were arriving from New York, including Ruth Adams. So, after a drink, we all went to bed, and got here bright and early today. I've been doing general color stuff today, like going to the Mayflower Hotel and showing how the huge Jefferson Day Dinner had to be canceled, and what they did with the food and such. I talked to Bob Hannegan at Democratic Committee HQ, too.

And now I'm pooped and hot and I think this profession is undignified. But one thing I know—I love you. Your own, your only ... WIFE.

* * * * * * * *

April 18, 1945

Dear Ellybelly,
FLASH! I saw the advance copy of this week's <u>Life</u> with the Roosevelt write-up. They treated it very nicely.
FLASH # 2! My name finally got on the masthead! It says: Managing Editor ... ; Executive Editor ... ; Assistant Managing Editors ..., ..., ... ; Senior Editors ... etc.; Associate Editors ... etc. etc.; Senior Researchers ... blah, blah etc. etc.; **RESEARCHERS: DOROTHY ANN MARCUS** and others.
I don't see why they made my name stand out so, for heaven's sake. After all, I'm just a lil ol' researcher.

After sneaking looks at the masthead all morning, I went out to lunch with Roz Mowrer. She married into the famous Mowrer journalism family, and is a researcher in the bureau here who thinks she's pretty hot, even though others don't. Roz had also invited the Society Editor of the Washington Post, *a dame of about 45, who said she liked Mrs. Roosevelt, but she just couldn't agree with her ideas about the Negroes. Grrrrrr. I spit in the milk of her mother. I obscenity in the juice of her prejudice.*

I couldn't let the remark go, and made a nasty pest of myself. She especially made me furious when she said the new administration will "put them in their place." Oh Ell—in the midst of this terrible war, why must there by such stupid people running loose with their hatred and ignorance and tight little mouths and beady little eyes?

* * * * * * * *

Washington, D.C.
May 8, 1945

My Most Wonderful Ellis,
How to begin a letter to you on VE Day? I feel very self-conscious, like the time I wrote a letter to my English professor at college. I feel I should say something philosophical. Mostly I'm wondering how much nearer to me this makes you. I'm thinking a lot of other things, too. I'm overwhelmingly sad and humble because of all the wonderful guys who had to die to make it possible. Guys like Teddy Feldmier from Little Falls, and Chester Mikus, who was my pal in the eighth grade. And then those millions of people whose lives are completely broken—homeless people and worse, those whose lives were snuffed out, or who were starved or tortured to death. I was looking through this month's Fortune *and there's a horrible painting in it. It shows a playground contraption—a pole with maypole-like rings on it, and little girls are whirling by on it, just like they would in any playground. Only the background is a bombed out town, and the pole is in the middle of a broken up*

street. And the little girls are frantically whirling around with too mature faces as if even playing were a horrible, hectic, terrifying thing. The name of the painting is "Liberation." I can't remember who did it, but God it's frightening.

It's very strange here in Washington. Practically no one is celebrating. Everyone seems pretty subdued while the papers say that Times Square was a mass of cheering, mad people.

This morning I hopped out of bed and over to the White House to cover Truman's press conference. He promised he'd give the photographers a go at him after his radio address to the nation. It got really hot in the Press Room. I went outside and stood in the hallway, and then the parade came by: Admiral Leahy, General Marshall, Jimmy Byrnes, my dream-boy-besides-you, Henry Wallace, and then Pres. Truman. I followed Truman in to face the lights and the cameras. Flash bulbs were flashing all over the place. "Mr President, will you please look this way?" Then the still guys moved out, and the newsreel guys took over. I was standing on a chair at the rear of the smallish room right in back of the cameras. Truman delivered the proclamation all over again, starting and stopping for the cameras. I gave him a "that's-the-spirit-Harry" thumbs up and he smiled at me.

After that I went up to The Hill. What an anticlimax that was! When they finally convened after calling the roll for at least 30 minutes to get a quorum, Mr. Speaker Sam Rayburn said a few generalities about Victory, Glorious Armies, Allies, Unity and "the fight still goes on."

He was followed by Minority Leader, Joe Martin, who said the same thing only longer; who was followed by Mr. McCormack who said the same thing only longer, louder, and with gestures.

This evening I listened to Toscanini conducting <u>Beethoven's $5^{\underline{th}}$</u>, and it was very strong and good. (Who do I think I am, Hemingway?)

Anyway, I fervently hope that Japan gives up without dragging the war on and on. I pray that the San Francisco Conference has been a success, even though the US insisted on seating Argentina and the Russians have locked up 16 democratic leaders of Poland.

How do the guys out there feel about things? Not the former Hollywood or writer guys, but real people. Let me know for I love you and want this terrible separation to count for something. I also pray that you stay put unless it's to come home to me.

With all my heart and mind and soul and body . . . Pooh

Teaneck, N.J.
July 27, 1945

Dearest Honeypooh,

I came back to New York to cover the Communist Convention, and waited for Earl Browder and pals to allow us to interview them and take pictures of their shindig. For three days the fotog and I sat and waited. Every once in a while the harried, hot, crumpled Press Secretary would tramp down the stairs on his way to the men's room and I'd pounce on him. "No pictures," he'd invariably growl.

I tried using logic. "We'll use bad candid pictures, and it would look much better if we had good pictures." But Commies are stubborn. So we waited some more. And the hell of it was that every time I got fed up with sitting around and marched the one block back to the office, back they would send me. "Marcus, get the pictures! Follow Browder to lunch; catch them when they get out of the meeting, etc." And so poor me and the fotog would go back and sit some more.

Yesterday, Saturday, a day I shouldn't have been working, I went back to Convention Hall early in the morning. One of the delegates drove up in a taxi. She was excited and said, "Did you hear about the Empire State Building?" And she told about the B-25 bomber that crashed into one of the upper floors.

I wanted to dash over since no one was in our office to cover it. What to do? Here was the biggest local story in years, but we were told to get pictures of the Communist convention or else. Naturally, I decided we should cover the crash. We dashed up to the office, got the only two press cards in the place, and were off.

It was spectacular. The day was rotten—misty, humid, rainy—

generally oppressive. Clouds were very low over the city, obscuring the tall buildings. And first we tried to get pictures of the whole building from 500 Fifth Ave. at 42nd St. But the mist entirely hid the top of the building. So we walked over to the Empire State. Four blocks on either side of it were blocked off by the police. People were crowded against the lines trying to see something. Those magic press cards got us right through the lines. The streets outside were a mass of fire equipment, emergency police trucks, ambu - lances, Red Cross canteens. On 34th St. pieces of glass, brick, stone and plane parts littered the street. There was one pile of wreckage half way down the street; part of the wing, all crumpled and yet bright aluminum with green and orange paint looking fresh and clean. Commissioner Walsh was there surrounded by a lot of news - men. I was set on going up to the 79th floor where the B-25 struck.

Inside, the police weren't letting anyone near the elevators. One bank had been put out of order by the crash, the ones going up to the 86th floor. But I knew press people were up there. So we went to a police captain and told him we had to get up there, and he said "Sure, go right ahead," and escorted us through the police to the elevators. It took us to the 67th floor, as high as it could go. From there we had to walk up to the 79th. It was quite hot and water from the hoses dripped down the stairways, but on we plodded. At the 79th floor, the place was a complete shambles. Someone told me I had better not go in because the bodies were there. I hesitated for a moment, but there were a lot of reporters there, and I figured if I thought I was a reporter I'd better prove it.

I went into what was left of the Catholic War Agency Welfare Offices with my eyes squinted, so that if I caught a glimpse of some - thing horrible I could look the other way. The water was about 3 inches deep up there and everything was black and charred, with rubble piled on the floor. The photographer told me the bodies had been placed in one part of the office, so I carefully avoided that part.

In the large office, the place was piled with parts of books. I guess they were sending them to soldiers overseas. I picked up some loose pages burned all around the edges. The walls, what was left of desks, were charred black. When the plane struck the gas tanks exploded, sending fiery cascades into the office—burning everything, including the office workers to a crisp.

Finally, out of morbid curiosity, I peeked at the bodies. I couldn't recognize them as bodies. They were just charred piles of something. Awful.

After Hal Carter had taken all the pictures he possibly could, we left. I had a kind of emotional reaction after we got down to the street. I felt dizzy and sick to my stomach. Those workers were volunteers. They had given up their weekend to do something charitable. Where is the sense in any of this?

I took a couple of deep breaths, and we rushed the stuff over to the dark room. I called Schrifte at home and told her we had covered it. She in turn called the editor, but I guess he had already gone to the office.

I had to turn the convention story over to another researcher who was called in so I could handle the research and editing for the Empire story. It's running for two and a half pages.

I didn't get through until ten o'clock last night. I came out to Teaneck and slept until 12:30 this morning.

And now it's time to go to sleep again. And I feel guilty because I'm thinking about how much I want you to climb in bed with me so that we could be as close to each other as possible, but another part of me is thinking about the families of those workers.

Remember how much I love you, and keep on sending those sexy, wonderful images of yourself to me.

D. Ann

* * * * * * * *

3925 Sig Photo Serv Co.
APO 958
San Francisco, Ca.
August 1, 1945

Dear Squeezable Yourself,
    I wish you'd make up your mind about whether I should keep on appearing to you or not. First you say I shouldn't because it dis-tracts you and makes you mopey and mooney. Then you say I should go ahead and do it because then at least you have some of me with you. Please let me know what to do. I have a couple of wonderful images of myself on the way to you now. Some of them are sexy and some are just plain ones. Which do you like best?
    As for your images which keep on cropping up in my mind, they are pretty great. Send a few more in that cream colored dress that unbuttons down the front. Send me a few more with your hair up. I especially like the ones where you muss me up and make me mad and then laugh at me. I love to hear you laugh. And send me one or two more of you when you've just awakened in the morning. And I could use a new one of you washing your hair. And, incidentally, you can turn the volume down a bit because they are coming through fine, although sometimes there's a bit of distortion. If you can manage it, send them out on a little higher altitude. I think they'll keep out of electrical storms that way.
    Last night we were sitting down by the ocean waiting for the jeep to come for us, and I saw a clipper ship heading for San Francisco. So I sent a couple of images on its wings. Let me know how these arrive. It's a very inexpensive way of sending them.
    One day soon I will come home and put my arms around you and never let you go. I want to make love to you in a million dif-ferent ways. I want to spend about fifty years trying out all sorts of ways of experiencing your being...animal, spiritual, social.
    I am a sensual man and you are a sensual man's picnic.
    Yr,
    Wellus

3925 Sig Photo Serv Co.
APO 958
San Francisco, Ca.
August 6, 1945

Dearest,

Your last two letters were wonderful. Your adventures in the Empire State Building and your difficulty with the Communists were pretty damn exciting. You are certainly getting your little fingers into the pie of what's going on in the world.

Speaking of which, the world is getting pretty near the Buck Rodgers stage what with the new atomic bomb. It's a fearful thing that atomic bomb. The paper says that one bomb is as devastating as 20,000 tons of TNT. In the hands of the wrong person that might mean the end of the world. Frightening thought.

I'm sorry to hear that Ida is not faring well. And of course I understand your decision not to return to the Washington Bureau. You want to be with her and she needs you. I hope Ray will be home soon, too, so that she can have all of you for a little while at least.

Ell

* * * * * * * *

Life Magazine
New York
August 2, 1945

Dearest Ell,

Ray's in this country! Wonder of wonders. He sent a telegram to Teaneck yesterday morning. Then this morning at 7 A.M. he called from Camp Patrick Henry in Virginia. He's <u>en route</u> to Fort Dix for a day of processing, and then that blessed 30-day furlough. God it will be good to see him. Poor Mom, she's in the middle of 12 new x-ray treatments, and feels awful, very weak and nauseous, and in a lot of pain. But her biggest concern is over. I'm so happy for her. Oh, won't it be wonderful when we can all have the ones we love home again!

* * * * * * * *

Life Magazine
New York
August 7, 1945

My Mostwonderfulwellus,
So you had a date with a nurse. And it was nice. And now you're nervous about my reaction to it. Well, I'm jealous—so goddamned jealous of that nurse I could wring her neck. She danced with you; talked to you; drank with you. It's a good thing you felt more lonely after the date. I know what you mean. I go to a get-together at someone's house and talk to someone. Maybe we dance. But at the end of the evening I feel so completely unsatisfied that by the time I go to bed all I've thought about is you. That's the time I miss you most, although it's a toss up between then and always. Maybe I should go on to other news.
My writing career is popping right along. Yesterday, with much fanfare, I was ushered into the office of the Associate Managing Editor, Joe Thorndike.
"Miss Marcus," said Mr. Thorndike, "I want you to write the captions for the Jerry Wald closeup."
"Thank you," says I. And that was that. Then Schrifte wanted to see me.
"You're going to write the Jerry Wald closeup captions," she said.
"Yes," I said. "Thank you." Then I went down to Bob Coughlan's office. He's the Closeup Editor.
"I'm going to write the Jerry Wald closeup captions," I said.
"Yes," he said. So with that I got the stats on the piece, pages of research (including the original manuscript, which was ten times as long as the final piece), closed myself in an empty office and wrote the captions. They consisted of 6 lines of 41 characters each, and 2 lines of 158 characters each. After reading all the research,

all I could write was this: "Wald runs off new film in projection room. Stickler for detail, Wald checks all costumes, etc." Terrific, don't you think? But wait. After I finished them and sent them into the copy room, I went back to my desk, and continued doing some research on the railroad strike. Bob happened to come by and said they threw the piece out at the last minute. Writing career——- pfffffphooey!

Gee—the atomic bomb. The news burst on us like a—well—atomic bomb. The thing scares the hell out of me. Everyone is talking about the new era—the era of atomic energy. But I just can't conceive of this thing. I don't understand it and it frightens me. My God, if it can destroy so much, what will happen if there is ever another war? This should be the strongest argument against war. We'll just have to learn to live together. If we don't BAAAAAAANNNNNNGGGGGG.

Dottie Ann

****

TIME & LIFE BUILDING
Rockefeller Center
New York,
Aug. 8, 1945

DARLING DARLING DARLING DARLING DARLING,
I CAN'T BELIEVE IT —CAN'T BELIEVE IT, NO I CAN'T. CONFETTI PAPERS TO YOU. HAPPY V-J DAY. HAPPY HAPPY. USING ALL CAPS BECAUSE I'M SO HAPPY. OH HONEY FACE!!!! Thing is—maybe this isn't V-J Day. Maybe no, maybe yes, but it can't be long now, and then ——-PEACE. MY WELLUS HOME AGAIN. FOR EVER AND EVER AMEN. Everyone here is going absolument crazee.

****

It is now about two hours later than it was when I wrote the first *paragraph. Now my feelings have skidded. War's still almost over. But how long will it be before you can come home?*

Of course Life is going mad. First they had to throw everything out for the atomic bomb. Then the mag was ripped to pieces because of the Russian war declaration. And now, everyone is standing by to make this issue la VICTOIRE. My particular con‐ cern seems to be to feed some research to John Field for a piece on Hirohito. Tonight I'm going on a round of the nightclubs with a fotog to see if we can get some reaction shots. The same old stuff— fat, stupid civilians who didn't do a damn thing for the war effort but make money—celebrating. Well, I didn't do anything, either. Nothing except give up for a while my dearest possession. But as long as it comes back to me in as good condition as it left, I won't mind at all.

The end of the war. It's almost too much to comprehend. I was talking to Lucy Hodges whose desk is next to mine. Her husband is in the Navy—been gone since last November, and she can't seem to grasp it, either. I can't help thinking how people must feel who have lost someone close. God... how awful. I'm so very thankful we've been so fortunate. Please be extra careful from now on because I'm a crazy kind of person, and I think of you falling on banana peels and slipping in the bathtub, and I get scared. If you'll just come back to me everything will be all right. I'll take care of you.

Haven't heard from you in days, but I guess you must be busy chronicling for all time how the brass in the Pacific Theater react‐ ed to the news. Well, take good pictures, but most of all take good care of yourself, because you belong to me. . . .

Dotpot

****

925 Sig Photo Serv Co.
APO 958 c/o PM
San Francisco, Calif.
August 15, 1945

Darling,

Two letters, which you wrote the day Japan started to surrender, arrived today. Both are tributes to your sensitivity and tenderness, and your feeling for this production we call Life. I mean Life in the sense of something to live rather than read.This may sound terribly literary and strained, but the emotion behind it is real. Every letter I get from you increases the feelings I have for you. I always look up from your letters and think . . . "Gee, she's wonderful."

It would be enough if you weren't wonderful. I'd love you anyhow because you'd still be Dot. But you are wonderful, and that means I get a bonus on top of loving you.

Everything is speculation these days. Japan seems to be stalling in making the peace. The war department talks of discharging five million men in the next year. High officials of every sort predict crisises of every sort . . . unemployment, inflation, lack of coordination in reconversion. President Truman charges Congress with providing eight million jobs. Everyone is wondering who will be sent to occupy Japan. Will it be troops from here? Will MacArthur's troops handle it? Both? If so where do we stand—the guys who are here?

I may be home in a month or I may not be home for eighteen months. Kind of puts a crimp in things. People are quiet and don't talk much. Everyone is waiting to see what is going to happen.

Wish I could be there for your birthday. I'm going to try to call. I love you.

Ellis

Teaneck
Aug. 17, 1945

Dearest Ellis,
   Tuesday night I caught the 7 p.m. train from Washington to N.Y. It was awfully hot and I hadn't had much to eat all day because I was busy digging up and interviewing Margaret Truman's friends for a feature I think I told you about.
   Anyway, I went to the dining car right away, and as the train started slowly out of Union Station whistles began to blow. Everything was muffled through the double train windows, but all the trains we passed were blowing off steam. And suddenly I knew it was really V-J Day!
   The waiter smiled broadly and said—"This is it. Boyoboyoboy!" But it was all so subdued. I had a fleeting impulse to scream, but it was only fleeting. I was half-heartedly eating a bad dinner when a red-faced, young-middle aged guy clutching a late edition of the Times-Herald *came in and was seated at my table. He looked very sour and distracted. The waiter and I kept smiling at each other, and we both couldn't bear this grouch. So finally the waiter said, "Well sir, it's all over!" And the guy said "What's over?" So we told him V-J Day was here, officially.*
   What a transition came over that guy. The paper he had been reading said the Japs were stalling, and he was thinking we'd have to drop more atomic bombs.
   *Right away he ordered two scotch and sodas—"one for the young lady." And then he noticed my wedding ring and asked if you were a soldier. He was happy for us, and toasted you and your quick return. He turned out to be what he called an ex-*Time, *Inc. husband. His wife used to be a* Fortune *researcher, but she was busy with two kids now.*
   Ray met me at the station and dumped a hatfull of confetti all over me. He wanted to see what it was like in Times Square. It was about 11:45 p.m. and since there weren't any taxis, we started walk-ing up 7th Ave. from Penn Station.
   New Yorkers had been celebrating all day long, much before the

83

official news. The streets were a mess of paper, confetti, pieces of cloth from the textile district, and people wandering around screaming.

I don't know what happens to me at times like that, but I can't seem to get with it. I feel completely isolated, as if I am standing outside myself looking on at myself and what's going on around me. Therefore everything I do is really play acting and forced and awfully self-conscious. I think Ray was feeling the same way, but he wasn't going to admit it.

So, like characters, we bought horns and blew them like mad and threw confetti around. It was very crazy in Times Square. Like New Year's Eve, only more noisy. I don't think Americans know how to celebrate <u>en masse</u>. Take the French. From the newsreels and all the accounts of their V-E celebration, they sang and laughed and cried spontaneously. But in the middle of Times Square there was a radio sound truck, and a poor fool was gathering a crowd around him pleading with them to sing "God Bless America!"

We walked all the way to the Time/Life Bldg., and I went up to see if there was any mail from you. No one was around. They had already provided for a V-J spread.

And suddenly there it was—the birthday package from you with that very swanky and symbolic perfume inside. <u>Je Reviens</u>! Oh honey soon, please.

Thank you thank you, but I really don't want to be 24. I hate birthdays. I don't want them to catch up with me because there's always a last minute reckoning and calculating to do just before I turn a new age. And I remember all the things I was going to accomplish and never did.

Let's have a baby when you come home. I have a terrific urge for a baby—your baby. God—I think about you and sex and—well I can't write it down. I just think about those things.

Ray and I wound up at Tracy and Jerry's. There were some whacky people there, and we sat around in the garden and talked until 4:30 a.m.

So now I'm on vacation, which will give me much more time to think about you and how much I love you. -Yours . . .

Life Goes On

HOTEL MOORLAND
Gloucester, Massachusetts
Aug. 29, 1945

Darling,
There's an orange, a white, and another orange rocker in front of me. Then a white railing, and beyond that the ocean. For as far as I can see it's ocean, deep blue that somewhere mingles with the haze of the paler blue sky.

This place is terrific, and the best part is that nothing is commercialized. No shootin' galleries or pop stands; no bingo games; just huge orange brown rocks, a sandy beach about a quarter of a mile from here, and the very picturesque town that smells of fishing boats.

Tracy is in a play at the Bass Rocks Theater right across the street. I'm so glad we finally picked up and left Teaneck. It's really difficult because Mom is so rarely well now. But Monday Ray piled the luggage in the trunk, locked the door, and off we drove.

We didn't want to get here for Tracy's opening because she was so unhappy about the play. So we got here Tuesday, and we're being frightfully extravagant and staying in $12 a day rooms. That includes meals, and they're very good. Honest, you should see me yet—fat I'm getting. Already since you left I've gained 5 lbs.

We saw the play last night expecting the very worst. Tracy had shown us the script before she came up here, and it was . . . terrible. The name, "Madame Svengali" should give you a clue. In the play Tracy is married to a dull banker who was married before to a hypnotist who, of course, comes back and tries to get her ex-husband back through all kinds of whacky shenanigans.

The play is impossible, but Tracy looked beautiful, and acted with complete charm and ease and grace.

Boy, if we couldn't write a better play than that . . .!
I miss you and long for you. All my love
Dotpot

TIME & LIFE BUILDING
Rockefeller Center
New York
Sept. 4, 1945

Darling . . .
Back from Gloucester, back at work and feeling miserable. Remember I told you I didn't have any hay fever because I had been taking injections? Well, one day, all the ragweed pollens and all the dust particles had a union meeting to discuss whether they should have a sit-down strike in my nose.

I must say, in all fairness, that a certain minority of particles (dust local 44 I think it was), said that it wouldn't be fair to do it inasmuch as I was the wife of a serviceman. But the majority said the war was over, and that you had been unfair to organized rag-weed because you were always praising my nose, and they voted to have the strike.

So they all got up my nose, and at a given signal from Moe Rags, president of the New York unit, they sat down. And that was the end of me.

My God, I've never had it this bad. All day long I sneeze and sneeze and drip water from my nose, and my eyes itch, and my head pounds, and I can't do a thing.

Right now I have two wet Kleenexes wrapped around my nose which works pretty well. But, of course, this makes everyone laugh except Goody Epstein, who just came over and expressed sympathy for me—even as she gave me a long research assignment on the steel industry!

So, even though I want to, I can't go into a long discussion about the letter you wrote about your postwar plans. It was a terrific letter, and I love you because you're sure of yourself—not in an arrogant or cocky way. And I feel that anything you decide is best and right and what I want to do.

I feel pretty bad now about those silly letters I wrote about wanting to be in the middle of things creative. It's just that being away from you so long, I've had to attach myself to something *(you're right, I need protection), so I allied myself with New York and the people who work here and my family.*

Everyone talks about the new and better magazines, plays, books, newspapers, better everything that'll come out after the war. I guess it's all just a big fraud—a way of compensating for the lack of security that everyone feels as a result of the war.

But I know that all I really want is you. And I want so much to have your babies, and live in your house and make of our lives something beautiful. And I know it doesn't make any difference what you do—whether it's plumbing supplies or play writing.

I have the feeling that we will always be creative. We'll have good music in our home, and we'll read things and discuss them, and I'll say to hell with the Wednesday Afternoon Bridge Club.

Well, we have a lot of discussing to do when you finally, finally come home. I love you very much.

    KEEERRRRCCHHOOOOO!

    peapot

Chapter 9

Beginnings And Endings

Looking back, it's hard to believe I wrote that letter to Ellis on September 4, 1945, in which I said, in essence, "Your home is my home; your people are my people; whither thou goest and whatever you decideth is okay with me." That's because, even though I couldn't wait for Ellis to come home, I was having a blast working for *Life,* and I wanted us to stay in New York. But with the end of the war, everything changed.

For women, there was a mad stampede back to the home. "Rosie the Riveter" threw down her tools and picked up her Mixmaster. WACS and WAVES hung up their uniforms and donned frilly aprons. Scores of smart, capable women who had worked so successfully during the war (including my friend Jean Murkland— bright, funny, talented, and on the staff of *Look Magazine*), left their jobs and the city, and fled to the suburbs to have babies and bake bread.

I did, too. Ellis and I moved to a leafy section of Pittsburgh called Squirrel Hill, and settled on the third floor of his parents' house on Ferree Street. For three weeks.

Maybe it was longer. It seemed longer, but I'm pretty sure that's all it was. We were so happy to be together again, so anxious to start our Real Life, that we didn't really think things through. We were swept up in the "back-to-the-home" hysteria overtaking the nation.

Besides, Ellis had studied for a year at the University of Michigan and two years at the Academy of Dramatic Arts in New

York before he was drafted. He'd been in the Army for five years, and even though servicemen had the opportunity to go back to school for free on the wonderful G.I. Bill, he was anxious to be on his own. He knew that making a living in the Theater was chancy—as was any kind of writing. Plus, his father was doing well in the kitchen cabinet business, and had invited Ellis to join him. I just wanted to be with him and do what he wanted to do. (Or so I thought.)

It made all kinds of sense. (Or so we both thought.) My father-in-law Harry was kind, easy going and generous. He paid Ellis two hundred dollars a week to learn the business which, unfortunately, Harry couldn't teach him. Harry represented manufacturers to contractors whom he had cultivated over the years, and he couldn't simply pass them along to Ellis. They wanted to deal with Harry.

I don't know. Maybe it could have worked. Then again, maybe we didn't want it to work. Ellis really wanted to write, and we missed the excitement of New York and our friends. But there was a deeper reason pulling me back. I knew Mother didn't have long to live, and I needed to be close to her. Ellis' mother had been sick, but she seemed to be better. I had no idea her illness would turn out to be fatal, too.

So, up in our third floor hideaway, I lobbied for us to rethink our plans as we made passionate love—which resulted in my becoming pregnant almost immediately. Ellis was receptive to both ideas: having a baby and leaving Pittsburgh, even though the two things didn't go together all that well. In fact, his parents thought it was foolhardy to start a family with no visible means of support. We had a small bank account from my earnings and his Army pay, but even if we hadn't had that small nest egg, we would have left. Have grown children ever listened to parents' advice?

Early in March 1946, we subleased Scottie Lanahan's fifth floor walk-up, just down the block from the St. Regis Hotel on East 55th Street, for fifty dollars a month. The rent was high, but so was our optimism. Scottie, who was F. Scott and Zelda Fitzgerald's daughter, needed bigger digs. (I didn't really know her. She was a friend of a friend.)

It didn't have a Murphy bed, but it had a Murphy kitchen. You opened doors to what should have been a closet, but inside was a teeny-tiny stove, teeny-tiny sink, and a likewise-sized refrigerator. There was also an ancient bathroom with a toilet that flushed when you pulled a chain which hung from the ceiling. I loved that apartment. The only bad thing was the anti-Semite who lived on the floor below and scrawled nasty things on our mailbox. We caught up with him one day on the fourth floor landing, and I started yelling at him and wanted Ellis to throw him down the stairs. But sensible, calmer Ellis simply glared at the guy, took my arm and led me away. I was disappointed, even though Ellis was right. After all, I was pregnant. He didn't want me in the middle of a brawl. But the bigot got the message, and there were no further incidents.

I tried to get my job back at *Life*, but there were too many returning veterans. However, someone on staff steered me to Joe McCarthy, who had been editor of the Army magazine, *Yank*, and had returned to New York to become the editor of *Cosmopolitan*. We had instant rapport, and he hired me to write two continuing features: "My Luckiest Day"(an as-told-to celebrity piece), and a not very controversial feature called "Both Sides of The Question," which debated such earthshaking controversies as which coast offered better living—East or West.

It was a creative time. We were expecting our baby in November. Ellis was writing a play, which his brother Marc wanted to direct, and his sister-in-law, Meg Mundy, was interested in starring in. Whenever I didn't feel up to writing one of the *Cosmo* features (because I was in our ancient bathroom upchucking), he wrote that, too. He also did some sculpting, and I did some free lance magazine articles. We had a wonderful group of friends, and played endless games of charades, and went to the theater, and ate in our 85-cent Chinese restaurant, and stayed up half the night talking.

But Mother was dying, and everything was filtered through that awful certainty. One of the reasons I wanted to get pregnant so soon after Ell got home was so Mother would be there when the baby was born. The terrible irony is that neither Ellis' mother, Amelia, nor my mother were there when Steven was born on November 20. For years—decades—I've wanted to share my children with my mother. All those times they've worried or scared me or made me deliriously happy and proud.

"Hey, Mom, Steve and John went to the Halloween Fair at Rio Vista as the front and back end of Thunderbolt-the-Wonder-Colt and won first prize! Oh—and Ellyn lost her first tooth yesterday, but we couldn't put it under her pillow because we think she swallowed it!"

No such luck. At least she knew I was pregnant. A few days before she died in June '46, she put her hand on my tummy and felt her grandson move.

My brother Ray was a brick during the last six months of her life. He got a job with Simon and Schuster, the book publishers, and commuted from Teaneck, spending almost all his free time with her. Tracy and I would come from New York just about every other day, but both my brother and sister shielded me from being there at the very end or, in fact, from being aware that the end was as close as it was. I guess it was because I was having a somewhat difficult pregnancy.

I hadn't seen Mother for two or three days around the middle of June. Then, early that Sunday morning, Ray and Tracy showed up at our apartment. I knew without their saying a word that she was gone. Ellis knew, too, and we just—all of us—fell into each other's arms and hugged, and I did that thing I do when something awful happens—retreated within myself and got very silent. I could see that they were upset by my reaction, so I took a big breath and said something dopey, which I also do at overwhelming times.

"Well," I said, "would anyone like some breakfast?"

They looked at each other—Ellis and Ray and Tracy—and then they looked at me. All of us looked perfectly awful, and suddenly we started to laugh. We laughed and laughed hysterically, tears streaming down our faces, helplessly gulping for breath, going off like crazy loons. And then it was over.

But it wasn't over. It has never been over. I still miss my beautiful, vibrant, somewhat mysterious mother who died when she was twelve years younger than I am now.

How does one deal with grief? The older you get, the more experience you have, but it's not the kind of thing one gets to be an expert at. Time, they say. Well, yes, time dulls; time softens the pain; time makes it possible to get on with your life. But time doesn't explain, or answer questions, or fill the void. I envy Orthodox Jews, devout Catholics, born-again Protestants, practicing Eastern Mystics, and anyone else with a sure-fire belief in the Great Beyond, because they know they'll see their loved ones eventually. They'll all be together one day, floating on rose-tinted clouds somewhere Up There. I love the idea. I love movies about it, too. I just don't believe it.

So summer limped on. The baby (who was turned the wrong way), finally righted himself, and I started labor pains in the middle of the night, of course, on November 19.

I was excited and very scared. All my life I'd heard about how horrible childbirth was, how painful, even dangerous. I kept thinking that by the time I got around to having children, the medical community would have improved things. But there I was, about to give birth, and I hadn't heard of any new and improved methods. This was something women did alone in those days. Daddies weren't coaches. There weren't any birthing and breathing La Maze classes. You went to the hospital and your husband could stay with you, but not when you were being prepared or examined, and never (Heaven forbid), when you were finally wheeled into the delivery room.

Poor Ellis. He didn't even get to be alone with me before I made it to the delivery room. Imagine (if you're not too young or haven't seen the reruns on the "E" channel), the birth of Lucy and Ricky Ricardo's baby, Ricky, Jr. Instead of the ever-present neighbors—ditsy Ethel and bumbling Fred—substitute my over-protective brother Ray and my over-dramatic sister Tracy, crowded into the room with Ellis and me, and staying there hour after hour as my labor dragged on.

They meant well. They worried about me. I had just lost my mother. So they hovered and comforted. They harassed the doctor, when he finally showed up, and the nurses, and drove everyone crazy. Especially Ellis. Oh God, how could I have let them do that? When, around nine-thirty that night, the orderlies finally came for me, Ray ran alongside the gurney until the swinging doors of the delivery room closed behind me.

I survived the birth. So did Ellis. So did Ray and Tracy. That was the last time the four of us had a baby, and it says volumes about Ell's patience, self-acceptance, and good humor.

In those days, after giving birth you were encouraged to stay in the hospital almost a week. I think it's a darn good idea. When my daughter had her kids they tossed her out of the hospital practically the same day. Sure it's a natural function, and the medical community has come up with some great new techniques. But to squeeze out of your body what feels like an enormous basketball, and then get up and go home to your other kids, and/or visiting family and friends with a newborn is dumb, not to say tiring, nervous-making, and possibly depressing. Seems to me there should be a compromise between lolling in bed for a week after giving birth, which makes you feel weak and less competent, and the current Pearl Buck method—which is like dropping the kid in a rice paddy, strapping it to your back, and continuing with stoop labor.

But in my day there was an even more quaint custom—hiring a baby nurse to see you over the first two or three weeks at home. Since I didn't know much about babies, I was happy to turn the baby over to the nurse when I got home from the hospital, even though her name bothered me a little.

She called herself "Miss Glorious Lamb" and when she answered the telephone she said, "Peace." Apart from that, she seemed just great with the baby—although she wouldn't let me near him. I figured that was the way it was supposed to be. But the longer she stayed, the more sullen and hostile she was toward Ellis and me, and the more she seemed to be keeping Steve away from us. So I asked her how come she felt like that. It turned out she belonged to an obscure religious sect which did not believe in procreation, and therefore she considered Ellis and me sinful. The baby was okay, she said, because he was as yet innocent. Well, that did it. Exit Miss Glorious Lamb with baggage, enter me as a mother with alarums!

It would have been okay if I'd simply been more relaxed, and hadn't taken the job of Motherhood so seriously. Or if Dr. Spock's revolutionary baby and child care book had been published six months before it was. The books I had read were much more scientific and rigid. Everything was done according to schedule. It was almost biblical.There was a time for feeding and a time for bathing; a time for airing and a time for napping. There wasn't any of this feed him when he's hungry, put him to sleep when he's tired nonsense. But this rigid schedule led to a lot of crying and that led to the Liverwright sisters, two elderly spinsters who shared our apartment building, but not our enthusiasm for our baby.

By this time, we had moved to an elevator building on West 58th Street, and the Liverwright complaints dominated my life so much that I tried to write a short story about it.

The Ladies Upstairs

Elderly unmarried ladies react to infants in one of two ways. Either they like them or they don't. It has become increasingly apparent that the two elderly, unmarried ladies who live directly above us do not like infants. However, I may be 50 percent wrong. In fact I have a sneaking suspicion that one of the Liverwright sisters really loves babies, but her affection is squelched by the other sister.

The reason I suspect this is that my actress sister appeared in a play in summer stock once in which she played a submissive character who was entombed in a vault by her sister with the same dominant characteristics as the older Liverwright sister.

My suspicions were further aroused the other day when I got on the elevator with my baby and the two sisters. The round, sweet-faced sister made cooing noises at the baby and waggled a finger at him.

"Isn't ums a little dear?" she inquired of her

sharp-featured, thin sister.

"No!" said the other, digging her long fingernails into her sister's arm. "He makes entirely too much noise." Thus rebuffed, the sweet-faced one cowered in a corner until we got out at our floor.

Since that time I have never seen the sisters, and I have only heard one of them. For all I know, the sweet-faced one may be entombed in a vault at this very moment.

However, if I said that I have heard one of them, that may be an understatement. My days are punctuated by sharp commands from her. She starts early in the morning when the baby, fresh from a 12-hour sleep, arises at 5:30 a.m., and screams with the sheer joy of being alive in this exciting world. Long before I reach his crib the first order of the day has been bellowed out. "STOP THAT SCREAMING!" screams Miss Liverwright in the hushed stillness of the dawn. Thereafter, throughout the day, a succession of commands follows one another: "STOP THAT HAMMERING! STOP THAT LAUGHING! STOP THAT CRYING! STOP THAT CHILD!"

At first I was indignant. Indignant? I was furious. Livid. I wanted to rush to the window and yell back. "Listen, you old bag, you make more noise than the baby!" (Actually I was going to use much more unladylike phraseology). But after the first rush of anger, I felt very sorry for poor, dear Miss Liverwright. She was, after all, an Old Maid. Perhaps she had had an unhappy love affair in the first flush of youth that had embittered her. Old, alone (except for her sweet-faced sister whom she kept in the vault), the world had passed her by. The playful screaming of the baby must sum up for her all the treasures of life that were beyond recall. . . .

I never finished the story. Steve finally stopped crying so much; the blessed Helen Viney came into our lives to help take care of him; I got pregnant again and went to work briefly; and we moved to Tracy's duplex when she left for Hollywood.

Chapter 10

For Better, For Worse, In Sickness And In Health . . .

From 1947 through 1950, the playground at the end of 57th St. and Sutton Place was a literary salon. Of course, it couldn't hold a candle to Virginia Woolf and her Bloomsbury pals, but we had some great discussions there as we watched our kids playing in the dusty sandbox cantilevered over the East River. And there were some interesting people, too.

Mary and John Cheever and their two kids, Susan and Ben, were regulars. John had been in the Signal Corps Training Film Center in Astoria with Ellis, and when we moved to Tracy's duplex on East 58th Street we were just around the corner from each other. The Cheevers lived on the corner of 59th and First Avenue, and John wrote in one of the windowless maids' rooms in the basement. How he could turn out such magnificent short stories in that gloomy space is hard to believe, but he came up for air once in a while and sometimes wound up in the small playground. I remember him as witty, WASPy, and repressed. But that didn't keep him from enjoying the company of people who were animated, argumentative, and passionate. I know he cared about me, but it was difficult to get to know him . . . well. His wife, Mary, was much more open and easygoing—and probably smarter (I think she thought so, too). Not that John wasn't smart. Mary was simply very, very smart. She was better educated than John, who hadn't finished prep school, and she eventually taught literature at Sarah Lawrence. I learned a lot from her during our playground seminars.

Patsy and Jules Bricken lived in the same apartment building as the Cheevers. (In fact, Julie's family owned the building!) Julie, who became a successful movie producer, and Patsy, who later raised horses in Ireland, were sharp, bright, and good company. But Patsy had this one bad habit—apart from wearing her husband's shoes to the playground. She was so enamored of her kids that she would nag me to do things like smell her two-year-old son Chuggie's breath. I'm sure Chuggie's breath was sweet, but hey, if I were going to smell a kid's breath (highly unlikely), I'd smell my own kid's breath.

Then there were the McKinneys, Phyllis and Duane, who had been actors in the Goodman Theater Company in Chicago. Duane had been a star in several "B" movies (using the name Michael Duane), before his Army service, but after the war he settled for a job as an art director at a small advertising agency. We shared a cottage at Fair Harbor on Fire Island with the McKinneys and their son Phillip in the summer of '49. That was where Duane first did his imitation of a male ballet dancer supporting an egotistic ballerina, which was the funniest improvisation I've ever seen. He was so talented and so frustrated. Maybe that's the reason he suffered a fatal heart attack just a few years later.

We had so many wonderful friends then. Ted and Jean Murkland had moved to Connecticut, and were raising their own vegetables and a flock of kids. Ted, who had been in the Signal Corps with Ell, went into industrial films. Jean went into homemaking with such a sense of ease and good humor it was a delight to visit them and stay the weekend. We'd put the kids to bed and drink martinis, and solve the world's problems. Or complain about them. We were at their home when the House Un-American Activities Committee was grilling the Hollywood Ten. I still remember our sense of outrage and helplessness.

I also remember that Jean was a flirt. She was cute with red hair, green eyes, a turned up nose, and, yes, freckles. But I wasn't crazy about the fact that she came on to Ellis, who was flattered. And I wasn't sure whether she was serious or not. So one weekend when we were there and the kids were in bed, and we were drinking martinis, and she was scrunching up her nose and laughing at Ell's jokes, and batting her eyes and acting like June Allyson in a college house party movie, I began paying special attention to Ted. I've never been a nose-scruncher or eye-batter, but I can look fascinated at what someone is saying, and soulful and even subtly aroused—and I gave Ted my undivided attention. We drank more martinis. Jean raised the flirt decibels, and I matched her nose scrunch for nose scrunch, eye bat for eye bat. The next thing you know, Jean and Ellis were kissing each other, and Ted and I were doing likewise.

Jean cried "uncle" first. I think Ted and I would have gone off to one of the bedrooms, and knowing Ellis, I'm sure he would have gone all the way with Jean. But she called a halt to the whole escapade by making a joke, and reminding us that we were all pretty smashed, and we had better eat dinner before we did something we'd all regret. In hindsight, I'm not so sure I handled that situation as well as I thought I had at the time.

Another couple we caught up with again was Muriel and Stanley Goldman. After Stanley came back from the Aleutians he went into his father-in-law's textile business. It was a much smarter way to support a wife and two children than writing poetry. They were great word-game players and theater-going buddies. I remember the night we saw T.S. Eliot's "The Cocktail Party," and stayed up until three in the morning discussing it. God, the theater was glorious then: Lillian Hellman, Arthur Miller, Eugene O'Neill, Tennessee Williams. I had a visceral feeling when I saw their plays. I don't think I've been as profoundly moved by anything in the theater since that time.

When I was pregnant with our second son we saw Tennessee William's "A Streetcar Named Desire." It was riveting. When the curtain came down, I sat in my seat unable to move. Ellis thought I was having a miscarriage, but I was simply overwhelmed by the power of the writing and acting. (Strangely enough the star of the play, Jessica Tandy, who lived in our neighborhood and whom I passed on Sutton Place many times on my way to the playground, didn't appear the night we saw it. Her standby, Uta Hagen, went on and was brilliant.)

Most of our friends were starting careers in the theater and in the infant television industry as writers, directors, and actors. One of the young women who had been in Ell's class at the Academy of Dramatic Arts, Toni Brown Kimmel, was appearing with Jose Ferrer in *Cyrano* as a pregnant nun. Not that the character of the nun in the play was pregnant—Toni was. As the play's successful run went on, Toni swelled beneath her habit more and more. I can't remember what happened first, the birth of Toni's daughter or the end of the run.

Ellis had been working on his own play, an adaptation of Mary Webb's novel, "Precious Bane." He had spent months on it, finally finishing it sometime in '47. He had been assured by his agent that he had the rights to the novel. Only he didn't. The J. Arthur Rank Film Company owned the rights to the novel. Somehow the William Morris Agency had been horribly negligent. The Agency tried to negotiate with the Rank organization, but it never worked out. It was devastating for Ellis. He had written a magnificent adaptation that had a good chance of being produced, and all he had to show for it was a beautifully written script to demonstrate his talent.

His brother, Marc Daniels, who was going to direct the play, knew how good it was. So when Marc began directing adaptations of Broadway plays on "live" television, he knew he could count on Ellis to write them.

Meanwhile, both Ellis and I were so impressed with the production of our first child, and Steve was so adorable on his first birthday, that we conceived our second son that night. I'm sure of it because exactly nine months later out popped John!

I don't think we ever would have considered a second child at that time if it hadn't been for Helen Viney. She came to work for us shortly after the exit of the baby nurse, Miss Glorious Lamb. They were as different as night and day. Helen was urbane, classy, very pretty, and very independent. She was mostly Black but partly Cherokee, with high cheekbones and bronze coloring. She literally made my day—if she came to work, which she mostly did, although I could never really be sure until she arrived. And then I could relax, and even think about going to work again.

I was still freelancing fluffy magazine pieces for baby magazines like "How Not to Name the Baby." But I yearned to sell the short stories I was writing to serious magazines. About the closest I came was a personally written rejection letter from *The New Yorker*. Encouraged by that, I asked John Cheever if he'd read two other pieces I'd written and tell me what he thought of them. He sent me the following note:

> Dear Dorothy,
> *(I hadn't started using my middle name yet.)*
> I was very glad to read these pieces. I can't say whether or not they are saleable, with any authority, and the word of an agency will be much more valu - able than mine. Such as it is, however, my word is that they are not. The story or character sketch about a woman animated by morbid anxiety will appear to be, I think, if you look back at your own experience, a too-familiar character. Baby-sitters, cooks, janitors, practical nurses and most of the peo - ple who read the Hearst press live wishfully in a world of rape, murder, suicide, fire, and blood. It has become a characteristic as undistinguished as the use of cigarets and to describe a woman in these terms is not enough. You have to determine what the roots of this anxiety are, you have to catch her at a more illuminating moment, you have to make a less arbitrary distinction between her anxiety and the human condition, for you live, after all, in a world where every backfire is, for 60 percent of the popu - lation, a portent of human disaster.
> The story about Little Falls seems to me charming and intensely personal, too personal, I think, to have much general appeal. It is your own business that your childhood was happy and the unwillingness of periodicals to produce what they have commissioned

> is not exceptional. I think these two points weaken, for a general audience, what is for your friends a pleasant story.
>
> I may not be making myself clear, or you may feel that I have misunderstood you; if you have any questions give me a ring, and I hope to see you very soon here, or in the playground or the trolley cars.

Of course, I wanted him to say they were brilliant and he'd personally speak to Harold Ross at *The New Yorker* about them, but I had to admire his candidness.

So I went to work for *See Magazine*. Never heard of it? Don't blame you. I think it lasted one or two years or less. I had taken to reading the classified ads. I was three months pregnant and restless. Helen Viney was showing up regularly to take care of Steve and clean the apartment, so I applied for the job of associate editor, and got it. It was a two-person staff—the editor/publisher and me.

See Magazine was a cheap rip-off of *Life*. Actually, it was mostly soft porn, with sexy pictures of well-developed young women in states of undress incongruously sandwiched between the text of serious articles such as the progress of the Marshall Plan. Thank goodness it was my job to solicit, oversee, and edit the "serious" articles.

I hadn't told the editor I was three months pregnant when I applied for the job, so I could see his puzzlement at my steady weight gain. Finally, it was apparent what my "problem" was, and we had a mutual parting of the ways.

John's birth was a breeze. However, the hospital left more than a little to be desired. I had the same OB-GYN as before. He handled a lot of theater people and showgirls, and his hospital of choice was The Park Avenue, which has long been out of business—and for good reason. I don't think they handled many births. Poor John Harry Marcus developed a raging case of impetigo in what passed for the hospital nursery. When my two sisters-in-law, Meg Mundy Daniels, and Miriam Marcus Cherin, took a look at him (covered with splotches of gentian violet over the impetigo), they didn't know what to say when they came back to my room. Ever the fatuous mother, I waited to hear how adorable he was. It must have been like going backstage after seeing a friend in a really bad play whose acting matches the writing. You say things like: "That was a performance!" Or "What an interesting performance." As I remember it, Miriam and Meg said: "What a baby!" And "Steve's going to have lots of fun with a baby brother."

By this time, Ellis was working on *The Ford Theater*, which preceded *Studio One*, and was the first hour-long drama series on television. Directed by his brother Marc, the show was produced by the Kenyon and Eckhardt Advertising Agency, and managed to get on the air once a month by the skin of its teeth (coincidentally, *Skin of Our Teeth* was one of the Broadway adaptations presented). Those were the days of "live" television when once the cameras started to roll whatever they recorded was broadcast. There was no post-production, no stopping—even if the set fell down, actors forgot lines or props were missing—all of which happened. The cast and crew had to have nerves of steel because show time was a harrowing experience. At the end of a production (having survived all kinds of malfunctions and disasters), Marc would stagger out of the control room drenched in sweat, his face beet red.

I don't know how he and the cast pulled it off, but they did and there were some memorable productions and wonderful performances: Lily Palmer and Frederic March in "Twentieth Century Limited;" Faye Emerson in "Outward Bound;" "Arsenic and Old Lace" with Ruth McDevitt and Jean Adair; Ronald Reagan and Grace Kelly in something I can't remember; and Fay Bainter in "Night Must Fall"—just to name a few.

Ellis teamed with writer Max Wilk on several of the shows, and on others with Norman Lessing, who became a kind of mentor. Norman, an extremely talented dramatist, is a Runyonesque character who loved horse racing. When they were working on a script he'd lure Ellis out to the track claiming he could think better—which wasn't exactly true since they'd wind up having to do "all-nighters" many times.

Max Wilk had been a classmate of our friend Ted Murkland at

the Yale School of Drama. His father was the East Coast head of Warner Brothers' story department, so Max was steeped in the lore of movies and theater. Max, who has written some wonderfully funny and knowledgeable books about the entertainment industry (<u>Don't Raise the Bridge; Lower the River</u>, etc.), was a worrier. A funny worrier. Everyone knows that writing doesn't make for steady employment, and that worried Max. Not that he worried about himself. He worried about his friends. To be specific, he worried about Ted and Ellis. We used to match notes with the Murklands. When he was with them, he'd worry about Ellis and how he was going to support his family. And when he was with us, he'd worry about Ted and how he'd make ends meet.

Ford Theater lasted a couple of seasons, and then Marc and Ellis worked on *Nash Airflyte Theater*, which was a semi-monthly, half-hour, live TV drama.

Life moved along at a busy clip. Exciting things were happening for Tracy in Hollywood, even though her marriage to Jerry was on shaky grounds. She was featured in her first film, "Actors and Sin," a Ben Hecht satire in which she played a sexy assistant to a Hollywood agent (Eddie Albert) who represented a hot, x-rated property written by an eight-year-old (Hecht's daughter, Jenny). It has become a cult classic. I saw it recently at a UCLA Hecht retrospective.

Ray had been involved with several women, none of whom could get him to the altar. After a year or so, he left Simon and Schuster and went to Europe to study on the G.I. Bill, but mostly to have fun—which meant getting involved with even more women.

I had neck surgery four months after John was born to remove a tumor (benign) surrounding my thyroid. And we bought a dog. We had driven to Bucks County to get away from the kids for a weekend. On the way home we passed a farm with a hand-printed sign announcing, "PUPIES [sic] FOR SALE." When we took Muffin, an eight-week-old Brittany Spaniel, to a vet in Manhattan, he asked us how much we'd paid for him. We told him twenty-five dollars.

"You bought twenty-five dollars worth of worms," said the

snobby vet, who didn't think much of our purchase. He never knew that Muffin, who used to "point" when he saw wooden ducks, lived to the ripe old age of eighteen.

During the summer of 1951 we shared a great house on Fire Island with Toni-the-pregnant-nun, her husband Jess Kimmel (who was production manager on Sid Caesar's *Your Show of Shows*), and their two kids, Tina and Peter.

The first day there was almost our last because, in the confusion of getting the kids, luggage, groceries, and supplies from the bay side to the beach side, we lost three-and-a-half- year-old Steve. Pandemonium!

Fire Island is a thin, long strip of land about a mile wide at Ocean Beach. At that time there were about eight or nine streets leading from the bay, where the water was deep, to the beach. Ellis and I took separate streets, and ran back and forth—going crazy with thoughts of Steve falling into the bay, or getting lost in the dunes and seaweed on either side of the small (and at that time isolated), community.

We found him and, of course, it wasn't the last time we were panicked by near disasters involving the children. As long as one is a parent it never stops. Twenty-five years later Ellis and I were awakened in the middle of the night by a call from John in a Guatemalan jail. He'd been picked up on some visa mixup with half a marijuana cigaret in his pocket. (After three days and a $1500 money order he was released.)

Back on Fire Island, it was a glorious summer of endless days on the beach with the kids, cool evenings on the deck drinking a new (for me) concoction of vodka and tonic, and weekend parties. I had only one slight problem—some minor but persistent pains in my tummy.

Ellis kept prodding me to find out the cause of the pain when we got back to New York. When I finally went to the doctor, he took it very seriously indeed. I was put through all sorts of tests, horrible barium x-ray studies of my intestinal tract, and consultations with specialists. I couldn't understand what all the fuss was about, since it only seemed to be a slight cramping and a small

105

amount of rectal bleeding.

My internist, Harry Taub, was a friend who lived in the same apartment building as we had before we moved to the duplex. Harry must have confided to Ellis how serious he thought things were, but he was quite vague with me. One would think I would have guessed it was the Big C—especially after the young and sympathetic associate of the specialist on my case said to me, "It's not necessarily what you think it is." I must have looked so clueless that he didn't pursue the conversation.

I'd always had a lot of confidence in my body. I was athletic, had a lot of energy, and had never been seriously ill. When I went for checkups, I was relaxed, even a little cocky: "You wanna see a healthy specimen, doc? Check it out."

Wow, did that ever change! In late November I was admitted to the hospital for a resection of the colon. They told me the truth—that they found a tumor, which had to be removed. But they didn't tell me the whole truth—that they suspected it was malignant, and that it may have involved the liver. I still felt confident. I previously had a small tumor removed from my neck with no consequences whatever. I fully expected the same with this surgery.

Tracy came in from California. Ray came back from Europe, and Ellis barely left my side. Very early one morning about a week after the first surgery, I woke up to find my friend and internist Harry sitting at the foot of my bed crying. And I still didn't put it together.

The tumor was malignant and had metastasized; the spleen had to be removed, and they weren't sure whether the liver was involved or not. Besides that, the lower intestinal tract hadn't reopened after a week—and if it continued to be closed, the surgeon would have to operate again to try to open it. It didn't open. The second operation, two weeks after the first, wasn't successful. After another week the doctors and surgeons were debating a third operation.

By this time, I didn't much care about anything except seeing my kids who were too young to visit me in the hospital. Friends rallied around, but I didn't want to see them. I glanced at their flowers and cards apathetically—but I did manage to enjoy a long and newsy letter from John Cheever:

Scarborogh, NY
December 20th

> Dear Dorothy,
> Mary met Sylvia Keefe on a crosstown bus a couple of weeks ago and she reported that you had been very sick but Sylvia's reputation as a news-gatherer is so shaky that we didn't believe the story until Ellis called on Sunday and told us how long you had been in the hospital. We were all very sorry to hear it.
> Things are about the same out here as they were when you saw them except that the swimming pool has been drained and everything has been buried in snow and ice. This is the first time that I have ever been responsible for heating a house and I spend a lot of time going around closing windows and turning down the thermostat. Mary is not cooperative. We have an infirm oil-burner that has collapsed twice. A man name Angelo Palumbo comes in and hits it with a stick and this seems to work, although we all dream about the hot radiators on 59th Street. On the first day that it snowed the children were terribly excited at the thought of going out to coast without having to ride an elevator and walk to Central Park but walking home from school yesterday Susie slipped on the ice, skinned her knees and began to brood about the cleared sidewalks on First Avenue. Our pleasures are mixed.
> Mary is, at heart, about the same but there has been a great change in her superficial activities. She sings soprano in the church choir and leads the procession up the aisle to the choir loft. The choir sang <u>The Messiah</u> on Sunday night and everybody went

with their children. It was pleasant, but Mary lost her bag of peppermints during the big chorus and since she was sitting in the front row everyone could see her rooting around in her robes and looking under her chair. Most people thought she was look - ing for her glasses; but I knew better. She has learned how to make a cheese cake and she makes cheese cakes for fund-raising food fairs. I heard her on the telephone, a few mornings ago, saying: "Well Mrs. Newbury, I think that brownies would be more welcome." It seemed a long way from the telephone conversations in town.

Ossining, because it is a service town, a river town, and a prison town, seems wonderfully apart from Westchester and it has, now at Christmas, a fine, lunatic atmosphere that I haven't seen since I left Saratoga. Griffin Hillikers, the one department store has a public address system for broadcasting carols and the one Santa Claus is municipal. He is an unemployed garage mechanic with ill-fitting whiskers and a small bladder. He keeps telling the children that he has to go and feed his reindeer. There is a big cardboard representation of the Nativity on the lawn of the Baptist Church and the streets—which are steep and narrow—are always crowded. Toys and Christmas trees are cheap and plentiful but I have to pay Angelo Palumbo five dol - lars every time he comes in and hits the furnace with his stick and so I never save any money.

Mary and Susie both send you their love. Benjamin—who thinks that he is a cute little dog— has nothing to say.

As ever,
John

Back in the hospital, the doctors asked if I'd like to go home for the holidays—even though I'd have to come back for more surgery if my plumbing continued to malfunction. "Yes," I said.

So, a couple of days before Christmas I went home with a temporary colostomy, tubes, clamps, and enough medical paraphernalia to supply a small clinic. My color was an off shade of green, and my energy quotient was minus zero and counting. I donned my cheerful Mommy face and hoped the kids wouldn't notice. But Steve, who had just turned five, was very sensitive and impressionable, and I don't think he ever got over how scary I must have looked and how close he came to losing me. John, aged three, was so involved with his imaginary friends who lived in his closet, didn't seem too affected.

Some people can't deal with illness. John Cheever was one of them. He came to see me about a week after I got his cheery letter. He tried hard not to look appalled, but for once his feelings were quite evident. He rushed off after the briefest of visits not wanting to "tire me," but plainly wanting very much to get the hell out of there.

How can I describe Ellis at this time without sounding cliche? He was a rock. He was loving, tender, caring, patient, protective, there for me. He nursed me. He suctioned the dreadful colostomy. He allowed me to feel and look awful, letting me know that he loved me anyway, and that green was his favorite color.

The holidays were miserable; I kept waiting for the blockage to open, but the damn thing wouldn't. I sure as Hell didn't want to go back to University Hospital and face another operation, and yet somehow, somewhere deep down I had this Mary Martin cockeyed optimism that things were going to turn out all right. (It's always people like me, who scoff at astrology and mystics and intuitive feelings, who sneak looks at horoscopes, and pay five bucks—at charities, mind you—to have palms read, and act many times on intuition.)

Harry Taub wanted to do another barium study in his office before I checked into the hospital again. And wonder of wonders, there on his cold metallic x-ray table, while the test was under way, the intestinal tract opened! It opened! Like the frozen tundra of the northern straits in Spring, it opened! I didn't have to have a third operation. All I had to do was go home and recuperate. I didn't know that they were still worried about my liver, and that I'd have to keep checking with barium x-rays every six months to see if there were any new polyps or tumors. This was 1952 and a lot of doctors didn't feel ethically bound to tell patients the whole truth, and Harry must have sensed that I really didn't want to know all the details.

Knowing I didn't have to return to the hospital, I recuperated fairly quickly. By the end of January Ellis and I were wrestling with another dilemma. The television industry was growing by leaps and bounds—and it was centered in Hollywood. Marc had already moved there. He was directing a new comedy he hoped might catch on called *I Love Lucy*. He and Meg had divorced, and he was now married to Emily Hosmer Daniels, who had been his assistant director on *Nash Airflyte Theater*, and was now the camera coordinator on the *Lucy* show.

And Tracy was there, driving her agent, her husband Jerry, her drama coach Elsa Schrieber, plus hairdressers, dressmakers, casting directors, writers and producers crazy because of her total inability to be where she was supposed to be when she was supposed to be there. (She was <u>always</u> late. Except when I was sick. Then she was there early in the morning, late at night, whenever she thought I needed her.) Fortunately, her terminal tardiness hadn't kept her from appearing with Bing Crosby, Donald O'Connor and Mitzi Gaynor in a fluffy musical called, "Anything Goes," but she was getting a reputation for being . . . difficult.

So Ellis and I wouldn't be without family on the West Coast, but we pondered whether we should uproot our kids, leave our friends, and move 3500 miles away to an uncertain future in an infant industry that hadn't exactly thrown out the welcome mat for us.

In February we packed up the kids and Muffin-the-dog, boarded the 20th Century Limited, switched to the Super Chief in Chicago, and were on our way to Lotus-land.

Chapter 11

Westward Ho!

I've only crossed the country once by train, and that was when we moved to Hollywood

It's a big country. Very big. After we stayed overnight in Chicago, we boarded the Super Chief, settled into our double roomette, and spent days and nights hurtling through plains, deserts, mountains and prairies. The kids were restless, Muffin was constipated, and Ellis and I were nervous. Were we making the right move? (Ellis didn't even know if I was going to live; I was blithely unaware of that problem).

Elliss' brother Marc met us in Glendale when the Super Chief pulled in. After three days and two nights on the train, we were a sorry bunch. I still hadn't fully recuperated; John was cranky because the barber on the train had accidentally jabbed him while giving him a haircut; Muffin hadn't "gone" since Denver; and Steve had come down with the mumps! Ellis somehow survived the trip, but he was concerned about the impression we were making on his brother, who was putting us up until we found a place of our own.

However, Marc and Emily, his bride of six months, couldn't have been warmer, more hospitable, or more helpful for the first week—maybe the first two weeks. They had a charming cottage on top of Horseshoe Canyon—high in the Hollywood Hills—surrounded by a lovely garden with a great view. But it was a small cottage, not meant for four adults, two small children (one with mumps), and three dogs (they had two boxers). Unfortunately, finding a house took much longer than we thought.

The kids and Muffin were very happy there. Steve got over the mumps and three-year-old John met some new and enthralling imaginary friends in the garden. There was Time Shouter and others named Excerbal, Loud Singer, and the Splosion Fish.

But Marc and Emily left for the set of "I Love Lucy" early in the morning and came home exhausted at night—wanting and needing peace and quiet, which was not possible with two extra adults, two small children, and a fairly large dog.

After five weeks, we finally found a house to rent. Everyone breathed a sigh of relief except John, who said that the Time Shouter wouldn't move into the new house. We promised John we'd let him call the Time Shouter and write to him regularly, so he agreed to leave his magic garden.

Recently, Emily showed me a Guest Book she has kept all these years, and there on the first page is the record of our visit. There's a list of all our names including John's garden friends, and under the column headed "comments" is the following: "We had a lovely weekend."

We rented an ordinary house on the corner of an ordinary street in what we thought was an ordinary section of the valley, Toluca Lake. It was an old two-story house, one room wide, with a pool and a tiny guesthouse. It was more than we wanted to pay, but Mother had left me some money and we decided to use it. We now had enough room to have Helen Viney live with us so we called her in New York and asked her to come. I held my breath until she said ... yes!

Other than the fact that the real estate agent neglected to tell us Toluca Lake was a "restricted community" (one of our new neighbors quizzed Helen about whether we were Jewish), we had a good time in that house. Money was tight. Ellis was having a difficult time finding work, but the living was easy. There wasn't much smog in those days. The weather was great. We had a pool, a badminton court, and wonderful Helen ensconced in the guesthouse to help with the kids and the house.

Since the pool was old and needed professional upkeep (which we couldn't really afford), I hammered a cigar box on the fence surrounding it with a sign that said: "Alms for the pool." Even though we entertained lots of friends and their kids (many of them fellow Easterners), no one took the sign seriously, and the box received only gag donations like Adlai Stevenson buttons.

I checked in with a new doctor, and everything seemed okay that first year. Better than okay since Ellis clicked with a story idea at Universal Studios, and wrote an original screenplay, *Ride Clear of Diablo,* starring Audie Murphy, Dan Duryea, Susan Cabot, and Abbe Lane. A recent catalogue of films calls it "an above average oater." Even so, after finishing it Ellis was out of work again. While he waited for another assignment, he took a job selling Muntz television sets from the trunk of our 1940 DeSoto.

"Mad Man" Muntz was the first of a long line of nutty TV pitchmen who lured clients with a "leader" set costing ninety-nine dollars. He'd give the call-in leads to his salesmen, who then went out to the client's home and sold him/her a much more expensive model. Since this depressed the salesmen a lot (because most of their customers were poor), "Mad Man" devised cheery compulsory sales meetings where gung-ho company songs were sung, and inspirational speeches were given. This added touch of lunacy drove the sales force (mostly out of work actors, directors and writers), to work harder trying to find jobs in the entertainment industry. It certainly worked for Ellis, who left Muntz after meeting Jon Epstein at ZIV Productions, and started writing for TV in earnest.

Meanwhile, I was still writing magazine articles—funny, serious, and mostly unpublished. I had read Simone deBeauvoir's electrifying book, *The Second Sex,* and felt she was speaking directly to and for me. Although I admire Betty Friedan enormously (I met her shortly after *The Feminine Mystique* was published) it was deBeauvoir who really started the modern women's movement.

Anyway, I thought I had a brilliant idea. Since Hollywood was a kind of barometer of our national customs and mores, I wondered how women were regarded in the movie capitol. Were they the first sex, the second sex, or just plain sexy? Were women treated equally in the industry? Did motion pictures reflect male chauvinism? I queried *Vogue Magazine* to see if they'd be interested in an article probing the issue. They were—with no guarantee of publication, and no advance. Undeterred, I set up interviews with several Hollywood luminaries: actors Ann Baxter and Ronald Reagan, writers Edward Anhalt and Ketti Frings. It was 1953. Here are some excerpts from that article:

Are Women The Second Sex In Hollywood?

"*A woman who is successful in this male-dominated industry,*" said Ann Baxter sitting cross-legged in her orange velvet slacks, "*has a tough time. When she arrives for a business conference, she doesn't want to be chased around the desk, but she doesn't want anyone to forget she's a woman either. This handicap of being a woman, which, I suppose, is a feeling of inferiority, is like a knife in her back. And when she's competing with men, she takes it out of her back and sticks it into them!*"

However Miss Baxter feels the problem modern woman faces is not inequality, but liberation.

"*We're so liberated we've bitten off more than we can chew.... There's no longer any stigma on a woman working if she wants to, and her mind is much more alive if she does. She's better for her husband, and her children, unless she's an actress. If I were a man, I'd never marry an actress. Instead of making a good home, she'd be off in darkest Africa making a movie.*

... It's like mitosis. A woman has to split herself two ways and keep the proper balance. If she concentrates too much on career, she won't have time for marriage and children. On the other hand, if she gives up her career for marriage, she's only half a woman. Here we are liberated yet emotionally and

biologically we don't want to be. We still want to be dominated by men, to feel their strength, whether we need it or not. We wanted out so to speak, and we got tossed out. Now the problem is how to get back in."

I left Miss Baxter feeling that she was aware of the problem but without a solution, and went to see writer/producer Edward Anhalt, who feels that the majority of women who reach the top in Hollywood pay a terrible toll in emotional stability.

"You see," he said, "women who are talented are aggressive, and they have to have excessive drive and will to get anywhere in Hollywood. With these characteristics, it follows that they begin to act like men emotionally, sexually, and every other way. Naturally men resent them. They want submissive women; they don't want to be 'taken to Atlantic City.' So you have a great many emotionally upset women out here."

Mr. Anhalt feels that movies reflect society and since, according to him, women occupy a secondary status in this country, he feels that motion pictures mirror this attitude.

"The major objective of the heroine in most movies is to marry for money. Any woman with a career is ridiculed. You've seen the Joan Fontaine picture a thousand times. She wears glasses all through the picture, but in the end she takes them off and goes to bed with Spencer Tracy. It's the old bit— my career or a child. I don't see why she can't have both."

Anhalt was discussing a type of picture that comes off the assembly line in Hollywood, but the subject of woman and her role in society is not always dealt with on a superficial level in films. With this in mind, I went to see Ketti Frings, who wrote the screenplay for one of the most adult films to reach the screen last year, "Come Back Little Sheba." Mrs. Frings feels that the sloppy housewife, Lola, whom Shirley Booth portrayed with such finesse, was a crystallization of the "second sex."

"I think Lola suffers a kind of trauma from terrible boredom. She represents, to me, the anguished cry of all women who yearn to be entertained, to be loved, to have contact with other people. The story exposes the need for communication between husbands and wives. If either could let the other know what he needed, perhaps there would be more cooperation and less of the age-old man vs. woman competitiveness."

... Re male chauvinism in the film industry, Mrs. Frings said, "Movies are controlled by men. There are just a handful of women producers, and I can only think of two women directors. Of course a director has to be a kind of dictator, and maybe that's a talent women lack. As for women screen writers, a lot of them get up to bat, but when it comes to the actual screen credits, they strike out. You have to play a certain game if you're a woman writer. You can't fight on an equal basis with the director or producer because you might endanger his manliness."

But according to Ronald Reagan with whom I chatted next, women can't emasculate men, because society has done that to them already. Looking extremely virile in riding breeches and boots, Mr. Reagan claimed that "the popular fiction shows man to be the second sex, a Dagwood who can't fix a faucet, whose children and especially whose wife is smarter than he."

Reagan saw no prejudice against women in the movie industry or anywhere else for that matter. "If women are getting kicked around," he said, "it's the most lovable kind of kicking." He was amazed that anyone had written a book called "The Second Sex."

"Any first year student of psychology knows that the guy in the saloon who takes one too many and then brags he can lick anybody has a deep-seated inferiority complex," he said. "The author should have realized that if men have made women feel inferior, it was just so much whistling in the dark."

I asked Mr. Reagan if he thought movies relegated women to a secondary role in society. "The only thing movies reflect is the desire for self identification on the part of the audience," he answered. "That's why we have all these action westerns. Men want to identify with the hero riding his horse hell-bent for leather."

I asked if he thought women wanted to see themselves waving goodbye to the hero as he rode off.

"At least they were there at the frontier," he said. "They weren't waving goodbye from the other side of the Missouri River. Women aren't made to feel inferior to men," he continued, "it's all a question of understanding them."

With this paternalistic statement ringing in my ears, I went home and asked myself a question. Just what is the status of woman in Hollywood? To reach stardom, the size and shape of the anatomy appear to be a lot more important than the size and content of the intellect. For women the sheer effort they make to reach the top in this highly competitive, male-dominated industry challenges their self-confidence.

As for non-acting women, the fact that they are pointed out with such pride by men indicates they are exceptions. True, women like veteran screen-writer Sonya Levine, top-flight agent Mae Baker, story editor Eve Ettinger, and lawyer Mabel Walker Willebrant are on an equal footing with men, but I

> *found they are forced to maintain a delicate balance between fulfilling their inalienable artistic rights, and ingratiating themselves with their male col-leagues.*
>
> *So in answer to my self-imposed question: is woman the second sex in Hollywood? I would have to answer—along with Mme. de Beauvoir I'm sure—an emphatic "Oui!"*

Not much has changed in the forty some years since that article was written. For the record, *Vogue* rejected it. They were more interested in what women were wearing than in what they were thinking.

So life went along. Adlai Stevenson got trounced by Eisenhower and we were treated to the McCarthy era. Toluca Lake, our subtly restricted community, had a large right-wing, uptight majority which, along with the alcoholic Wisconsin senator, saw sinister plots hatching all over the place. One day when I picked Steven up from the first grade, he was clutching a flyer in his hand. It was a call to arms from the Rio Vista Dad's Club, urging parents to attend a meeting in which we would learn about COMMUNISTS IN OUR SCHOOL!

Early on, the few of us in the neighborhood who were ardent Stevensonites, or at least anti-McCarthyites had found each other and formed a tiny "cell." Chief among us was Dan Mainwaring, a gifted screenwriter and novelist who had written the original script of *The Invasion of the Body Snatchers*. He had signed a brief in support of the "Hollywood Ten," and was having difficulty getting work as a result. He and his delightful wife Sally, who had been a dancer in George White's "Scandals," lived across the street from us, and we had become good chums in a very short time. Then there was Oliver Haskell, who ran an after-school program for kids called Haskell's Rascals; and the wonderful Robesons, David, whose Grandfather had served in the Civil War, was a writer/musicologist/philosopher, and his activist wife, Naomi.

We gathered at the Dad's Club meeting place—the banquet

room of a popular French restaurant—and sat together, waiting for the Dads to name names and tell us who the "Big Bad Commies" were. The place was overflowing with concerned parents. After all, none of us wanted our kids taught by Russki-loving, card-carrying, Red zealots.

After a routine greeting from the president of the Dads, and the reading of the minutes, the treasurer's report, etc., etc., they finally got to the meat of the evening: "The Report on Communists in Our School." According to them, they had made an investigation of all of the elementary school teachers and staff, and had come up with one name, the assistant librarian who was—gasp—a card-carrying member of the American Civil Liberties Union! There followed a heated discussion about what to do about this traitor among us, with our small unit deliberately overlooked when we raised our hands to speak.

David Robeson, the most civil among us, finally got the chairman's attention, and pointed out that it was customary under Robert's Rules of Order to recognize anyone who wanted to speak. Whereupon I got up and, in a quavering voice (due as much to anger as to fear), said something to the effect that President Eisenhower was a member of the ACLU.

The meeting finally broke up after a resolution recommending the termination of the librarian passed overwhelmingly. Our group retreated to the bar as members of the Dad's Club and their spouses left a wide space between us. Every once in awhile they'd glance at us with real hatred. One young mother said to her husband, "Who let those Communists in?" We truly felt like outsiders that night.

But I got even with them. I started volunteering in the PTA. I became a den mother. Ellis managed a little league team; I wrote and cast the PTA show—and some of these same people were delighted to be a part of it. Mickey Rooney and Judy Garland were right. There's nothing like putting on a show to get people together. I got to know them; they got to know me. And the strange thing is—we found we liked each other, we really liked each other. But I still wouldn't want my sister or brother to marry one of them.

Speaking of my brother and sister, we were together again

because Ray moved to Los Angeles to become a story analyst for Warner Brothers. Tracy's career was flourishing. She starred in *Queen for a Day* with Scott Brady, and in a rootin' tootin' western, *Fort Defiance*, in which she was the only woman in a cast of sixty-five including Dane Clark, Peter Graves, and Ben Johnson. It was shot in the desert in 125-degree heat, and in one sequence she had to endure a wild chase riding in a stagecoach with no front or rear suspension. For some reason her stunt double wasn't used and poor Tracy wound up in the hospital with a strained back. ("If only I'd sued them," said she recently, "I'd be a multi-millionaire today.")

Tracy and I were becoming even closer. I wasn't intimidated by her friends anymore. In fact, her friends became my friends, and vice versa. I accepted her dazzling beauty and persona and developed my own style—a cross between Jo March (as played by Katharine Hepburn) in *Little Women*, and the *Broadcast News* character created by Holly Hunter—at least in my own mind.

Still, I was feeling bored and unfulfilled. I loved being a wife and mother, but I knew there was more to life than writing unpublished articles, buying lamb chops, attending PTA meetings, and being a sounding board for Ellis' story ideas. Oh yes—and undergoing surgeries. Because in the next four years THEY had discovered more polyps (benign) in my colon which required two more operations, which weren't nearly as bad as the original surgeries, and from which I recuperated quickly.

Mostly I felt physically fine; I simply yearned to be involved in something stimulating, fun, challenging!

So I became an actress.

Tracy invented me.

It happened on the Griffith Park public golf course. She knew I was feeling out of sorts, and she also knew I had loved acting in college—plus I was a whiz at playing charades. She decided I should join an acting group, change my name, and borrow some of her East Coast acting credits to get an agent.

I hardly protested—even though it was outrageous and I was scared to death. But it sounded like a hell of a lot of fun and it was certainly challenging.

We decided I should use my middle name, Ann (which I've kept from that time on), and use the surname Spencer, which had a certain serendipity with her adopted name, Tracy.

So, just like that, Ann Spencer, actress, was born.

Chapter 12

I'm Ready For My Close-up, Mr. De Mille, Are You?

Tracy knew Richard Boone, an excellent character actor who starred in several TV series (*Medic, Have Gun Will Travel*), and who, in the mid-fifties, rented space over the Brentwood Market and formed an acting workshop with a group of colleagues. Most of the group were from New York, had theater backgrounds, and wanted a place to work at their profession between jobs in television and movies.

Then there was me. My last theatrical outing had been a scene from *The Front Page*, done as a lark with a couple of fellow copy boys from the *New York Daily News* for the John Golden Auditions in 1943! Actually, we were semi-finalists, but nothing much came of it except a questionnaire from Republic Pictures asking if I could ride a horse. I eagerly responded "YES!" but I never heard another word from them.

Nevertheless, Tracy was determined I should join Dick's group. So she called him and told him about her talented sister, Ann Spencer, who had done this and that in stock and whatever on the subway circuit in New York (her own lesser credits), and had just moved to the West Coast, and was looking for a place to work. Dick was very cordial and invited me to join the group.

It was a dedicated and serious group of actors. Beside Boone, I only remember a few of them: James Whitmore, Lamont Johnson, Maxine Cooper, Warren Stevens, Gene Reynolds and someone who became a good friend, Mary Gregory. I think Mary knew I was playing at acting, but she never let on. We lived close to each other, so I would drive her out to Brentwood every week—especially since she was pregnant.

One night, I was terribly excited when I picked her up because we were going to do a scene from *The Mad Woman of Chaillot*, my first "work" before the group. Mary didn't think she should go. She thought she might be experiencing the onset of labor. According to her, I had a semi-fit.

"You can't have your baby now," she says I said. "What about tradition? What about 'The show must go on?'"

Good sport that she was, Mary went to class. We did the scene. I drove her home, and two hours later she went to the hospital and delivered a baby girl.

The only other production I remember working on in that class was Ibsen's *Peer Gynt,* an opus I never understood, which was okay since I had a non-speaking role frolicking as a peasant with Gene Reynolds. Gene had been a Muntz TV salesman with Ellis, which propelled him into a distinguished career as a producer/director. (Among other TV shows, he was the producer of M*A*S*H). At this writing, he is president of the Directors Guild of America.

Class was okay, but I was anxious to get a real job. Tracy tried to tell me I needed to work on the basics: motivation, imagery, energy and all the rest. She encouraged me to attend a class she was taking with Michael Chekhov, who had been head of the Moscow Art Theater for gosh sakes, and a fascinating actor himself. But I was restless. Sink or swim, I thought. Fish or cut bait. Either you've got it or you don't. I was ready to play anything: Medea, Anna Karenina, Blanche Dubois!

My debut was a little less auspicious. It was a walk-on (actually a run-on), in an hour-long anthology on NBC, which I got through nepotism. My brother-in-law Marc was the director and he was kind enough to cast me. I was an extra, a reporter in a horde of other media types, in a scene in which we ran after some celebrity or other. There were a lot of other extras on the show. One of them was Boris Sagal (*Married with Children* Katie Sagal's Dad), who became a talented director. We rehearsed for three days. That is to say we sat around the set, and I listened to them talk about how awful their agents were, and how they all had just finished leads in an independent movie, and how the stars of the show we were working on couldn't act their way out of a paper bag. I loved every minute of it, and acted more bored and more incredulous at playing an extra than any of them.

There was nowhere to go but up. In my next part I spoke! True it was only one line, but to me it was as exciting as the transition from silent movies to talkies. Spencer speaks—almost as momentous as the post World War II publicity about Clark Gable being back and Greer Garson getting him. The line I spoke, "They found the body near Greenbrier Trestle," has become a rallying cry in our family. It stands for—discovery! The solving of mysteries! The ongoing challenge of life!

I don't think I was ever serious about acting, but I was having an awful lot of fun running around town trying to get jobs, having professional pictures taken, and working every long once in a while. Meanwhile, Ellis was trying to establish himself as a writer in an increasingly large and more competitive pool of television writers who were crossing over from features and Broadway.

He wanted me home. He wanted me there for him, cheerleading him on, taking care of the house and the kids. There was also the question of my health—I'd had a couple more colon resections—which took a much bigger toll on him than on me, since I still wasn't aware that I had had cancer, and that it might still be lurking. We had a few rocky scenes when tensions would bubble to the surface, and we'd blow up at each other. The only time there was violence, I caused it, pummeling Ellis and ripping his shirt off. But our arguments were usually brief and low key, and we both spent a lot of time saying, "I'm sorry" and making up. I always liked that part.

But there was also the pressure of money. Or lack of it. Mother had left me a sizable amount for those times, but we had spent it on summers at Fire Island, renting the house-with-pool in Toluca Lake, and paying for the services of wonderful Helen Viney. Now it was up to Ellis to keep us afloat.

I'm Ready For My Close-up, Mr. De Mille, Are You?

We had to find a more modest house to buy for practically nothing down, and for which Ellis could get a G.I. mortgage. We could have bought the Toluca Lake house for $18,000 (hard to believe these days), but our friend and neighbor Dan Mainwaring said the foundation was rotten. Besides, it was a little steep for us. We finally found a house in Studio City less than two miles away and in the same school district, so that the kids wouldn't be uprooted. The house was definitely more modest, only two bedrooms and one bath—no pool, badminton court, guesthouse, but charming. It was an old stucco Spanish-style house with a red tile roof, and a living-room with a tall, beamed ceiling. It cost $13,250. We needed three thousand for a down payment, which we borrowed from Ell's Dad and one of my Uncles.

And we had to say goodbye to Helen Viney, who was anxious to be on her way since James Mason and his wife wanted her to work for them.

With a much smaller monthly outlay, Ellis was able to relax and devote his time to writing instead of worrying. His credits were piling up: *Mr. District Attorney, Science Fiction Theater, I Led Three Lives, December Bride, Ellery Queen, Highway Patrol,* and many more. In fact, he was so relaxed he began writing small parts with me in mind, and then he'd lobby the producer to give me a shot. And many times the producer, more often than not a friend of ours, would offer me the part. Small parts, but as everyone knows, there are no small parts, only small actors.

Except that I was and have always been small, and the parts, though varied, stayed small. I played a farmwoman who was being held hostage by the bad guy in the next to last scene in *Highway Patrol*. Pursued by Broderick Crawford, the villain would crash through the back window and I'd get to say, "He went that way, officer. There's a shed out back!" "Ten-four, ma'am," Crawford would say on the run. That was it.

Then there was the memorable night I invited friends over to watch an episode of *I Led Three Lives* that Ellis had written and I had a small part in. We gathered in the living-room in front of the television set, drinks and *hors d'oeuvres* in hand, as the show began. I was in the first scene playing the part of a German Communist, who was welcoming Philbrick (Richard Carlson) into our cell, one that was about to blow up a US army installation.

"Thees vay," I said in a fake German accent. "Kuminzee!"

Well, the guests broke up. They laughed, roared, did everything short of slapping their knees. I was so awful that Ellis and I laughed, too. Maybe I just wasn't cut out to play a German Communist. I certainly couldn't blame my performance on the writing, which was excellent. Could it have been the direction? I don't think so.

I did do some reasonably professional work. I spent two delicious summers at the Laguna Playhouse appearing in *Time Out for Ginger,* and two forgettable original plays, which I've... forgotten. We rented a house on the beach. Ellis commuted on the weekends, and Steve and John had a great time being watched over by one of Ray's lovely girl friends, Sandra Johnston. What a great way to spend the summer—swimming in the ocean, sun bathing and picnicking on the beach all day, and then performing in a real live theater at night.

The following two winters I appeared at the Sombrero Playhouse in Phoenix, Arizona. I even got good notices, which said I was believable and quite moving as Natalie Landauer, the German-Jewish student of Christopher Isherwood in "I Am a Camera." The stars of the play were Joanne Dru, who was wonderful as Sally Bowles, and her husband John Ireland, equally good as Isherwood.

The Sombrero Playhouse was a winter stock company that recycled Broadway hits. Richard Charleton ran it with Ann Lee and among the staff were two women steeped in theatrical tradition who had traveled with the Lunts—Alfred and Lynn Fontaine, for years. One ran the box office and the other, Charva Chester, was the stage manager. They were the ultimate professionals.

"Five minutes to curtain, Miss Spencer," Charva would call out as she knocked on my dressing room door. I felt I was an actress at those times. The assistant stage manager the year I did *Camera* was a young man named Mark Heron, who later married Judy Garland.

Before my entrance, he would adjust my hat at just the right rakish angle, and I'd step out on stage feeling like Julie Harris!

The next year I did *The Seventh Season* with Leo Fuchs, and stayed on to appear with Edward Everett Horton in *The White Sheep of the Family*. That was quite an experience. We had rehearsed the play all week without Horton, who was off doing the same show with another cast in Florida. The day before the opening, he flew into Phoenix, swooped down on our dress rehearsal, and changed EVERYTHING! He grabbed each actor one at a time (including Laura LaPlante, the silent movie star who was in the cast), and ran us around the stage changing our entrances and exits, our moves, line readings—everything! He was wonderful and crazy. The show was a great success.

One of the biggest boosters and backers of the Sombrero was a jolly, large, very wealthy woman who went to every opening, laughed loud and long at the comedies, and shed many a tear at the dramas. Her husband was equally enthusiastic, not about the plays, but about the actresses. He was lurking outside my motel room late one night when I returned after a performance, lurched at me, and began to grope. He was quite drunk, so I was able to push him away, get my door open and slam it shut in his face. Luckily he didn't try it again.

Besides that, going to Phoenix the two or three times that I did was a treat. It meant leaving Ellis and the kids for two weeks, but by this time Steve was ten and John was eight and Irma Wilson came to our house every day to keep things running smoothly. Irma was very different from Helen Viney, much more traditional and old fashioned. And wise, and warm, and caring. But she would never separate the laundry, which made most of our clothes come out in shades of puce and mauve. Ellis called it "color by Irma Wilson." She was also the only person I know who got a traffic ticket for driving on the L.A. freeway too slowly.

After a stint in Phoenix I'd come back to Hollywood clutching my notices—if they were good—hoping to get better roles in TV. But the parts continued to be small, and I found sitting around a set for hours and hours waiting to work a bloody bore.

Then one day, I went to my internist, Dr. Robert Kositcheck, for the results of the latest barium x-rays. THEY had found yet another polyp in my colon, and I needed another abdominal surgery—the fifth!

"Wait a minute," I said. "Isn't this getting a little redundant? What's going on here? How come I keep growing these things? Isn't there some other way beside surgery? How about diet? How about eating nothing but sweet potatoes or kelp or tofu?"

Kositcheck lowered the boom.

"Don't you realize what you had?" he asked me. Obviously I didn't.

"Cancer," said he. "That's why we have to keep checking, and that's why we have to get rid of these things as soon as they appear."

I don't know what else he said that late afternoon. All I remember is that I was going to die. Cancer. I was thirty-six years old, and I was going to die.

The doctor's office was in Beverly Hills. I had to drive over Laurel Canyon to get to Studio City. There's a magnificent vista stretching to the San Gabriel Mountains as you cross Mulholland Drive and start down the canyon into the valley. It was a smogless day. The sun was setting. I had never seen a more beautiful sight. But I wasn't going to see it much longer. I wasn't going to see my kids grow up, either. No grandchildren, no golden anniversary . . . no Ellis.

I don't know how I got through dinner that night or waited until the kids went to bed, but once I was alone with Ellis all my panic and terror spilled out. He was wonderful, but even his strength and love couldn't erase the truth. I had cancer. I was going to die.

Dr. David Rosenbloom, the surgeon, told me that was not necessarily true. That the two previous surgeries I'd had since arriving in Los Angeles had not shown any malignancy. It had only been the original polyp that had been cancerous. He also explained that if I kept on developing polyps in the colon, it was possible the doctors could miss one, which could become malignant. His advice was that my colon had to go.

I'm Ready For My Close-up, Mr. De Mille, Are You?

First of all, I wasn't reassured that would be the end of the cancer, and secondly—no colon? I knew what that meant. I'd had a temporary colostomy back in New York. I didn't want to spend the rest of my life (however short it might be), with one of those dreadful bags hanging out of me.

My old pattern went to work as I tried to deal with what was happening by not dealing with it. I blocked my feelings. I became physically hyper—roller skating, playing ball, riding bikes with the kids, acting as though everything was normal. But kids know, certainly husbands know, and my brother and sister knew, too. And finally. . . finally I knew I had to exhale, to open up, to let my feelings out—the fear, the anxiety, the anger—everything that was bottled up inside me.

I had one illuminating experience with a far-out psychologist who got me to deal (at least that one time), with my father's suicide. It was such an overwhelming experience that I never went back to him. But I was seeing another unconventional doctor, Louis Druckman, who practiced group therapy. Ellis, Tracy, and Ray were in different groups, and we'd all meet once a week and have a ball doing psycho dramas—which I never took seriously, which is the way I usually deal with serious things.

Dr. Druckman also conducted private sessions, and I began to see him twice a week just to test the water.

I also made arrangements for the surgery. Dr. Rosenbloom assured me I would not have to have a colostomy. He could remove the colon without having to resort to that.

The operation was scheduled for early summer, and I sailed through it. It was a combination of things: the support of Ellis and my brother and sister, the skill of Dr. Rosenbloom, the ministrations of Dr. Druckman (who made me feel worthy and unafraid—temporarily, at least), my competitive nature—don't you dare knock me off yet, and luck.

In three weeks, I was swimming in the ocean. In four weeks, I was sitting in the doctor's office for a post-surgical checkup, and read an article in a news magazine in which the survival rate of cancer patients was discussed. It said you were considered a survivor if you lasted five years. I panicked. I had already survived more than five years since the initial cancer. Did that mean I could die next year and still be considered a survivor?

Even though Dr. Rosenbloom was reassuring, he, like most doctors, did not want to be pinned down absolutely. Or at least that's the way I interpreted what he said when I asked him what the article meant. What he said was, "You're fine; don't read articles."

Why shouldn't I read articles? Was there something even more scary I might learn? Does "you're fine" mean I'm fine for now, but that only lasts a limited time—like a warranty?

Back to Druckman. That's what I should have done, but I didn't. Instead I worried. And hid it. And got an idea. I'd always wanted another child. If I told the doctor I wanted to get pregnant, he'd have to tell me the absolute truth about my condition. I was either truly okay, or there were still doubts. So, the next time I saw Dr. Rosenbloom, I told him about wanting another baby. I think he was getting a little upset with me—Mrs. "Don't Take Yes for an Answer."

"Why do you want another child?" he asked. ""You already have two children; you've just turned thirty-seven; you've just had major surgery."

I persisted. So he shook his head, let out a sigh, and said "Be my guest."

The next step was to discuss it with Ellis. But I was afraid. I knew he'd think it was a dumb idea—if not for health reasons, then because it would be starting all over with an infant when the boys were just getting to be independent.

I didn't want Ellis to know my reasoning—that if there were any doubts about my condition, the doctors wouldn't let me conceive. I didn't want to burden him with the fact that I was still afraid. Plus, I did want another baby, even though Steve and John were almost adolescents.

So I chickened out and didn't tell Ellis. Instead I threw away my diaphragm.

In a couple of months I was pregnant.

Chapter 13

Miracle On Camellia Avenue

Since we were going to have another child, we needed more space. Ellis and I looked for a house with at least three bedrooms that we liked—and more important that we could afford—but everything was either too old and needed work, or too new and made out of stucco that glittered. So we decided to add on to our existing house on Camellia Avenue. Mistake!

We had a deep lot with several fruit trees in the back, which absolutely delighted me—except when the fruit ripened. When that happened, it was like the pot of porridge in the fairy tale that went on cooking and cooking and boiling over because no one could remember the magic word that would stop it. Suddenly, we'd be inundated with tons of ripe peaches, plums, and apricots—and everyone else in the neighborhood would be, too, so you couldn't give them away, or eat them all, or 'put them up' in preserves unless your name was Smucker. So I didn't mind too much that the trees would have to be removed to make way for the addition. Or that the ugly two-story garage had to come down to make way for a carport.

An architect friend of ours, Teddy Grensbach, who later became architect to the stars, drew up the plans (which he labeled Ann 'n Ell's Lanai for some reason known only to him). We were all set to begin after Ellis chose what appeared to be a reliable construction company. Wrong!

I imagined a crew of strong, bronzed, young carpenters swarming over our house and grounds, so I was totally unprepared for the lone, aged man who showed up to do the work. And that was only the beginning. In the middle, after the back end of the house had been ripped open, the construction company went bankrupt! There we were with a tarp separating our bedroom from the back yard, and the rainy season commencing.

I had never seen Ellis so mad. Apoplectic. Luckily he had taken out a completion bond, and even though it took four times as long as it should have, what with hiring lawyers and threatening to sue, the addition was finally completed.

Meanwhile, life in our lean-to was almost normal. We even went to the theater one night, but halfway through the play Ellis had to rush me to the hospital because I started having severe abdominal pains. I was terrified I was going to lose the baby, but I didn't. It was an intestinal blockage due to scar tissue from all the surgeries—probably exacerbated by the pregnancy. After they got that horrible abdominal tube up my nose, down my throat, and into the intestine to decompress it, I was okay. I stayed overnight in the hospital just to make sure, and the next morning I felt fine. I had the feeling that Ellis wasn't so fine, though. I had put him through a bad time, but after that night the pregnancy thrived.

Which is more than I can say for my acting career. It simply dissolved by mutual consent between the Industry and me. Although I did make a farewell appearance in the Walter Reed Junior High School PTA Show of 1959, singing a Noel Coward song with original lyrics: "Bewitched, Bothered and . . . Pregnant, Am I!"

Shirley Henry and I had a lot of fun writing that show. She was wonderfully talented, witty, bright, a great friend. And she was a professional. She wrote special material for nightclub acts, especially for the MacCreas—Gordon and Sheila.

My best friend at that time was Rhea Wiseman. Both she and Shirley had daughters in the same class as Steve. Rhea was an absolute delight. She was somewhat older, and during the war had an important job as second-in-command of the rubber industry in Akron, Ohio. After the war she was absolutely content to be a wife and mother. I don't think she was ever restless or bored. Then again, maybe she was but never let on. But it puzzled me that this brilliant, capable, accomplished woman with a master's degree in psychology from Columbia, who had done such important work, seemed totally content to dabble a bit in volunteer politics, and look after her husband and daughter.

Sometimes I envied Rhea because I couldn't settle down like that. Freud was right when he asked, "what do women want?" Or at least what do <u>some</u> women want? There I was with two great kids, a wonderful husband and a baby on the way—and I wanted more. What a spoiled brat. I loved being with Rhea, and talking to her about anything and everything the way best friends do. I loved having lunch with her, going to Club 22 for Democratic Women with her; swimming in her pool, talking about books, kids, husbands, whatever, but I continued to feel restless.

I tried painting. Virginia Taylor, the mother of one of the Cub Scouts in my den was a gifted painter, so I took a class with her. But I was too competitive to enjoy it because everyone seemed to be more talented. Especially a woman named Rita. Virginia said Rita was a natural primitive and she wouldn't touch her work—it was that exciting. I thought Rita's paintings were awful. Every portrait looked like a Yeshiva student. I don't have anything against Yeshiva students, but when she turned black bongo drummers, American Indians, and delicate old ladies into Yeshiva students, something was out of kilter.

Then someone mentioned a playwriting class at USC. It sounded interesting. I was gliding along smoothly in my pregnancy. Ellis was writing for more prestigious television shows. The boys were doing well in school, and Irma Wilson had started separating the laundry so that our underwear was Rinso White again. So I enrolled in the class, figuring I could always drop it if it didn't work out.

Marvin Barowski taught the class. He had worked in the theater, written screenplays, taught at USC and UCLA, and was not only charming and cultured, but a gifted teacher. I fell in love with the class, the medium, and Marvin. He was so knowledgeable about the theater, so urbane—a true Renaissance man whose lectures were witty, practical, and inspiring.

I couldn't wait to get to class, and began writing a one-act comedy almost immediately. Then I got bogged down with exposition and plot, and happened on a *Theater Arts Monthly* article by Jean Kerr, which addressed this very subject. Said she—not only should you write about something you know (Marvin had said this, too), but if you're writing a comedy, you have to make the exposition funny.

I tossed out the one-act and started over again. With Marvin's encouragement, I poured my heart and soul into a three-act comedy called *A Woman's Place*. It was somewhat autobiographical, about a woman with a hard-working husband and two cute sons, who yearns to be more than a wife and mother. She writes a play on the kitchen table—which has a chance of being produced on Broadway, but only if she goes to New York for an indefinite period of time to work with a collaborator who happens to be her former lover. She's torn between her husband and kids who need her, and a promising career that beckons.

It was a good play. Marvin Barowski thought so. I wanted Ellis to think so, too. I didn't want to feel guilty about the time I'd spent writing it, the way I had felt guilty pursuing my ephemeral acting career. So I breathlessly handed him the completed script one night—and the first thing he did was sharpen several pencils before starting to read it. And then he made notes, starting on page one.

I know he was trying to be helpful. After all, he was a professional writer with dozens of writing credits by this time. But I didn't want that kind of meticulous criticism. I wanted him to read it and look at me, awestruck. I wanted him to tell me it was wonderful, terrific, and that old standby, marvelous! But that wasn't Ellis. He never did like the third act.

I finished the play by the end of the course in June. Less than a week later, one of the best ideas I had ever had came to term. On the fourth of July 1959, Ellyn Tracy Marcus was born! It was the easiest birth of all. Two labor pains, and out she popped, my beautiful baby girl. And what a symbolic date. Independence Day. I was free from fear at last.

Ellis and I were ecstatic. So were Steve and John. So were Ray and Tracy.

Miracle On Camellia Avenue

We brought our baby home. The addition to our house was complete. We had even added a pool out back. I forgot about my play. I wasn't restless anymore. June Cleaver, the Beaver's mom, became my role model. I was content being the Happy Housewife, even though I began to bore all our friends. I remember one dinner party in particular at writer Henry Sharpe and his witty wife Jean's house. We arrived a little late because I had to nurse Ellyn before we left. I sat down in the midst of the Sharpes' bright, thirty-something guests and launched into a cute baby anecdote. Suddenly, as if on cue (and it probably <u>was</u> rehearsed since Henry wrote comedy), everyone got up and left me sitting on the sofa alone. Point taken. I was even boring myself.

So I went back to my Selectrix (I had finally mastered the electric typewriter), and began writing again—after giving my play to friends who knew actresses who might be interested in it, hoping to get it produced. While I waited, I wrote short pieces about the kids. I still like one of them from that period:

Should Mothers Have Brains?

My sons think I'm dumb. Oh, they love me enough, but lately I've noticed a growing condescension in their attitude towards me. Once they thought I was Mrs. Answer Lady. Now they ask me fewer and fewer questions, and those they do are much more practical like "Where's my catcher's mitt?"

Sociologists have been wondering lately whether woman is the second sex. I'm beginning to feel that this is not an academic question in our house. To be more precise, there is a definite feeling of male superiority here, and the thing that rankles is that it is an attitude I have carefully cultivated over the years.

I am merely reaping what I sowed when the boys were young, and their egos were tender and malleable. In those days, the most respected word in childcare was 'permissive,' and the id was thought

135

to be delicate and easily damaged. But the pendulum has swung back, and now the idea is to be less permissive so that youngsters will learn to adjust to the realities of life. Realities such as women are smart, too.

Now they tell me. Who was in charge a decade ago when they had me doing everything in my power to assure that the two large-size boys who sit at the dinner table today have a decided psychological advantage over me? I, who nurtured their egos as carefully as I fed their bodies, find myself being admired more for my cooking than my intellect!

Does my husband do anything to counteract this falsehood? Au contraire. He sits at the head of the table, a David Susskind-like moderator of our nightly symposiums, which masquerade as dinner conversation. Steve is Dr. Teller, John is Dr. Oppenheim, and I'm Billie Burke!

Why can't I be Madam Curie or at least Margaret Chase Smith? I'm as up on current trends as the next layman, and even though science has never been my cup of tea, I read Werner Von Braun in This Week, and I can hold up my end of the conversation. But no, we have to persist in this silly game, which I helped to create, that mother is a nice lady but not too bright.

For example, we'll be having a delightful discussion about rocket thrust and I'll be sitting there arranging some exciting facts I've gleaned from Time Magazine, when one of them will upset my whole thought process by asking a ridiculously simple question. Cherubic John, sipping chocolate milk through a straw will turn to me and ask:

"Do you know what holds the milk in this straw?" Suddenly the three of them are all looking at me the way we look at our one-year-old.

Obviously this type of question should be treated with amused scorn. But what do I do? I stick to the script, and barely refraining from crinkling my nose, ask fatuously, "No, dear, what does hold the milk in the straw?"

"Air pressure," John answers with a look of incredulity and pity.

I'll never forget the night they found out I didn't know what makes the front doorbell ring. We were engaged in a discussion of the electron mobilities in gasses as applied to thermal equilibrium, when one of them said that something was as simple as the electric buzzer.

"What's so simple about that?" I asked. The three faces turned toward me again. Right away I should have told Steven to eat his cauliflower. Instead, I had to sit through an oversimplified lec-ture on alternating currents and magnets geared to the kindergarten level.

Madison Avenue would be proud of the image I have projected, and even though I try to break away from it now and then, it continues to haunt me. Just last week, inspired by the recent political debates between Kennedy and Nixon on television, I made a renewed effort. When I was asked point-blank by one of my sons to explain the Pythagorean Theory, I did-n't hesitate a moment.

"I'm glad you asked me that question," I answered staring levelly into his eyes two inches above my own.

"Let me make it perfectly clear. Let me set the record straight once and for all on my views on this important theory. I think we should all be aware in these times of the Pythagorean Theory — one of the truly great theories of this or any era—although as a theory there are those who do not accept it, and I want to state here and now that they have every right to their opinions. But this reminds me of something I've been wanting to ask you. How come your room is such a mess?"

Was he impressed by this candid answer? Not at all. In fact, no matter how brilliant I might appear, it wouldn't make any difference to either of them. It is simply too late. If I wanted to create a different image, I should have thought about it down through the years as I deliberately let them trounce me in every game of chance, skill, or intellect merely to build up their egos.

For who but I, feigning ineptitude, let their pudgy little hands jump four of my pieces on the checkerboard? And who was always stuck for answers to riddles so amusingly easy as what do you call a truck that carries cows? Who taught them how to keep score in tennis, and then got beat the first set? Who showed them the chess moves one day and proceeded to lose the queen on the fourth move?

The pattern was set a long time ago. Billie Burke I wanted to be, and Billie Burke I remain. I can only hope that when some Radcliffe girls get their hands on my sons they will be kind.

As for me, I have been blessed with another baby, and therefore another chance. This time I am determined to start out on the right foot. Already I am building better block structures, and my finger paintings, in all honesty, are far more creative. The only problem is the new baby is a girl!

Erma Bombeck had nothing to fear from me since I didn't sell that piece, either.

But something very exciting did happen at this time. Sheree North, who had just starred in *The Lieutenant Wore Skirts*, and was under contract to Twentieth Century/Fox, agreed to try-out my play,

A Woman's Place, at The Sombrero Playhouse in Phoenix. Richard Charleton, the owner/producer at The Sombrero called from Arizona and the plans were firmed up.

I was ecstatic. It would go from Phoenix to Broadway. Watch out Jean Kerr—here I come!

Chapter 14

Broadway Unbound

I didn't make it to Phoenix. Late in the afternoon, the day before I was to leave for rehearsals, Richard Charleton (who will forever live in infamy), called to say he was canceling the production. He was sorry. He was terribly embarrassed. I had his deepest apologies, but the playhouse had only been involved in revivals of Broadway hits. He had never mounted an original play, and he simply got cold feet. Cold feet! I was numb all over. Crushed.

It was getting dark outside. It had begun to rain. It never rains in California, in spite of what Cole Porter said about its being cold and damp. I grabbed an umbrella and left the house. Other than illnesses and deaths in the family I had never been as miserable in my life. I walked around the block in the wet and gloomy night. No one walks anywhere in Los Angeles, even on a bright, sunny day. I was desolate and letting it all hang out. I stopped on the corner of Aqua Vista (apt name), and Valley Spring Lane, and watched the rain reflected in the street light, remembering that time on my sled in the park in Little Falls. And I promised myself that I would never ever let anything that didn't have to do with the health and well being of my family get to me like that again. Which might not have been such a good idea because that's exactly what I've always done, and this promise only reinforced the way I've put a wall between me and my feelings since my father's death.

Soon after that self-pitying, depressing walk in the rain, Tracy rode to my rescue.

Tracy had formed a workshop of actors, writers, and directors at the Desilu Playhouse on the Paramount lot. Getting these three talented groups together was unique on the West Coast but, along with other professionals including Ray Bradbury, she did a number of staged readings, scenes, and seminars. So, when she offered to do a workshop production of my play, she pulled me out of the doldrums. By this time she was separated from Jerry, and her current boyfriend, Jack Doner, directed and played the husband. Gene Roddenberry's wife, Majel Barrett (who was Nurse Christine Chapel in the original *Star Trek*), played Amy, the restless housewife-turned-playwright. There were some other wonderful people in the cast: character actress Peggy Rae, and doughty Barbara Morrison (who had played the Madam in *From Here to Eternity*).

It ran for two weeks, and I was there for every performance. God it was fun! Not only that, it got some good reviews, and convinced Ellis' agent, Gordon Molson, that I was serious about writing, and he offered to represent me.

My first pitch session was for a sitcom starring three chimpanzees. I guess you could call it high-concept. One thing you couldn't call it was high class. But, hey, it was a network prime-time comedy, and I would have done almost anything to get a chance to write an episode for it, though I wasn't quite prepared for what Ezra Stone, the producer had in mind. The series was called *The Hathaways*. Besides the chimps, it starred Peggy Cass and Jack Westin, playing a childless couple raising the chimps as their kids. My brilliant idea was that one of the chimps has to have her tonsils out, and the crazy, mad, wonderful romp that ensues.

Ezra saw the possibilities and said I could have the assignment, <u>but only if Ellis would write it with me!</u> Was this rampant chauvinism, or simply his fear of taking chances with a new TV writer? Whatever it was, Ellis agreed. I swallowed my pride, and we had an absolute ball writing *"Say Ahhhh."* Every morning I'd drive to his office, which was over Manny Dwork's tailor shop on Santa Monica Boulevard, and we'd dazzle each other with our wit and humor. It was a breeze, a piece of cake, such a high that we found ourselves making love on the desk!

Ezra liked the script, too, so we pitched a couple of other stories, and he gave us two more assignments.

The second script wasn't quite as much fun. It was still exhilarating for me, but Ellis and I were beginning to have "creative differences." Then Ell was asked to testify before Senator Thomas Dodd's committee on TV violence (same old, same old—this was 1961), and we decided I should finish the script on my own and he'd "go over" it when he got back. So I went blithely on, enjoying my independence, and marveling at my comic talents.

When Ellis got back from Washington a few days later, I picked him up at the airport. On the way back to the office, he told me about his harrowing experience in our nation's capitol. Seems one of the committee members, Sen. McClelland of Mississippi, had asked a few of the Hollywood witnesses, including Ellis, to drop by his office for a chat and a drink. Ell got there a little late. The booze was flowing, and the Senator was reminiscing in his heavy southern drawl about his days on the bench in rural Mississippi. While Ellis was helping himself to refreshments, he thought he heard the Senator describe someone in his story as a "Jew-boy." He couldn't believe it. Forcing down his anger, he joined the group around the Senator's desk just as the word came out again, "Jew-boy!'" McClelland was talking about one of his cases, but Ellis was too upset to pay attention.

"I couldn't sleep that night," Ellis said. He knew he had to do something, say something, but what?

The next morning, they met in McClelland's office before the committee hearing got under way. Ellis, heart pounding, was determined to challenge the Senator.

"And damned if he didn't use the ugly description again," reported Ellis, "only this time I was able to translate what the senator was actually saying. It wasn't Jew-boy; it was jur-or!"

We were laughing about the story when we reached the office, and then I handed Ell the finished script I'd written while he was away. Again with the sharpened pencils and the notes starting on page one. The collaboration wasn't working.

By the time we got around to our third script, we were not only not making love on the desk; we were barely speaking to each other. It was either the marriage or the writing partnership. A no brainer. Somehow we finished the script, and didn't collaborate again for almost twenty years. But our marriage flourished.

We celebrated our seventeenth anniversary that year, and we were giddy with happiness. Here we were practically middle-aged with an adorable baby daughter and two bright teen-aged sons. Ell's career was on a roll. He was in demand, writing for better shows, and I had just signed a deal for multiple episodes of *Please Don't Eat the Daisies.*

We had dinner in a *faux* English tavern called "The King's Arms" in Toluca Lake, and got smashed on Brandy Alexanders, which we ordered for old time's sake. Ellis presented me with a Manny Dwork sideline specialty: trashy, hand-painted underwear. I still have it—red satin panties with a hand-painted Oscar and the legend: "For seventeen years of outstanding performance in the field of entertainment."

In the parking lot, Ellis took a swing at a man he said had been flirting with me throughout dinner. He missed, but they both fell down anyway. It was a memorable evening.

And a memorable couple of years. It was Camelot. For Kennedy, who was in the White House, too. It seemed as though all was right with the world. The Civil Rights Movement was getting under way. Young people were asking what they could do for their country, and signing up for the Peace Corps. Of course, there was also the Bay of Pigs fiasco, and the escalation of the "military advisers" role in Vietnam, but good things seemed to outweigh the bad. I was healthy, and began to trust my body again. We were both working, and we had a lot of stimulating friends.

There was brilliant Bruce Geller, who created *Mission Impossible,* and his charming, beautiful wife, Ginny; *Star Trek* creator Gene Roddenberry and Majel (my erstwhile leading lady); big, gentle, vastly talented Sam Rolfe, who gave us *Have Gun Will Travel* and *The Man from U.N.C.L.E;* his wife, Hilda (who was—and is—scrappy and argumentative and very, very bright); and

Christopher Knopf, an enduring friend and extremely gifted writer, and his then wife, Bette, sane, centered, and a marvelous hostess. Chris, several years younger than Ellis, had the tiniest office over Manny's tailor shop. It was so small Chris tacked up a sign on the door: "ELEVATOR." Chris feels that Ellis helped him get started on his successful career, acting as his mentor along with the resident writer/guru, Walter Newman.

We were all enjoying the good life—and then came November 23, 1963, Kennedy's assassination. Almost everyone alive at the time has a searing memory of that terrible day. I was watching four-year-old Ellyn and her friend, Mara, splashing in the pool as I tried to come up with a story for *Lassie*. I heard the bulletin on a portable radio, and I had one of my typical no reaction reactions. The awful news was confirmed. I heard it. I believed it, but it didn't register. I didn't feel a thing.

I got the kids out of the pool, left them with Irma, and drove to Rhea's house. She was a wreck, tremendously emotional, shocked, devastated. When was it going to hit me? I still wasn't feeling anything.

I suggested we get out of the house and we drove out through Malibu Canyon, turning off on Stunt Road before we reached the coast. Rhea was in tears. I was steady as a rock as I negotiated the hazardous twists and turns on this old movie location road where they used to film Buster Keaton and Harold Lloyd car chases.

In fact, it didn't hit me until about the third day of national mourning, when Ellis and I were watching the funeral ceremonies in the rotunda of the Capitol on television. John-John saluting, and Carolyn and Jackie touching the catafalque. That did it.

How distant it all seems now. Even the speculation about what might have been or what might never have happened if Kennedy had gone on to a second term: the bloody escalation in Vietnam, the riots and protests—Nixon!

Eventually the classical music and news documentaries gave way to commercial television, and life went back to normal—almost. I went back to writing stories for Timmy and his dog *Lassie*; Mark and his pet bear *Gentle Ben*; and Uncle Spiffy and his nutty campers at *Camp Runamuck*. In the mid-sixties, Ellis and I switched agents, signing with Robert Eisenbach, who continued to represent me for the next twenty-five years.

Bob gave my play to Paul Monash, who was producing *Peyton Place,* the extremely popular nighttime soap based on Grace Metoulious' naughty novel of the same name. Even though my play wasn't racy or sexy, I was hired, and joined a talented group of staff writers working in a Hansel and Gretel-type building on the 20th Century Fox lot.

There weren't any reserved parking spaces for writers in front of the building. There never are. Years later, when I was serving on a negotiating committee for the Writers' Guild during a bitter strike, I brought the subject up. Big Hollywood Mogul Lou Wasserman, sitting on the other side of the table representing management, pounced on my request as one more example of the pesky, frivolous demands of writers.

Back on the Fox lot, I parked in Frank Sinatra's space for as long as I could get away with it. The job was great fun. Sort of like the days I'd read about when Dorothy Parker, Hemingway, F. Scott Fitzgerald, and Faulkner were selling their souls writing for the movies. We had a writer's table in the commissary, too, and endless bull sessions in each other's offices, practical jokes galore, intramural romances (I just flirted—nothing serious), and lots of money for not much work.

The way we perpetuated that was slightly outrageous. The writers would meet with Story Editors Del Reisman and Nina Laemmle about once a week. After a pleasant social hour of drinking coffee and sharing gossip, we'd have a general discussion about the story. Then Del and Nina would write outlines, and assign two writers to each half-hour episode. The trick was to get your assignment from Nina Laemmle, a bright and attractive Englishwoman who loved to discuss literature, art, music, the theater, cultural mores—anything and everything under the sun. I could spend an entire day with Nina (with time out for lunch off the lot), supposedly discussing the half an episode I was assigned to write—when there was hardly any need for that, since she had already worked out all of the problems in her outline.

145

I joined the staff just after Mia Farrow left the show wearing her precious locket—which was supposed to show up on someone else at a future date under very mysterious conditions. I can't remember if it did or not. But a lot of excitement left the show with Mia's departure, and to generate another love interest for Ryan O'Neal, Leigh Taylor-Young was added to the cast. It worked, too. About the second week she was on the show she and Ryan disappeared for several days, finally showing up—married!

Also to generate interest and excitement, a black family moved to Peyton Place to integrate the all-white cast. Of course, Percy Rodriquez wasn't just any middle-class black man. He was a neurosurgeon. Ruby Dee played his wife. Glynn Turman was their son. What a cast! And what a waste. Because after Percy saved Ryan O'Neal's life, and after Ruby chitchatted with Dorothy Malone about recipes, and after Glynn talked school athletics with Chris Connelly—there wasn't anything for them to do. Meanwhile, I was having a blast, and feeling guilty making so much money for so little effort. So I wrote a memo to Paul Monash stating the obvious—that we had segregated the black family, and there should be more stories for them.

Paul took the memo very seriously. He hired Ossie Davis as a consultant on the show. Not only that, but he held me up to the rest of the writing staff for having the best interests of the show at heart. You can imagine how popular that made me with my buddies, although I think they forgave me in time.

After five years on the air, going from twice a week to three times and back to two, Peyton Place finally ran out of steam—or should I say steamy stories. The last ten weeks a very young writer, Ken Hartman, joined the staff. But even his fresh and wonderful talent couldn't stop the inevitable. It's always sad when a show folds. It's like a graduation. You've had good times and bad; done some good work and some not so good; met and made friends with people with whom you'll never have quite the same relationship.

Meanwhile, Ellis, who had written scores of television shows by this time (including *Streets of San Francisco, Ben Casey, Mission Impossible*), got tired of facing the blank page, and accepted a job offer from his pal Perry Lafferty, who was head of programming at CBS, and became a network executive producer. This meant he had to switch sides, and become one of "Them," a network "Suit," the Enemy. Because he was unique, knowing first hand what it meant to create, write, and produce a television show, he was one of the "good guys" at the network. I've never met anyone who knew him in that capacity who didn't find him reasonable, helpful, cooperative, a pleasure to work with. He was, simply, being Ellis.

The kids were growing up. Ellyn was ready for school, so I looked for one that had a full time kindergarten program, not the two-hour-and-twenty-minute public school program. I found one close to our home in the un-chic section of the San Fernando Valley—unaware that Oakwood was the private school of choice for the offspring of Hollywood's elite. So for the next several years, Ellyn had stars like Joanne Woodward and Paul Newman dropping their kids off for sleepovers (along with their pet snakes). They were awfully nice, too, not the snakes, the people.

Steve and John had started in the public schools, and by this time were in North Hollywood High School. (I think Cher was a year or two ahead of Steve but Steve, being Steve, doesn't remember her.)

Our two sons were the best of friends, discovering Ayn Rand together, and joining the organization her disciple Nathaniel Branden founded. As a bad practical joke, they, along with some of their buddies, told the Mormons who came to proselytize one day that they were interested in joining the crusade, and actually went out and did God knows what door-to-door. They also were fans of Esperanto, the universal language they thought would bring lasting peace to the world. Too bad it didn't. They were definitely bright, and probably a little nerdy. Not athletic, although Steve made the B tennis team. And fell in love. With the daughter of one of my best friends. They were in the 11th grade, and it lasted through graduation and into college.

Brother Ray, that Lothario, had still not made any emotional commitments, going from one terrific woman to another, each one becoming my potential sister-in-law and good friend. He almost did the same thing with jobs, going up and down the coast of California writing promotional pamphlets and books touting the business, cultural, and residential opportunities of various communities; working as a writer's agent for a while, and finally going back to UCLA to complete courses for his bachelor's degree, which he never got due to WWII. After that, he enrolled at Cal State Northridge for a graduate degree in English, and got a job teaching at UC Santa Barbara—where he quickly became one of the most popular English instructors. He also became the faculty advisor/chaperone of one of the campus sororities.

And what of sister Tracy? She was still being Tracy in a Tracy kind of way—gorgeous and glamorous, stopping heads at studio commissaries—where she might be lunching with Cary Grant, having tumultuous affairs (not with Cary, but with the wrong men), and driving producers and directors nuts by never being on time on the set, and always being in the midst of some emotional trauma.

I worried a lot about Tracy because her life was so stressed, so wildly dramatic and chaotic. I consulted my wise friend Rhea, who told me there was nothing I could do about it. Sort of like that AA thing—accept what you can't change. Rhea said it was the life Trace had chosen, and if she wanted to change, she would. Hmmm.

I was freelancing once again after *Peyton Place* was canceled. For a while I teamed up with Joe Bonaduce, one of the most opinionated men I've ever known. We wrote several episodes of *The Debbie Reynolds Show*. Joe made my collaboration with Ellis on *The Hathaways* seem absolutely idyllic. I mean, Joe was impossible: domineering, manipulative, politically right-wing, a chauvinist caricature—and yet he made me laugh. He'd arrive at my house in his van (Italian opera blasting from his cassette player), and we'd spend hours arguing about politics, Vietnam, the women's movement, child care—anything and everything to keep from getting down to work. But we turned out some pretty funny scripts, especially a two-parter called *To and From Russia With Love*, a rip-off of *Ninotchka*. (If you're going to steal, steal from the best!) My health was good, and I felt fine.

But something was happening to Steve. He was growing quiet, withdrawn, and uncommunicative. He and Ruth seemed very much in love their senior year in high school, but I knew he was terribly troubled by something that he couldn't, or wouldn't, talk about. He shunned his other friends, even John. Still, he managed to become a National Merit Scholar, pull down a perfect SAT math score, and was accepted at Cal Tech in Pasadena. Ruth enrolled in Pomona College, and they continued to see each other as often as they could.

John, sensitive and creative (attributes not always appreciated by classmates), wrote poetry, read a lot, and studied Japanese at UCLA while still in high school. He graduated a year and a half after Steve, and went to Berkeley. Ellyn was only six and never really got to know her brothers until years later (and then only John), because they traveled such different roads from that time on.

It wasn't until John and Steve were in college that Ellis and I finally found our dream house at the end of a cul-de-sac in Sherman Oaks. It wasn't that impressive from the outside, but once we went through the front door we both knew this was "it." There were glass sliding doors along two sides of a spacious living-room, dining room, and family area that looked out on lovely lawns, shrubbery and a pool. There were two wings—one of them had a large space for an office that had been the previous owner's art studio. We bought it and moved.

Irma Wilson, sage, friend, and caretaker, took one look at the much larger new house, and decided to retire. So we bestowed Steve's Falcon on her, and bid her a fond farewell. We hired a new live-in housekeeper and moved. Anna Reina had never worked as a housekeeper. She was a lovely, shy, well-educated young kindergarten teacher who had just arrived from El Salvador. She quickly became a member of the family.

Shortly after our move, at the insistence of Jacqueline Smith (a daytime executive at CBS who was a friend and colleague of Ell's), I met the wunderkind, Fred Silverman, daytime programming chief. It was a poolside luncheon meeting at the Beverly Hills Hotel, and I couldn't help thinking I had stumbled into a real-life chapter of Budd Shulberg's *What Makes Sammy Run*.

Chapter 15

Tune In Tomorrow

It was the summer of '69. Vietnam was tearing the country apart. Nixon was president, but he wouldn't have been if Bobby Kennedy hadn't been assassinated. Riots broke out at the Democratic convention in Chicago the summer before, which helped sink Hubert Humphrey's campaign. In between freelance assignments, I was "Another Mother for Peace"—which was about as effective as Nixon promising to end the war.

Steve and John registered for the draft with student deferments for the time being. Steve, still troubled and non-communicative, broke up with Ruth, and transferred to the University of Wisconsin. He said it was because Cal-Tech was an impossible pressure cooker, but I think it was because he wanted to put distance between all of us. I began to realize what was bothering him when my doctor told me Steve had been calling with questions about my original malignancy, and the hereditary nature of colon cancer. In fact, the doctor was upset with Steve's incessant calls, and said Steve needed help. But how do you help someone who refuses to be helped? Steve was obviously suffering from a terrible phobia, but refused therapy. Refused, even, to acknowledge the problem. His way of coping was to do medical research on his own—and to get as far away as possible from Ellis and me, both physically and emotionally.

John was at Berkeley at the height of the Haight/Ashbury scene: making love not war, smoking grass, nibbling on psychedelic mushrooms, sitting in, getting tear-gassed, and ignoring classes. After one particularly nasty anti-war confrontation between the students and the National Guard, I wrote a letter to then Governor Ron Reagan wondering if there might be a better way to deal with student unrest than tear gassing them by helicopter. I got a form letter back saying, in essence, no. I think Ron would have enjoyed nuking them.

One night, John was swept up in a mass arrest, and spent a night in jail. Shortly after that, he left Berkeley for an odyssey that took him across the country, to Canada, Mexico, and eventually the foothills of the Pyrenees in France.

Meanwhile, back at the ranch house in June of '69, I was preparing to lunch poolside at the Beverly Hills Hotel with Freddie Silverman. I entered the hotel the back way through the tennis courts, and there, by God, was Katharine Hepburn rallying with the pro—a good sign.

I was escorted to Freddie's cabana where Jackie Smith was waiting for me, her finger to her lips since Fred was on the phone. He stayed on the phone for the next twenty minutes, his back to me, while Jackie and I looked at the menu and whispered to each other.

Freddie was furious with whoever was on the other end of the line in New York. He still hadn't turned around, but from the rear he looked a little pudgy, young, and very mad.

"Goddamn it, the announcement was supposed to be in the f—- trades yesterday, and it isn't even there today! I'm not gonna stand for it. You tell PR to get their asses in gear or else!"

The tirade went on for another several minutes.

When he finally got off the phone, he couldn't have been sweeter, gentler, or more charming. He looked even younger from the front. He was in his late twenties, and had been head of top-rated CBS' daytime programming for several years. The reason he was mad, he explained to me, was that an announcement was supposed to have been made the day before that he had been named a vice-president of the network. (It came through the next day).

Jackie had done some great groundwork with Freddie, telling him about my *Peyton Place* experience, and what a good writer I was. Fred didn't seem particularly impressed, or maybe his mind was still on the missing announcement, because he abruptly went back to the phone to complain to someone else, leaving me to munch on my Cobb salad. (I hate having important meetings during meals. First, you have to decide whether or not to have a drink. If you do, will it muddle your thought process? If you don't, will you appear stuffy? Then you have to decide what to eat, all the time trying to make light and witty chatter. Then your food comes, and you have to cut and chew, and things get stuck in your teeth, and other things fall in your lap—or worse. So, long ago, I came up with Cobb salad for lunch. It's practically predigested and you can eat it and make conversation at the same time.)

Jackie thought I'd be a natural to write soap opera, even though I didn't know beans about the medium. I never watched them, and, like people who don't, I felt superior to those who do. So I didn't care that the meeting hadn't gone well. In fact, I was sure I'd never hear from Fred again. But a couple of days later, Ellis called from his office at CBS to tell me he had invited Fred to dinner (at Fred's request), and was that okay?

Fred arrived with a four-foot stack of scripts from the soap *Love is a Many Splendored Thing*.

"How soon can you start as head writer?" he asked.

"Wait a minute . . . wait a minute," I said. "I don't even know what a head writer does."

" Write the show," said Freddie,

" What else?" I asked.

" That means the bible, three or four long-term interconnecting stories, the daily outlines, and the scripts—with the help of a couple of staff writers. So when can you start?"

"But . . . but . . ." I sputtered, ""I don't know the show or the characters or the stories."

"So read the scripts," he said pointing at the stack, which had grown another six or so feet.

I don't know what made him think I could do it. All I know is that I was scared to death, and made all kinds of excuses to delay things. Ellis and I had planned a trip to Europe in July during his vacation. I still had to finish a script for *The Debbie Reynolds Show*. Fred wouldn't take no for an answer, and insisted that my agent could negotiate the deal while we were in Europe. I looked at Ellis. He told me it was my call, and went off to make Freddie's favorite drink, a Tanqueray gin martini. Fred followed him to the bar. I followed Fred. We all drank martinis, and suddenly headwriting a show I'd never seen in a medium I'd never worked in didn't seem like such a big deal.

But we still went to Europe that summer. Ellyn went to Camp Roosevelt and had a blast. John was hired to drive a truck from San Francisco to New York with a buddy, who misjudged a tunnel in New Jersey and sheared the top off. Needless to say, they weren't paid for the job. Steve, meanwhile, was researching hereditary cancers in the U. of Wisconsin's medical library, and teaching sailing on the side.

After meandering through the English countryside, eating our way through France, and motoring down the coast of Italy, Ellis and I reached Rome—where a cable was waiting for me. Bob Eisenbach had negotiated a terrific deal for me to be head writer of *Love is a Many Splendored Thing* (at an unheard of salary), starting the week after our return home.

We were at the Rome Hilton, at the fancy bar high atop the city, celebrating my good fortune. And I had a panic attack. The bottom fell out of my stomach. My heart began to pound.

I was taking over a show I hadn't watched, in a medium I'd never worked in, and I'd be responsible for delivering five scripts a week!

"This is crazy," I said to Ellis. "I can't do this. Why did I let this happen? What am I going to do?" By this time I was hyperventilating.

"What's the worst thing that can happen to you?" Ellis asked, calm as a cucumber. And then he answered his own question. "You'll get fired."

It was the perfect thing to say. It put everything in perspective. Were our sons getting shot up in Vietnam? Had a grizzly snuck into Ellyn's tent at camp?

With our new prosperity, we hired Arturo, a private tour guide, for the rest of our trip through Italy—and came home in time for Tracy to throw a great birthday party for me.

I remember that party very well. I felt so blessed. My health was good. I had a wonderful, high paying, challenging new job, and here was Tracy with this lavish catered affair around her pool with all our friends. In a moment of wild abandon (after a lot of champagne), I semi-stripped and jumped into the pool! Ellis was the next one in, and then seven or eight guests followed. One of the guests (who hadn't jumped in) was an amateur astrologer. She made a bet that the people who jumped were either Leos or Pisces. Except for me she was wrong, but it was a wonderful party.

And then reality set in. For the next four years I was embroiled in the trials and tribulations of San Francisco's Donnellys, Elliotts and Chernaks, churning out almost a thousand scripts for LIAMST (short for *Love is a Many Splendored Thing*).

Of course I didn't do it alone. I gathered a terrific writing staff, albeit an eclectic one. First, I persuaded Ken Hartman, the gifted young writer from the last days of *Peyton Place* to join me. Then I called Ray at UC Santa Barbara, and ruined what would have been a brilliant career in academe by telling him he could make more money in a month writing LIAMST than he could in a year teaching English. Rounding out the staff was my ex-brother-in-law, Jerry Adelman, aloof, intellectual, but a very good writer and still a close, personal friend. None of us had written for daytime dramas (a more dignified term by which "soaps" are known), maybe that's why our stuff was so good.

Or maybe it was because the production team and the cast were so talented. Or a combination of both, because we really clicked and turned out a good show.

People are always asking soap writers how we come up with "all those stories." We borrow from all over: everything we've read, everything we've seen in the movies or on stage (David Jacobs, creator of *Dallas* and *Knot's Landing,* calls this "paying homage to"), everything we've lived through, the life stories of every person we've known. Same as Charles Dickens and Jane

Austen, who would have been terrific soap writers.

On LIAMST we did a full range of stories dealing with contemporary themes: Vietnam and its divisiveness (we made a popular character a draft resister), drugs, wife-beating, rape, artistic freedom, racism, politics. You name it, we wrote it—including a story about blind, pregnant Iris who had an irreversible, malignant brain tumor. Sure we were soapy. I wrote it, and then sat in front of the TV set with tears streaming down my face when pregnant Iris climbed the ladder to place the angel on top of the Christmas tree, and realized her sight was finally gone! I was moved in spite of the fact that the episode (which was taped "live") ended with an agonizing close-up of Judson Laire the distinguished actor who played Iris' father saying, "You mean my daughter is not only blind and pregnant, but can't see!?"

How could we save Iris, played by radiantly beautiful Leslie Charleson—who had changed her mind about leaving the show, and had signed on for another year? Brother Ray came up with the answer; laser surgery up her nose! A total figment of his imagination, which has since become a commonly used surgical technique.

LIAMST was produced in New York at the CBS Studios on West 57th Street, but we wrote it in Los Angeles. That meant frequent trips to New York for story conferences, which didn't bother me a bit. In fact, I loved those trips.

In those days, networks didn't have scores of channels and cable systems competing for audiences. There was no downsizing, no penny pinching. Talent was treated lavishly. First-class air travel, limos to and from the airport, suites at the Plaza. And in New York there was John Conboy.

Conboy was the executive producer of LIAMST, and the most elegant man I've ever known. But nervous. He was very young, and very tall, and very determined to make it big in the Industry. He was also a perfectionist, who drove everyone crazy except me, because I was still operating under Ellis' dictum: what was the worst thing that could happen to me? Getting fired? Hey, I was good—as good at head writing as Conboy was at running the show—so we not only liked each other, we respected each other. And we had a lot of fun. Conboy took me to the best restaurants in town. He could even get a table at Elaine's. When we went to the theater, we had house seats. But the pace was tiring, so in the morning (before our semi-hysterical story conferences with Freddie Silverman and the ad agency people), I'd pop a Dexymil, and John, anxious about the meeting, would take a Valium. That way our metabolisms would meet in the middle.

I had several interesting encounters with fellow passengers during my frequent flights to New York. On one trip, Katharine Hepburn and George Cukor were sitting across the aisle. Stewardesses were kneeling at her feet as though she were royalty, which, of course, she was. I felt like genuflecting myself, although I'm not the type, but I was anxious to talk to her because Ellis had written a wonderful screenplay, and Hepburn would have been perfect for the lead.

So I screwed up my courage and approached her.

"Excuse me," I said self-consciously, "I really hate intruding, but my husband has written a screenplay . . ." and I gave her a clumsy but brief description of the Marya Mannes novel *THEY*, which he had adapted. She could have easily brushed me off, but she was terrific. She told me to drop it by her Murray Hill brownstone.

"The kitchen door is usually unlocked. Just stick it inside."

She not only read the script quickly, she sent Ellis a personal letter complimenting him, and suggesting it would make a better play than a movie. She signed the letter "K. Hep." What class!

Another time, I sat next to an important-looking, WASPy CEO. When he found out what I did, he asked why so many of "my people" were in the entertainment industry. I'm not sure why his question ticked me off, but I guess it was his fatuous stereotyping of Jews the way I'm sure he assumed all black people had rhythm. I wasn't about to give him a pat answer.

"Maybe it's because 'my people' were excluded from so many other industries, and professions, and schools, and clubs for so many generations by 'your people,'" I said more than a little defensively. But I wasn't about to let it go at that.

"Maybe it's because 'my people' were outsiders for so long we've developed more sensitivity, and that's made us more philosophical, more inclined to self doubt, to looking within, to wondering what life is all about. Or maybe it's simply that 'my people' are more talented and creative than 'your people.'"

I don't think the CEO wanted an in-depth response. He spent the rest of the flight buried behind his *Wall Street Journal*, while I tried to figure out how to save blind, pregnant, fatally ill Iris.

The other fun thing about my frequent trips to New York was seeing our old friends Muriel and Stanley Goldman, and Martha and Tom Keehn. The Goldmans had a fabulous apartment on Park Avenue, and two bright and precocious daughters. Meanwhile, Martha and Tom had been doing good works in India, Africa and the Far East for various organizations such as The Rockefeller Foundation, and World Education, and managing to have six children along the way. In between far-flung postings, they'd stay at the old homestead on Tennis Place in Forest Hills.

I remember one time when we all met at the Oyster Bar at the Plaza on the eve of one of their assignments to some far-flung post in the Third World. Stanley was convinced that mild-mannered Tom was really an undercover agent for the CIA, and tried to get him to admit it. But, through many martinis and dozens of oysters, Tom remained steadfast and denied it.

Meanwhile, the story conferences continued—sometimes in Sherman Oaks in my home office, or around the pool. Freddie and Mike Filerman were joined by a very talented newcomer in their department, Phillip Mandelker, who was shy, and funny, and talented, and didn't say much, and who went on to become an innovative and talented producer of excellent TV movies before his untimely death.

By this time Anna, our novice housekeeper, had gone back to teaching in El Salvador (or so we thought), and Gabriela Flores took her place. Gabriela's specialty for lunch during the many story conferences was tuna-fish salad. Exclusively.

In fact, Gabriela served tuna fish salad to the visiting CBS executives so often that Mike Filerman took revenge. The next time I arrived in New York and was registering at the Plaza Hotel, I was handed a very large, official CBS package. Thinking it contained important documents that needed immediate attention, I opened it at the registration desk—finding a can of tuna and a can opener inside, and an invitation to "do lunch" in my suite! I got back at him, though. I still have a picture of him floating in an inner tube in my pool, cradling a bottle of Pepto Bismol after one of our dyspeptic story meetings.

Soap actors are wonderful. Many of them are seasoned Broadway actors. Many more get a start in soaps, and go on to star in films and primetime television. Some of the actors in LIAMST did exactly that: Donna Mills, David Birney, Bibi Besch, Andrea Marcovicci, and Paul Michael Glaser to name a few. It was agony writing their characters out of the show, and even worse recasting them.

But the show had to go on, and it gobbled up so much material that Freddie Silverman decided that we needed another core family to broaden the playing field. I came up with the Chernaks, a Polish-American, blue collar family, headed by a widowed mother whom I described as large, ethnic, and speaking with an accent. Elitist Conboy ignored the description. He insisted on an uptown type to play Mama Chernak, and cast the elegant Diana Douglas—who was as much like an ethnic, blue collar Pole as Princess Di.

Fred Silverman left daytime to become head of primetime programming for CBS. Mike Filerman took Fred's job for a few years, and then he, too, went West into nighttime TV. Conboy and I stayed on for a year or two until he took off for greener pastures in Hollywood, and the show was finally canceled. I spent the next several months writing a TV movie, and developing a new soap for Spelling/Goldberg. The movie, which had something to do with a mail plane crashing and the consequences of undelivered letters, aired to slightly less than critical raves.

The soap never saw the light of day. Like the huge Spelling hit *Beverly Hills 90210,* which aired some twenty years later, my soap, *Henderson High,* was about the lives of the students, teachers, and parents in a southern California community. Oh well. Shortly after that the folks at Proctor and Gamble hired me to write the long running soap *Search for Tomorrow*. During this time our son John was doing a hippie version of Kerouac's on-the-road by visiting Berkeley friends in various communes from New Mexico to New York City, where he sometimes played his flute in subway stations for loose change. One time he played in the fountain square in front of the Plaza Hotel when I was in town for a story conference. He tried to visit me, but was stopped by the management. I didn't blame them. He was bearded and grungy—holes in the soles of his shoes, his untucked, wrinkled shirttails flapping out of ripped jeans (before they were chic); but at least they checked with me—just in case he <u>was</u> my son. I assured them he was, and they allowed him (using the service elevator), up to my room. He bunked down in the lavish sitting room of my suite that night, and the next morning (since he couldn't appear in the hotel dining room), I insisted he order breakfast from room service. The bill was twenty-seven dollars. I don't think he had eaten in weeks. In fact, he enjoyed eating so much that he became a stevedore on the Brooklyn docks for several months after that before he took off for Canada, where he worked with disturbed kids in a Canadian government program.

Steve started the Fall semester at the University of Wisconsin, went on a ski trip to Iron Mountain, and broke his leg so severely that he had to drop out, and spend the rest of the semester recuperating at home. He was still uncommunicative (at least with Ellis and me), so I was glad Anna, our housekeeper, was there to cheer him up. She taught him to speak Spanish fluently, and when he could hobble around a bit, they went to movies and concerts. Steve being Steve and Anna being Anna, they were very secretive about their growing relationship. (It has always puzzled and hurt that they thought we would disapprove). When Steve went back to the University in Madison, Anna told us she had to go back to El Salvador. Surprise! She wound up in Madison with Steve. They were married soon after, although it was more than a year before they told us.

Tracy, who had never enjoyed acting (why else had she thrown so many roadblocks in her way with all her talent and beauty?), threw her energies into teaching. And she was sensational. All that training—from Madam Ouspenskaya to the Group Theater, Lee Strassberg, the Actors Studio, and Michael Chekhov—paid off. She rejected some of it (Strassberg mostly), borrowed some (from Chekhov, especially), and filtered it through her own sensibilities and intelligence—and young actors and professionals responded. She started with a few students, but as word-of-mouth spread she became one of the hottest, most sought after teachers in Hollywood. With the help of gifted actor Martin E. Brooks, whom she met when they both appeared in a LA repertory production of Chekhov's *The Seagull* (she played Arcadia to his Trigorin), she opened a small studio in Beverly Hills. Before long, she moved to larger quarters.

Ellis left the network to become an executive story consultant for the TV series, *Executive Suite*, and when that was canceled, he wrote for other top primetime series.

And then tragedy struck. My two closest friends, Rhea Wiseman and Shirley Henry, died within two weeks of each other. Unbelievable, almost unbearable that these two wonderful women were stricken with cancer in the prime of their lives, and at the same time.

Rhea became ill when her daughter was pregnant with her first child. It was the story of Mother and me all over again.

Shirley was devoted to Rhea (I had introduced them years before), and she spent hours and hours with her. I was so busy writing about the fictional problems of my soap characters that I had to steal time to see her, but when I did she was as upbeat and stimulating as ever. We had marathon gab fests that became monologues when she lost her voice because of the cancer. She miraculously regained it during her daughter Robin's visit from New Haven, and was able to have a joyous baby shower for her.

Shirley was there, and appeared to be fine, but shortly after she was stricken with colon cancer and went downhill quickly. Unlike Rhea, Shirley refused to see most of her friends during her illness. She died two weeks after Rhea.

Why did they call her the Gibson girl? Mother shortly before her marriage.

Dad was handsome, sensitive and sometimes troubled.

Here we are in front of the Buick touring car: Mom, Dad, Tracy, Ray, and me.

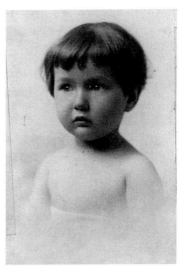

Me, age 9 months.

Tracy was starring on Broadway and about to go to Hollywood while...

I was planting a "Victory Garden" at Western College, and...

Ray began a 4-year stint in the Air Force. He visited me at college before he was shipped off to Europe.

Marriage at 22 after a whirlwind romance with a dashing soldier.

We honeymooned at a most appropriate resort, Schroon Lake!

Our beautiful kids: John, Ellyn and Steven.

We...did it! Jerry Adelman, Daniel Gregory Browne and I get our just desserts, winning the Emmy for *Mary Hartman, Mary Hartman*.

Celebrating high ratings with the cast of *Days Of Our Lives*. (I'm on the left)

With cadets on the set of *Women At West Point*.

On the set of *The Life And Times Of Eddie Roberts*, the show Ellis and I created, wrote, and produced.

At my desk at Lorimar when I was supervising producer of *Knots Landing*.

John's family: In the Garden near the Dome of the Rock, Israel. Left to right: Jacobo, Carmen, Paola, Ellis, Etienne, John.

Steve's Family: Anna, Kevin, Steven, with Uncle Ray.

Ellyn's family: left to right: Bill, Ben, (me), Katie, Ellyn.

Fun in the sun with my siblings Ray and Tracy.

Hamming it up with Tracy.

Ray and his wife Mary Ellen, with me.

Singing Sondheim's "I'm Still Here," at my 50th college reunion.

With good friend Suzanne Childs (attorney, broadcast journalist, writer).

Partying with Donna Mills and producer John Conboy

Lifelong friend Martha McKee Keehn.

Michelle Lee and me at the opening of *The Art Of Dining* produced and directed by Tracy.

My favorite picture of Ellis taken at Marina Del Rey, California.

Ellis with his brother, director Marc Daniels, and sister Miriam Cherin.

Ollie and me.

I was grateful to be working at a demanding job, hoping it would keep me from brooding. It was hard to accept the fact that we were losing our contemporaries. That same year, both Ted Murkland and Stanley Goldman died. Unbelievable.

Work was a great distraction. The wonderful thing about writing soaps was that I controlled who lived or died. So I tackled my job on *Search for Tomorrow* with fervor. *Search* was the longest running soap on the air, and Mary Stuart was on it from the beginning. She was its shining star. She survived countless fatal illnesses, almost a dozen marriages, divorces, widowhoods, affairs, intrigues, kidnappings, false accusations, murder trials, and other disasters too numerous to mention. With her indomitable spirit she prevailed through them all, keeping her blonde good looks (with the help of a few nips and tucks), and was the center of every major story. Until I arrived. At least that's what she thought a few months after I'd taken over the show, when she ran into me at a restaurant.

Ellis and I were having dinner at a charming small cafe on Melrose Avenue, when she spotted me and sailed over to our table.

"Why," she asked, "do you hate me?"

"What?" I asked, dumbfounded.

"Oh, don't play the innocent with me," said she. "You have deliberately refused to write stories for me. You have me standing around. . . <u>reacting</u> to other characters' problems; drinking coffee in <u>other</u> people's kitchens; holding my <u>stepdaughter's</u> hand while <u>she</u> lies on a hospital bed waiting for <u>her</u> test results!"

People were staring at us. They recognized her of course. And they must have wondered who could have caused their heroine, the selfless and courageous Jo, such anguish. I mumbled something about not hating her at all, that I admired her tremendously, and escaped before the mob came after me.

It wasn't my fault Mary wasn't the "tent-pole" character she had been. I was ordered by the guys who ran the show to concentrate on the younger people.

And there were a lot of guys running the show: Bernie Sofranski, the executive producer; Paul Rauch, the head of CBS daytime; Bob Short and John Potter from Proctor and Gamble; and

Milton Slater, from the advertising agency. All male except for *moi*. It's so different now. These days story meetings are decidedly gender friendly. And in daytime, almost all the executives are women.

My favorite story on *Search* involved a character, played by Morgan Fairchild, who had been involved in the mercy killing of her fatally ill, rich father-in-law. Actually she didn't do it, but it sure looked as though she had—and the ambitious D.A. was determined to nail her and send her up the river. Which he did. So we did "Women Behind Bars," paying homage to the old Ida Lupino film. Polly Holliday played the tough prison inmate leader. When Morgan tried to foil Polly's attempt to escape, Polly locked her in a meat freezer—where she almost became a Birdseye product before she was rescued. I guess you had to have been there.

We did more plausible material, of course, and we not only had the highest rated soap on the air, but our writing team (including Ray, Ken, Jerry, plus Joyce Perry), won the Writers Guild Award for best written serial that year, 1974. I had a lock on the job, but then an opportunity came along that I couldn't refuse. Norman Lear beckoned.

He wanted me to co-create a satirical soap about an autoworker's dysfunctional family in Ohio, a soap that turned out to be *Mary Hartman, Mary Hartman*.

Chapter 16

The Truth About Mary Hartman's Waxy Yellow Buildup

I think I was the writer of last resort on Norman Lear's new project in 1975—and I got in through the back door. Well, maybe it was the side door. At any rate, he had just about given up finding a writer to implement his idea for a different kind of soap opera—though his stubborn chief of staff, Al Burton, kept looking.

Al ran into my agent, Bob Eisenbach, in the men's room at the Beverly Wilshire Hotel, and that's how I got to meet Norman. Not in the men's room, but in his office in the Metromedia Building on Sunset. Norman was wearing his signature outfit: a cashmere sweater, a white porkpie hat, and Fumanchu mustache. Al was there, too, as Norman explained his concept, a soap on two levels. One level would satirize the medium, the other would hook the audience with characters and stories on a realistic level. Obviously, since it was a Norman Lear project, the stories would be controversial—all Norman's shows were. But with *Mary Hartman* Norman wanted to be outrageous.

The concept sounded logical enough. The soap would be built around an autoworker's family: Tom, his wife Mary, their adolescent child, plus Mary's parents, sister, and neighbors. A typical, ordinary, blue-collar family living in a small town in Ohio. But there was a stipulation. It was what Norman insisted on happening the first week of the soap. And it was so bizarre that it had driven half the comedy writers in Hollywood screaming from his office.

They heard the pitch and told him: A) It wasn't funny; B) It wouldn't work; C) He'd never get it on the air; D) If by some chance he did get it on the air nobody would watch it; and E) "Let me outta here!"

What was this vision of Norman's that had freaked out all those writers? He wanted to open with the mass murder of a neighborhood family including their goats and chickens.

It was Norman's litmus test. If, on hearing this outrageous stipulation, a writer used any of the above-mentioned A) through E) comments, the meeting was over. I wanted the job so bad I sat glued to the chair when I heard it. I did not bolt. I did not gasp. I even managed to laugh.

"Wonderful!" I said. "What a great way to start," I added shamelessly, intuitively realizing that Norman (like every other writer I've ever known including myself), loves to be flattered.

Norman and Al looked at each other. I hadn't run screaming from the room. I passed the test. I was given the material that had already been created by novelist and comedy writer Gail Parent, who had come up with the original concept of dramatizing the everyday life of a dysfunctional auto worker's family. One of the documents was a hilarious and defining scene between the housewife and a door-to-door salesman that totally captured the essence of the *Mary Hartman* character. But after creating and describing the other members of Mary's family: her bored auto worker husband, Tom; libidinous sister, Cathy; and clueless parents, Gail left on a long book tour and had nothing more to do with the show.

In the coming weeks as I struggled to deal with the material, create the story lines, flesh out the family, and invent the neighborhood characters, I realized those other freaked out writers who had failed the test were right. There isn't anything funny about the massacre of a family of five—even (or especially), if their goats and chickens are included.

I wasn't having much fun, and Norman wasn't much help. He was busy with his other shows, and he had so many negative reactions about the concept from other writers that I don't think he felt I could bring it off. Neither did I. I knew I needed help, and I knew

The Truth About Mary Hartman's Waxy Yellow Buildup

where to look for it.

Ken Hartman had changed his name sometime between working with me on *Love is a Many Splendored Thing* and *Search for Tomorrow*. He had flirted with all sorts of New Age philosophies and other non-establishment practices, numerology being one of them. So he re-christened himself Daniel Gregory Browne because the letters added up to some special number that was supposed to be good for him, I guess. Whatever, he was still a brilliant writer, and I desperately needed him to help create the rest of the characters and get the show on its feet.

I also recruited Jerry Adelman, whose weird, eclectic sense of the absurd fit in perfectly with the style of the show.

The three of us solved the problem of how to make the mass murder palatable and even funny by not showing it, and simply having Mary and friends react to it. We fleshed in Mary's family, the Shumways, and created Grampa Larkin and the other characters: the neighbors (in particular the Haggars, would-be Country/Western singer Loretta and Tom's best chum Charlie); Sgt. Foley, Coach Leroy Fedders and his wife, Jimmy Joe Jeeter (the eight-year-old evangelist), and his slick dad Merle; Ed and Howard (the homosexual couple), and all the others.

After Daniel, Jerry, and I finished writing the Bible (the long-term stories), we wrote two weeks of scripts—ten half-hour comedy soap scripts. The first two half-hours—during which the massacre, Grampa Larkin's flashing, and Tom's impotency occur—served as the pilot. But that's not what sold the show. The waxy yellow build up on Mary's kitchen floor sold the show. Daniel Gregory Browne was responsible for writing that scene. Mary was in the kitchen with her sister Cathy, listening to their favorite soap. When it was over Mary said:

MARY

How do you like the floors? See that glow?

CATHY

What glow? You mean that waxy yellow buildup?

MARY

(PICKS UP CAN)
What do you mean? That can't be waxy yellow buildup. Read the can.

CATHY

Mary, you're looking at a waxy yellow buildup.

MARY

I'm not. I'm looking at a label that says that can't be.

CATHY

Mary, I'm your sister; I'm telling you it's not waxy buildup there . . . it's a waxy buildup <u>there!</u>

MARY

These people turn out a million cans a week. Who am I suposed to listen to, you?
(SFX: WAIL OF A SIREN PASSING BY OUTSIDE)

CATHY

Mary, I'm telling you that's a waxy yellow buildup.

MARY

It does look a little yellow.

Joan Darling directed the pilot and assembled an unforgettable cast. All along we had written the part of Mary Hartman with one person in mind, Louise Lasser. But Louise didn't want to do a soap. After all, she'd starred in several of her ex-husband Woody Allen's memorable movies, including *Bananas*, and *Everything You've Always Wanted to Know About Sex*, as well as Ingmar Bergman's acclaimed TV drama, *The Lie*. Besides, she said she "didn't get" the concept, the character or the series.

But Louise Lasser <u>was</u> Mary Hartman, i.e., Mary Hartman filtered through Louise's brilliant, fractured psyche. And Louise had

The Truth About Mary Hartman's Waxy Yellow Buildup

more to do with creating the character than any of us. It was Louise who gave Mary that blank stare. That slow, earnest, deliberate way of speaking. She even invented her wardrobe: the puffy-sleeved little girl/housewife mini dress, the braided hairdo and bangs. And no, that wasn't her real hair. She kept her brown hair tightly bobby-pinned underneath a reddish blond wig.

I had a little difficulty relating to Louise. I don't think she completely trusted me. I don't think she trusted Norman, either. Norman and I were old enough to be her parents, and both of us felt as protective toward her as parents do with their fragile offspring. She certainly brought out the "Jewish Mother" in me. I kept wanting to hug her and tell her everything would be all right. . . "and afterwards we'll all go to the House of Pancakes." Louise was terribly thin and I nagged her to. . . "eat, Louise, eat."

When she finally agreed to do the series, all the other characters fell into place.

Mary Kay Place was the perfect Loretta Haggers, Mary's best friend—a blend of dogged determination and sunny optimism in the face of every conceivable catastrophe we could dream up, from her car crashing into a station wagon full of nuns on the way to Nashville causing her to become paralyzed, to discovering that the baby she was carrying was not a fetus but a fibroid tumor (which she insists on naming Charlie, Jr.). Every adversity only added to her repertoire of Country/Western songs (for which we loved writing lyrics). Not for a moment did she doubt she would be a superstar, never once entertaining the thought that her talent was anything less than divinely inspired.

One of the reasons for her super confidence was the total devotion and support of her husband Charlie, her "good ol' baby boy" her "precious bedtime toy," who believed in her as much as she believed in herself. Dan and Jerry and I saw Charlie as a real hunk, but in one of Norman's typical risk-taking twists, he went the other way and cast older, balding, bespectacled Graham Jarvis—which turned out to be a terrific idea.

Mary's parents, Martha and George Shumway (Dodie Goodman and Philip Bruns), and her oversexed sister Cathy

(Debralee Scott), kept Mary in a constant state of perplexed denial.

At first, we couldn't decide the sex of Mary's only child, finally settling on a prepubescent girl. We gave her an ordinary name but Louise didn't like it. She thought for a moment and then breathed out another name . . . "Heather." Of course. It was just right. A lovely, subtle, gentle name at total odds with the cranky brat who makes Mary's life as miserable as she can. Claudia Lamb played her to a tee.

Victor Kilian was the semi-senile, poignant Grandpa Larkin, whom Mary related to better than anyone else in her family. And that included her husband Tom, played so organically by Greg Mullavey. Poor Greg, he was so good as the earnest breadwinner, dressed invariably in his Fernwood High varsity jacket and baseball cap, but he was totally overshadowed in the media and on the show by Louise.

Which I could totally relate to. Because I felt Daniel, Jerry, and I were totally overshadowed and ignored, too. Even before the show went on the air, a great deal of publicity had been generated in which we weren't even mentioned. It was Norman Lear's show all the way down the line. According to the media, he had created the whole thing. Daniel, Jerry, and I were some "veteran soap writers," who had filled in the numbers.

That made me mad. So I challenged Norman about it. The wonderful thing about Norman is that if you confront him with the truth, he agrees with you. He's not defensive; he doesn't try to blame someone else, he simply does the right thing, or (in this case), almost the right thing. A day or two after our meeting a full-page ad appeared in the trades:

FIRST CAME THE WORD . . .
The "veteran soap writers" widely credited as having "something" to do with Mary Hartman Mary Hartman are in fact the very gifted, insightful and vastly experienced
ANN MARCUS
JERRY ADELMAN

# The Truth About Mary Hartman's Waxy Yellow Buildup

DANIEL GREGORY BROWNE
and Program Consultant
OLIVER HAILEY

The ad went on to mention the "brilliant directorial talents of Joan Darling and Jim Drake," and the actors.

So why did I say he "almost" did the right thing? Because, even though he said we were talented, he failed to mention that we were co-creators of the show. That we invented a lot of the characters, and wrote the pilot. Am I quibbling? I don't think so. Credits are a writer's best friend. So much so, that I blew a chance to give enough credit to Daniel Gregory Browne who was so important to the creation of the show. We shared the 'created by' credit, but I also had another credit: Head Writer. Dan wanted another credit, too: From The Neck Down. I was too uptight to go for it, but I wish I had even though I don't think the Writers Guild would have allowed it.

Mary Hartman premiered on January 6, 1976. Ellis and I hosted a small party at the house to watch it. Jerry and Daniel were there as we lowered the lights and turned on the set. The corny theme music started, and Dodie Goodman's voice could be heard from our collective childhood calling out, ". . . Mary Hartman . . . Mary Hartman!" We were off on the most exhilarating and exhausting experience of our lives.

We knew it was good, but we weren't prepared for the overwhelming reaction to it. *MH2* wasn't just a hit, it was a mega hit. In no time at all, it became addictive—a "pop culture craze," as *Newsweek* put it, ". . . a sort of video Rorschach Test for the mass audience." Everyone was talking about it, or writing about it. Critics were comparing it to the best of Chekhov, Cervantes, James Joyce, John Updike, and Ingmar Bergman. *Mary Hartman* stared out from the covers of every popular, glossy, high and low brow periodical in the country. And inside there were long analytical pieces on the meaning of it all. Ted Morgan in *The NY Times Magazine* wrote:

> "No longer merely a television program, MH2 has become a cultural event, in the same league as those other sociological signposts that culture watchers and think tanks and Whither America specialists are always on the lookout for to help us explain ourselves."

He went on to describe an extension course at UCLA (not the only college course based on the show):

> "The participants, including dramatist Abby Mann, will discuss 'the dreams and nightmares of the American people as they are reflected darkly, through the glass of Mary Hartman—can a culture survive a nervous breakdown . . . ?"

The *Times* then quoted Harold Freed, the coordinator of the *Mary Hartman* course, as seeing *MH2* as an example of what he called:

> "The Society of the Spectacle, in which television reduces all of life to a meaningless spectacle that can be turned on and off. The waxy buildup on Mary Hartman's kitchen floor, where stunned and defeated she sinks down again and again, becomes the equivalent of Sartrean nausea . . . Mary's uneasy feeling that things should be different is a form of existential awareness. She is a divine omen indicating misfortune."

Wow, I thought, so that's what we're writing. And I thought we were just trying to be funny and tweak a few noses.

The more notoriously successful the show became, the more interested Norman became in it—and the more time he spent with us. In the beginning, Dan and Jerry and I had been left pretty much on our own. But once the show was in production, and especially after it enjoyed such a spectacular reception, Norman neglected his other shows to spend hours and hours and hours with us. This was both wonderful and terrible.

We had daily story conferences—which were tape-recorded, and ran into eighty or more pages of transcripts (keeping an army of typists at work through the night). But there were only three of us writing the five scripts each week, and what with participating in marathon story meetings, reading the transcripts, writing the outlines, and then writing the scripts, we were always in a state of hysterical exhaustion. On the other hand, Norman (who wasn't writing scripts or outlines), remained fresh as a daisy, and very funny and inventive. He was especially fond of thinking up quirky ways to eliminate characters he didn't like. When he decided Coach Leroy Fedders should go, he browbeat us into coming up with a bizarre exit. But the light bulb went on over his head first.

That was the best part of those meetings—Norman acting out one of his ideas. This time it was "The Death of Coach Fedders." First he set the scene: The coach has a bad cold. He's been home taking cold medications and sipping Jack Daniels, but Mary insists he come over for a bowl of her homemade chicken soup. Warming up to the improvisation, Norman talked through a stuffy nose. He bent over the imaginary huge bowl of soup Mary places in front of him, first taking another Seconal and another swig of bourbon. As Mary and the coach's wife gossip, Norman-as-Leroy gets drowsier and drowsier, unable to keep awake, and unnoticed by Mary or his wife. Then Norman started reaching for the back of his shirt collar, trying to pull his head up out of the imaginary soup bowl. He almost does it, but his head keeps dropping lower and lower until it finally plops into the bowl of soup, and he quietly drowns. We all applauded. That was one of the easiest scripts I ever wrote. All I did was describe Norman's inspired pantomime.

Other characters exited in bizarre ways, too. Eight-year-old evangelist Jimmy Joe Jeeter was electrocuted when a TV set fell into his bathtub; Mary's father George disappeared behind the blind spot in the rear view mirror of his car.

As the meetings grew longer (plus the transcripts), and the pressure to keep the show at as high a level as possible, I lobbied for another writer. Playwright Oliver Hailey, who was the program consultant, sat in on the story meetings and contributed ideas. But his main function, God bless him, was to protect our scripts from the actors once they got to the set. He did this in the most diplomatic way, by spending hours on the set listening to the actors' gripes and complaints with patience and fortitude, and only as a last resort agreeing to a line change here or there. He had no time to write scripts. His wife, Betsy (who went on to write the literate bestseller, *A Woman of Independent Means*), joined us around the story conference table, too, but she wasn't interested in writing scripts.

But I had someone in mind. Peggy Goldman, the daughter of our good friends Stanley and Muriel, had come out to the West Coast to seek her fortune as a writer. She graduated from Vassar, and worked on the editorial staff of *Esquire* for two years, but always wanted to write for television. She sent Ellis and me a couple of spec scripts, which we thought were excellent. So we were delighted when she made the move. I arranged for her to meet Norman after I got back from a ski trip to Vail with the family. I had been working nonstop for six months, and desperately needed the time off. Peggy came along, too. Ever the jock, I decided to try an expert trail and broke my wrist. Peggy broke her ankle.

When we arrived at the meeting with Norman, my arm was in a sling and Peggy was on crutches. Avuncular Norman fell in love with crippled Peggy on the spot, and gave her a script assignment. She aced it, and became the fourth member of our writing team late in the season.

We were at the point in the series where Loretta's career had taken off to such a degree that she was invited to appear on *The Dinah Shore Show*. Our mission was to find some way for Loretta to self-destruct on Dinah's show so that we could get her back to Fernwood and Mary's kitchen. What could she do that would guarantee the end of her career? What outrageous thing could happen?

We were sitting around the conference table, the tape recorder dangling from the ceiling recording every wild and crazy idea we could come up with, but nothing worked. Norman was as tapped out as the rest of us. Then Peggy mumbled something almost under her breath. Had I heard right? Was one of the words ". . . anti-Semitic?"

Norman heard it, too, and his eyes lit up. "What did you say?" he asked, almost pouncing on her. Peggy's voice dropped even lower. We all leaned toward her.

"Well, Dinah is Jewish and maybe Loretta can make some comment, totally innocent . . . but anti-Semitic . . .?"

Peggy sort of let it hang there. Norman loved it. We all loved it. And it worked. Loretta blows her career when she tells Dinah how much she appreciates the Jewish agents and promoters who have helped her, and then gushes: "I can't believe those are the same people who killed our Lord."

As the first season (all 124 episodes) was nearing the end, Louise was wearing out. It was insane for her to do a completely new script five times a week for twenty-six weeks. But that was Louise's fault. She insisted on appearing in every episode. I tried to tell her how impossible it would be, that even in the common, garden-variety soaps lead actors appeared three times a week, max. *MH2*, being a satirical comedy, was much harder to do. Did she listen to me? No. Did Norman overrule her? Noooo.

Come to think of it, they were probably right, because what would an episode of *Mary Hartman, Mary Hartman* be without Mary Hartman? But that didn't make it possible. Yet gutsy Louise hung in—even after The Incident.

I was in the office late one afternoon when the phone rang. It was an inquiring reporter wanting my reaction to Louise being busted by the Beverly Hills cops, and jailed for disturbing the peace, possession of a controlled substance, and (seemingly right out of a *Mary Hartman* script), nonpayment of two traffic tickets—one of them for jay walking! I denied everything, said there was some mistake and hung up. But it was all too true.

According to Louise, she had gone to a charity boutique to buy an antique dollhouse for her wardrobe mistress's birthday, but the clerk refused to accept her credit card. Louise, who had the flu and a temperature of 102 degrees, refused to leave without the dollhouse. The clerk called the cops—and the rest appeared in every major media outlet across the country.

It wasn't all that serious. She only had a tiny bit of cocaine in her purse—less than 80 milligrams, or six dollars worth. She was placed on probation on the condition that she see her psychiatrist three times a week. (Actually that may have reduced the number of visits she was already making). So everything turned out to be all right, although no one suggested going to the House of Pancakes afterwards.

Louise's nerves were fraying. Things got kind of weird around the set, especially when Louise suggested to Dan and me that what happened to her should happen to Mary. If Louise was the chicken and Mary was the egg, we now knew which came first. Louise also suggested a way to end the first season that was very much in tune with both Mary and herself. Mary, she said, should have a nervous breakdown. She was right, of course, and we set about to make it happen.

Because of the enormous popularity of the show, we were able to get a commitment from David Susskind. So, we had Mary chosen as America's Typical Consumer Housewife, a film crew document a typical week in her life, and sent her to New York to face a panel of experts on Susskind's show—a feminist, a consumer advocate, and a media expert.

Mary arrives in New York to do the show and gets mugged. She loses her identification and credit cards, so when she tries to buy an antique dollhouse, the clerk won't sell it to her. Just as in real life, she refuses to leave without it—and winds up in jail. But that was only the tip of the iceberg. Back in Fernwood, Tom's lost his job and has become an alcoholic. Heather has brought home a joint from school—and wants to wear a string bikini, platform shoes, and join an all-girl band. Her mother is on a bus to Columbus, with her recently discovered biological father, a Choctaw Indian who, along with 28 other Indians and a collapsible teepee, is going to stage a protest over fishing rights. And her sister Cathy has run off with a Catholic priest. All that on top of everything else Mary's gone through—from being held hostage in a

The Truth About Mary Hartman's Waxy Yellow Buildup

Chinese laundry by the mass killer to her doomed affair with Sgt. Foley . . . no wonder she flips out.

During the last episode of the season, Mary/Louise gave a bravura performance and went bonkers on the David Susskind Show. She ends up back in a Fernwood hospital for the mentally challenged.

And Daniel, Jerry, and I were nominated for an Emmy.

Chapter 17

What's The Worst Thing That Can Happen To You?

These days the Emmys are awarded by the Television Academy of Arts and Sciences in the fall, but in 1976 the ceremony took place on May 17. It was held at the Shubert Theater in Century City, and it was hot. Very hot. Daniel, Jerry, and I were nervous. Very nervous. And excited.

The guys rented tuxedos for the occasion—stylish, light-colored ones with velvet lapels, ruffled shirts and oversize bow ties, that you might have expected to see on Sonny Bono. I went shopping for something smashing to wear, but I bought the first gown the saleswoman at Saks showed me, a bland chiffon beige thing, with a matching jacket trimmed in ostrich feathers.

Those were the days when the awards went on, and on, and on. (There's been a real effort recently to shorten the ceremony, although people still complain about the length of the Emmys and wonder why the show can't be as brief as the Tonys. But, when you consider the amount of TV programming there is, compared to the vanishing theater on and off Broadway, it's a wonder the Emmys haven't been turned into a miniseries.)

At any rate, we waited and waited for our category to be announced, which wasn't until almost the end. We were sitting in a side aisle, being slowly oven-roasted by the broiling TV lights, when Danny Kaye was introduced to make the presentations in our category. We weren't competing against anyone, because *MH2* was unique—a five-times-a-week, non-network, non-primetime show, which couldn't be judged against any similar series since there weren't any. It had been nominated in what was called a "special classification of outstanding individual achievement."

Which meant the Academy could give us the Emmy or withhold it.

What we were holding was our breath as Danny Kaye presented the first award to Johnny Carson and his producer Fred De Cordova for *The Johnny Carson Show*. After their gracious acceptance, Kaye picked up the next envelope. He opened it. He took forever to look at it before announcing that the next Emmy was awarded to the writing team of *Mary Hartman, Mary Hartman* . . . Ann Marcus, Jerry Adelman, and Daniel Gregory Browne! We won . . . we won! What a delicious feeling. I did the whole bit, hugged Ellis, hugged Dan and Jerry, hugged Al Burton who was sitting next to us, danced down the aisle to the podium and then I thought . . . "Oh my God, what am I going to say?" By this time, we were on stage shaking hands with Danny Kaye, who gave each of us an Emmy. Then it was my turn to say something to the people in the theater, and the millions watching on television. I felt hot and sticky and rumpled; my makeup was caked. I clutched at the droopy feathers on my jacket.

"I've been waiting so long I think my ostrich died," I said. There was polite laughter. Then I thanked Ellis and my family and Al Burton. But I forgot to thank Norman or Louise or anyone else connected with the show. But hey, I was giddy. And besides, Daniel did that, and Jerry did, too.

Tracy said later that during the presentation the camera cut to Norman, who was sitting with *Maude* star Bea Arthur (who had lost the "Best Comedy Actress" Emmy to Mary Tyler Moore earlier in the evening). According to Trace, Norman looked grim. He could have been upset about Bea (who went on to win several Emmys in the years following), or maybe Tracy wasn't wearing her glasses and he looked perfectly fine. Then again, it could have been an omen.

Nevertheless, it was a good time for all of us. Ellis, who was serving a second tour as a CBS program executive, planned a luxurious cruise of the Greek Islands to coincide with the end of the MH2 season. Ellyn was finishing her junior year at Oakwood High School. Steve, married, was living in Santa Monica and had gone back to school for a graduate degree in Physics at UCLA. John was in Chiapas, Mexico, in a serious relationship with Carmen, an ex-Marxist, ex-student, and talented artist. Tracy's classes were thriving, and she was directing Equity-waiver productions at her studio. Ray, who had stepped into the head writing job at *Search for Tomorrow* when I left, had just sold an idea for a TV movie to Warners that was based on *The Bridge of San Louis Rey.*

A week after the last show was taped; Ellis, Ellyn and I were winging our way to Venice, where we boarded the cruise ship. I was feeling almost as bubbly and confident as Loretta Haggers on her way to Nashville before the car crash. I had won the Emmy. I was embarking on this glorious, sun-drenched trip down the Dalmatian coast, and then island hopping in the Mediterranean. And the best part was the satisfaction of knowing I was going back to a second season of a smash hit, the most talked about, popular show on TV! When my shipmates found out my connection with *MH2*, I became a minor celebrity. I basked. I slept a lot and ate a lot, and was an ardent sightseer.

I loved the Greek Islands; the blue/green harbors, the stone steps and glittering white houses with their flowering patios. The lobsters on Mykenos! The antiquities both on Sicily and the Greek mainland. It was all wonderful, even the fact that Ellyn developed a serious but doomed crush on the handsome, married, First Mate. Ellis and I held our breath, tried to keep a discreet distance, and hoped for the best. She handled it pretty well, considering.

I got back home rested, refreshed, and eager to tackle the further adventures of *Mary Hartman*, happily ensconced in the hospital for the mentally challenged. There were all sorts of marvelous avenues to explore. There was even a possibility that Gore Vidal would appear on the show as himself to record Mary's treatment and recovery.

I knew we had to get cracking. The start of production was drawing nigh, and we had to have stories approved and scripts written. But Norman was not only hard to pin down, he did something very strange while I was on the cruise. He went to New York, and, on the spur of the moment (his favorite form of action), hired Tom Eyen, a young and gifted playwright, to join our writing team. Only he hadn't told me. In fact, he never told me. I went to the office one day and there was Tom, as nice as could be, charming and confused. Very confused. Tom had never written for television. He had no idea what it meant to turn out five scripts a week. He didn't know how the stories were constructed, how the weekly outlines were developed, or how the daily scripts were written—the form, the pace, *nada*. It's hard enough to go from one medium to another when there's no pressure. But to go from the leisurely pace of play writing to the cauldron of writing on a five-times-a-week TV show is next to impossible.

Tom was panicky. Norman wasn't. Norman wasn't concerned about Tom's distress, our lack of settled story lines, or the imminent start of production. He wasn't concerned about anything. At least as far as I could see.

Then Al Burton explained it all to me. He invited me to lunch, and told me Norman wanted me off the show. I stared at him blankly. It was a *Mary Hartman* stare. What Al said didn't compute.

Poor Al. Poor me! What an indignity. If Norman wanted me off the show, let's face it, FIRED!—why didn't he tell me himself? Al hastened to soften the blow. Norman didn't want to fire me. He simply wanted to move me from *Mary Hartman* to another show, a show I'd create, another half-hour soap.

That didn't help. I was furious. Enraged! I didn't want to create another show for Norman. I had already co-created a show for Norman. *Mary Hartman, Mary Hartman*! It was my show as much as it was his show. I felt like throwing a temper tantrum in the restaurant. I wanted to yell and kick and scream. But I never act on those impulses. Besides, Al wasn't at fault. He was only the messenger.

I went home and called Norman. Him I yelled at.

"Norman, godammit, how could you do this to me?" I screamed.

"I've worked my ass off on the show. You never would have gotten it off the ground if it hadn't been for me! Is this the way you repay me? Kicking me out! Slamming the door in my face! Not even having the guts to tell me yourself?!"

There was a moment of silence on the other end of the line. Then Norman said, in a very surprised and hurt voice, "You don't understand. It's just a simple, lateral move. No one said anything about letting you go. If you want to leave, I'll certainly pay off your contract, but I have a really good idea for another comedy soap I want you to write."

"What idea?" I yelled, wanting to kill. "I thought of it while I was shaving this morning," said Norman. And I knew he had because that's the way he works. I was torn between wanting to throw the phone across the room, and hearing what his great idea was.

"It's a reversal of the way things are," said Norman. "Instead of men being the first sex and women the second, we do a 180. Women are the predominant sex, men are the second sex."

"That's your idea?" I yelled. "Who are the characters? What's it about?"

"That's up to you," he said.

I wanted to tell him to take his idea and shove it. I wanted to tell him how hurt and angry I was, and how rotten and uncaring I thought he was. I wanted to tell him to pay off my contract, plus a million or so for emotional distress—but I didn't. Why? Because I'm probably the most competitive person I know—and I needed to prove to him that he'd made a terrible mistake. That I could take his one-line idea and turn it into something wonderful. Then I'd dump him, and he'd be sorry. Actually, what I wanted to do most, was to choke him.

Instead, I accepted the challenge to write another pilot.

This was the age of Transcendental Meditation. Deep down, I thought it was a bunch of hooey, but I paid a couple of hundred bucks on the chance it might help me cope with the rage. For hours, I sat in a darkened room, rested my palms upward on my thighs, breathed deeply and evenly, and mumbled my mantra—which I can't remember, but which sounded something like: "Yo Kimba . . . . hubba, hubba, hubba." Then I sat and created the characters and story lines, and wrote the pilot for *All That Glitters*—with very little input from Norman, although he took half the "created by" credit. I gave TM and my mantra a helluva workout through that trying time.

Norman offered me the head writing job on the new series, but I turned him down because I was still so angry, in spite of all my "yo kimba-ing." Besides, he had hired an executive producer who had run the National Endowment for the Arts, but didn't know beans about how to run a TV show. I was quite pleased when the series only lasted 13 weeks.

As for *Mary Hartman, Mary Hartman,* it lasted another year before it segued into *Fernwood 2Nite,* when Louise Lasser left. *Fernwood* limped on for another two years, and then fizzled out. Though I can hardly be objective, even after twenty years, I think the first year of *MH2* was the best. It went downhill after that, and there are those who think (me, for instance) that one of the reasons is that I wasn't there, heading the writing staff.

Daniel Gregory Browne, Jerry Adelman, and Peggy Goldman stayed on, but their talents were diluted by the addition of several new writers. Dan, whose brilliance, edginess, and grasp of the contemporary scene had done so much to create the ambiance of that first year, must have been held in check somehow. As for Jerry, his abrasive wit, which had been responsible for Merle Jeeter's Condos for Christ (among other things), also got him banned from story meetings.

But in my heart of hearts, I think they really needed me. I grounded the show in reality and made it all work. And I wrote funny, too—over fifty scripts that first year, as well as the story lines and half the outlines.

It took a long time to get over my bitter feelings. I certainly didn't live up to the vow I had made fifteen years earlier. So much for vows. I would have made a terrible nun.

The irony is, Norman wasn't even aware of how I felt. It's difficult to get even with someone who doesn't have a clue you feel wronged. And the double irony is that I like Norman. Now.

After a couple of years passed, and my dentist informed me I had stopped gnashing my teeth in my sleep, and wouldn't be needing caps on my molars, I would greet Norman with hugs and pecks on the cheek whenever we met at Hollywood functions. He still calls every once in a while to say he's been thinking about me and how am I? And I admire him not only for his talent, but also for putting his money where his mouth is:People for The American Way, The Equal Rights Amendment, and tons of other good causes. Once his consciousness was raised—mostly by his late ex-wife, Frances, and their daughters, he's been very sensitive to the Women's Movement. But it took time.

I remember a particularly spirited *MH2* story conference at which I'd been really sharp. When it was over and the others had left, Norman and I were alone for a while. He told me I had contributed so much that afternoon, and he felt so enthusiastic about me... "I could fuck you!"

Emancipated woman that I was, did I tell him off? Hardly. I was thrilled. I thought it was the nicest compliment he ever bestowed on me.

Norman and I remain friends. Maybe acquaintances is a better word. But he's still clueless about my contribution to *Mary Hartman*. We had lunch about a year ago, and he asked what I was doing. I told him I was working on a comedy.

"Oh," said he, "I didn't know you wrote comedy."

Norman... hello?

For some reason my experience on *MH2* reminds me of the 1940's British war film *Mrs. Miniver*. At the end of everything Greer Garson had been through, she goes to church in a bombed out chapel. As the congregation sings the opening hymn, the camera angles skyward through the bombed out roof to follow a flock of doves disappearing into the sun-dappled clouds. That let us know that Greer was at peace. And so am I, because that's how I'm going to remember *Mary Hartman,* as a trying but beautiful experience.

Only, dammit, I can't. Because in my fantasy the picture doesn't end there. My version ends with one of those doves peeling off and flying back to the bombed out church, where it lets loose just as Norman, one of the congregants, looks up. Now I've got it out of my system. Now I'm at peace, too.

So Ellis was right that night in the Rome Hilton bar when he comforted me by asking the rhetorical question ". . . what is the worst thing that can happen?" Getting fired is the pits, but it ain't fatal.

Chapter 18

Back To The Future

As the sun set over *Mary Hartman* and *All That Glitters,* I was at liberty—and milking it for all it was worth. Offers came in to head write daytime soaps, but I turned them down.

Like a character out of a Joan Didion novel, I drove the freeways with nowhere special in mind. We were between beach houses, but I have a deep and abiding passion for the ocean, and I'd drive out with Ginger and Max, our two lovable mongrels, and take long walks thinking about nothing at all. (Tracy has a habit of asking me what I'm thinking about when I stare into space. She refuses to take "nothing" for an answer, insisting I'm deep into some troubling inner angst.)

I wrote a couple of freelance scripts for prime-time dramas, and the story for a TV movie called *Having Babies II,* in which I created a character named Dr. Julie Farr, an OB/GYN. The story was the dilemma faced by the good doctor when her teenage niece becomes pregnant. I wanted to explore the pros and cons of abortion, especially the hysteria surrounding pro-lifers who were, even then, blocking clinics and threatening doctors and patients. Fat chance. It became a watered-down version that hardly dealt with teenage sexuality, and certainly not abortion. But the main character, Julie Farr, was "spun off" into a series of her own called, unremarkably, *Julie Farr, MD*. Susan Sullivan played the lead, but the show didn't last very long.

Back To The Future

I was elected to the Board of Directors of the Writers Guild, the aggressively feisty union representing screenwriters, which proved to be both stimulating and mind numbing, depending on who had the floor. It gave me a chance to know some very articulate screen writers (with impressive credits), such as Mel Shavelson, Daniel Taradash, Fay Kanin, Ed North, Frank Pierson, Alan Burns, Bill Froug, and others. Ellis had served on the Board a decade before I did, and knew all the old timers. Some, like Dan Taradash and Ed North, had been in the Army Training Film Corps with him. At this point, Ellis had just about had it, again, with being a "suit" at CBS. It was a thankless job. If a network executive is inventive and his/her creative input is good, the show runners take credit. If the show is panned, it's because the network "interfered" with their creative process.

Our children were not children anymore. Steven finished the academic courses for his Ph.D. in physics and atmospheric sciences, and was writing his thesis and teaching at UCLA.

John's relationship with Carmen evolved into a serious commitment. They arrived from Chiapas with Carmen's adorable two-year-old son, Etienne, and were married at the tiny Rudolph Steiner Christian Community Church in North Hollywood.

I thought my two Latina daughters-in-law would become close friends, but I wasn't aware of the subtle prejudices that abound among our neighbors to the south. Steve's wife Anna is a light-complected El Salvadoran, who came from a family of doctors, lawyers and businessmen. Carmen is Mexican and dark; her lovely parents were school teachers but this didn't seem to make any difference to Anna.

I was dismayed to discover the pecking order in Central America. The El Salvadorans look down on the Guatemalans, who look down on Mexicans. Good God, what is wrong with the people who live on this tiny sphere? Just as scientists are discovering what could be signs of ancient living organisms on Mars, the Iraqis are annihilating the Kurds. The Bosnians, Serbs, and Muslims are cleansing their territories of each other. The Protestants and Catholics are blowing each other up in Ireland; the Israelis and

Palestinians, the Tutsis and Hutus... it's all pretty discouraging.

John, Carmen, and Etienne didn't stick around long. They took off for France planning to settle in the foothills of the Pyrenees where there were several small, international communes of likeminded young people who raised children and food, made Music and Art, and "did their own thing."

Ellyn graduated from high school, and we traveled back East to look at colleges. After canvassing the New England campuses, we drove to Little Falls, my old hometown. I hadn't been back since that ill fated, never published *Life* photo essay. Instead of running me out of town as I half-suspected they might, the townsfolk were extremely cordial and hospitable.

We stayed with the son of Mother's good friends, Judge Bloomberg and his wife Dorothy. Henry Bloomberg was the District Attorney of Herkimer County, and had bought ex-mayor Tanzer's lovely old house—where I had had lots of sleep-overs with my pal Chappie Tanzer.

Few of my childhood friends still lived in Little Falls, and half of Main Street was gone—replaced by a nondescript mall. Dad's old store was in the half that remained, but it wasn't a clothing store anymore. It was a gloomy service center and hardware emporium.

I loved growing up in Little Falls, and I wanted to share that feeling with Ellyn, who responded in her own sensitive way. I know she dug the ambiance, which was so different from the San Fernando Valley. She was struck by the vibrant colors—the greens and reds and golds, by the rolling grassy hills, the tree-lined streets, the friendliness of the natives. We were having a special time, until I undertook my second mission for returning to my roots. I wanted to visit my ailing Uncle Mort, Father's youngest brother—the last of his generation, who was in a nursing home in Utica.

But Uncle Mort didn't want to see us. He had no interest at all. In fact, I don't even think he came to the phone when I called from Little Falls—which, of course, made me more determined than ever to see him. So I drove up alone, leaving Ellyn behind. It was depressing. This was my fun-loving, athletic, young Uncle—who used to bike the twenty-two miles from Utica to see us on the weekends. Sometimes he'd show up in a roadster with a splendid, spirited F. Scott Fitzgerald-type woman, and Ray and I would pile into the rumble seat and go off on some wonderful adventure with them—like skinny-dipping in Ilion Gorge. Now he was terribly sick and weak, and even though he wasn't old (my God, I think I'm about his age as I write this), he had given up and was dying. There was nothing I could do to ease his sense of despair or raise his spirits. Was this some melancholy, depressive gene showing up late in his life? Was it related to whatever caused my father to take his own life? Or was it the result of the path he had taken on his own? After all, he had never married. His siblings were gone. Was he simply waiting his turn? Thinking back, it makes me angry because he had never taken any responsibility for his life. He could have married. He could have lived a meaningful life with at least some sense of fulfillment or accomplishment. But he just meandered along, clerking in his brothers' store without taking much of an interest in it (or anything else), and now there was nothing to show for it. At the time, though, I wasn't angry, I was devastated. He hardly acknowledged me. He was beyond caring about, or being interested in, anything. I couldn't wait to get out of there. When I did, I went to the first liquor store I could find, bought a half-pint of something awful, and sipped it on my way back to Little Falls—trying to obliterate my sense of dread, which I'm sure had a lot to do with the unfinished business of my father's suicide. I had been eleven years old then, and unable to deal with it. And now I was a grownup and equally helpless to do anything about Uncle Mort.

Ellyn and I left a day or so later. She decided she didn't want to go to college thousands of miles from Ellis and me, so she opted for Berkeley. I was glad. A month or so before she left, we took a long hike around Hansen Dam in the Valley. I was always concerned because she was practically an only child, being so much younger than her brothers. I worried about how she'd cope without us. What if—God forbid—we perished in a plane crash? Call it the Jewish syndrome, but if I'm not working I tend to dwell on the possibility of all sorts of disasters. So I brought the subject up rather gingerly. She rose to the occasion splendidly. She assured me she could handle things, and I should quit worrying. Of course I didn't, but it was nice to hear her say that. She was going to be fine away from us. Ellis and I were the ones who found it difficult to see the last of our birdlets leave the nest.

I got heavily involved in work. I was still refusing to consider head writing a daytime soap when Betty Corday, owner and Executive Producer of *Days Of Our Lives,* called. I told her I wasn't interested. She insisted I meet her for lunch. We met in one of those small, dark, wood-paneled restaurants on Riverside Drive close to the NBC studios in Burbank where *Days* was produced. Betty was a pretty woman, with a mature figure, who teetered on spike heels. I was afraid she'd fall off, but she maneuvered on them just fine.

"What would it take to get you to head write *Days?*" she asked right off the bat.

I was flattered. It was nice to be asked, but I really, truly didn't want to head write a soap again. I thanked her, but reminded her I had told her no on the phone. She brushed that aside.

"What if I could make it an overall deal with Columbia?" she said. "A deal that would include developing prime time TV series and movies?"

It sounded wonderful. Too good to be true. Which it was. I knew, and she knew, that if I were to head write a one-hour soap (five hours of drama a week), I'd hardly have time to go to the bathroom let alone dream up, write, and produce a new series or a movie. Actually, she was appealing to my ego, and it was working. There had to be a way to do it. Suddenly, I had a flash that wasn't menopausal. Ellis! We hadn't worked together since our love-on-the-desk collaboration on *The Hathaways* sixteen years before. He was bored at the network and was thinking of quitting. But what about his ego? Would he want to be piggybacked onto my deal?

I discussed the idea with Betty, anyway. I told her (small fib) how much Ellis and I wanted to work together again. That she was catching him at just the right time, since he was ready to leave the network. If a deal could be worked out, I could head write the soap, and collaborate and consult on other projects. Betty said she'd talk to Larry White, head of Columbia TV, and get back to us.

So it came to pass that Ellis and I moved into a suite of offices at Columbia, and began a three-year working relationship that was productive, exciting, and lots of fun.

It marked a subtle turning point in our relationship. Ellis had long since regarded me as his professional equal. Now he had to deal with the fact that my career had taken off—and somewhat eclipsed his. It takes a special kind of man to deal with a wife he's mentored, encouraged, and supported, who is suddenly in a position to do those things for him. With things reversed, so to speak, it could have been a touchy situation, but Ellis was a special kind of man, and working together this time was an epiphany for us—especially when our late night comedy serial *L.A.T.E.R.* got on the air. But that didn't happen right away.

As Ellis began setting up our development operation, I plunged into *Days of our Lives*. I took over the reins from Pat Falken Smith, who had been with the show on and off (mostly on), since its inception in 1965. It's one thing to be in at the beginning of a soap; quite another to take over after a show has been running for years. There's all that back story to cope with, all those characters to untangle, all those complicated plot twists—such as who is married to whom, who had he/she been married to before, and whose evil twin had slept with which orphan who turned out to be who's long lost sister whose baby had been adopted by which parents who had been killed in what freak accident caused by whose brother who was being tried for manslaughter by whose ex-vindictive lover who's also the District Attorney and the biological mother (unknown to her) of the defendant?

But *Days* was a solid show, with a wonderful cast, and Pat Falken Smith had left it in good shape. I'm not exactly sure why she left, but after she did, she sued everyone connected with it—including her ex-husband, NBC, Columbia, Betty Corday, and eventually Ellis and me. If I ever knew a litigious person, it was Pat, who went to court as often as some people go out for a frozen yogurt.

"It's nothing personal," Pat told us.

"Of course not," said Ellis, who promptly hired our own lawyer because he didn't trust the network or the studio to protect us. I think the suit was eventually dropped, or maybe it was settled, or maybe it's still in litigation. At any rate, no one seemed to get mad at anyone, and Pat was back on *Days* after a couple of years—and many years after that Ellis worked with her.

Meanwhile, I was in charge of the story and the writers. I would have kept those already on staff, but they felt loyal to Pat (or maybe they were afraid she'd sue them), and declined to stay on. Which was fine with me, because it meant I could hire some of the people who had worked with me on other soaps. Ray came aboard—along with Rocci Chatfield, Mike David, Joyce Perry, Laura Olsher, and Elizabeth Harrower, who eventually plotted my overthrow.

H. Wesley Kenney was the Co-Executive Producer of the show, which he ran most efficiently in a genial, good-natured way that made for a happy cast and crew. And head writer. Wes had excellent credentials. He was a graduate of Carnegie/Mellon, had directed and produced plays and television (including *All in the Family*), yet he was the most unpretentious producer I've ever known. And energy! That man could go from dawn 'til whenever existing on coffee and junk food, and still maintain a low cholesterol count and an athlete's blood pressure. (I know this because we took from the same Beverly Hills internist).

He arranged for me to meet the cast my first week. I sat in a dressing room on the second floor of the studio like some sort of headmistress, as they filed in for one-on-one discussions. It was a lovely, talented cast—some of whom are still there. Unfortunately, Macdonald Carey (who was the head of the Horton clan), died a few years ago. But Frances Reid, the redoubtable Alice Horton, is still there, and can still move me whenever I catch a glimpse of her on the show. Susan Seaforth is there, too, along with her real-life and stage husband, Bill Hayes. This remarkable duo, the Lunts of the soap world, never age, have never lost their talent, and send me a birthday card every year!

Deidre Hall, who plays psychiatrist Dr. Marlena Evans, is still aboard, too, after a number of timeouts for TV movies and prime time series. When I met her that first week, I discovered she had a real-life twin sister. Wow! Here was a chance to do an "evil twin" story without the star having to double the twin part. I think that was the storyline the fans got the most angry about. Andrea Lovell Hall, Deidre's sister, who was a Florida teacher, was cast as Dr. Marlena Evans' sociopathic, drug-abusing, failed-actress sister Samantha, from Hollywood. (The fact that Andrea wasn't a professional actress worked for her in the part). I concocted a story in which Samantha ruins her sister's life because in her twisted, evil way she blames Marlena for her own failure. Not only does she break up Marlena's romance with Don Craig (Jed Allan); she sleeps with him while pretending to be her sister. And when she's about to be discovered, she slips her sister a mickey, gets her committed to a mental institution by switching identities, and then has her subjected to electric shock treatments!

The fans went crazy. They hated what was happening. They promised never to watch the show again. They said they'd boycott the sponsors. Only they kept tuning in—making the ratings higher than ever. We were nominated for Emmys two years in a row.

I'll always be ambivalent about soaps. In order to maintain high ratings, the storylines have to be melodramatic and soapy, closer to *The Perils of Pauline* than *Anna Karenina*. Yet there have always been other stories that conscientiously deal with cutting-edge social issues, and soaps are often way ahead of their snobbish prime-time cousins in dealing with controversial issues.

Pat had left me with an interracial story on *Days*. It was developed honestly, with both sets of parents as well as the lovers dealing with their hopes, fears, and emotions. I wanted to continue with it; to have the young people marry and then dramatize their problems, but there was no way the network, or the sponsors—or the fans—would allow it. Just as with the abortion story for the TV movie, this story was aborted. The beautiful young black college student was given an opportunity she couldn't refuse, a full scholarship to a medical school that just happened to be thousands of miles from Salem. She left for school, and was never heard of again.

While I was churning out the soap, Ellis was busy shepherding our production company's other projects, and I tried to keep my hand in. One of the projects was a pilot for CBS called *Paradise*, a sitcom set in a trailer park on the outskirts of San Diego—with the requisite collection of oddball inhabitants. The idea originated with Merrill Markoe, who had arrived from Berkeley and contacted me during the last of my *Mary Hartman* troubles. We had a vague connection through her parents, who were best friends with Ellis' sister's husband's brother and his wife. And if you can figure that out you're a better person than I, Gunga Reader.

Merrill was (and is) enormously bright and funny, although a bit weird and quirky, and I hired her briefly as my underpaid assistant when I was working on *All That Glitters*. Unfortunately, *Paradise* was not picked up by the network, but Merill was destined for bigger things, and went on to become Dave Letterman's head writer and significant other, among other achievements.

At about this time, we read an article in *MS. MAGAZINE* about the first women cadets at West Point, which we thought would make a good movie. When we took the idea to the Columbia long-form executives, they told us that the producing team of Jim Green and Allen Epstein already had a script in the works on those pioneer women cadets. But when their script fell through, Green/Epstein asked if we'd be interested in writing our version.

We went to West Point to research the project, with preconceived ideas about the kinds of people who were in the military or would choose soldiering as a profession—especially the women. Instead, we found (both among the cadets, male and female, and the faculty) a group of capable, bright, and articulate people who were interesting, personable, and fun to be with.

It was a wonderful experience, and a pretty good movie starring Linda Purl, Andrew Stevens and Jameson Parker. Ellis did the major work on the script, going back to West Point when the movie was in production for rewrites, while I stayed home chained to *Days of our Lives*.

It was clear, though, that Columbia was waiting for me to come up with a late-night comedy soap in the vein of *Mary Hartman*—

no small order. The task got easier when I was tossed out as head writer of *Days* by a combination of my own stubbornness and a wonderful, wacky intrigue uncovered by our executive assistant, Chris Kevin. Live by melodrama, die by melodrama!

There are plays within plays behind any production, be it a soap, series, or film. Writers are as insecure as actors or other crew members (with the possible exception of directors, the Saddam Husseins of productions). Backstage, paranoia rules, disastrous rumors abound: the show's about to be canceled, your part is being written out, the head writer is getting axed which means the writing staff is out, too. And this is apart from the jealousies, affairs, backbiting, favor-currying, upstaging—normal activities which are par for the course. Most people at work on a show are very much aware of who's in, who's out, and who's involved in the latest intrigue. Except me. And it's not because I'm above it all; it's because I have some unique gene missing. An intrigue gene? Whatever it is, I'm always the last to know the latest gossip.

Evidently, though, our executive assistant, Christine Kevin, had intrigue genes up the kazoo. She <u>always</u> knew what was going on, and to whom. When she got wind that a certain memo had been written that was highly critical of the way I was handling the show, she set about to find the perpetrator <u>and</u> the secret memo. So one night she stayed late, waited until Betty Corday's assistant had closed the office, and snuck in! She opened a locked drawer with a letter opener (or maybe a wax mold of the key?), and found the damaging evidence. It was a long letter to Betty outlining how I was ruining the show by not being true to the characters and other like atrocities. It was well written, and some of it was true, even though our ratings were excellent and the show was doing well. But it had been written by someone I had hired, a member of my writing staff, and that wasn't nice.

I never got as mad about it as Chris and some other members of the writing staff, who, of course, found out about it through whatever means they found out about everything. I didn't even want to fire the "perp" because she was a good writer. At the same time, I was beginning to lose interest in the grueling job.

I think the longest I've head written a soap is three years—at which point I get cranky and argumentative, and pick a fight with the network or the Executive Producer over a story I stubbornly insist on writing, which they refuse to do. So they fire me. That's exactly what happened with *Days*. I wrote a story about one of the beloved characters who was a Vietnam veteran about to get married. A few days before the marriage, a beautiful Vietnamese woman shows up with her six-year-old child, who was fathered by the beloved character.

"No!" said Betty Corday.

"No!" said the Network.

I dug my heels in. Ellis, Ray and I went to Mammoth for a long weekend ski trip. It snowed and snowed. Up over the windows of our cabin. It snowed so much we couldn't ski, and all of us were getting cabin fever. I called the office and was told that Betty was trying to reach me. I called Betty and she said I had to come up with another story. The Vietnamese story was a definite no-go. I refused. She fired me.

This was a couple of months after the stolen memo caper. The perpetrator of the memo became the new head writer. I went to her milestone 75th birthday a year or so ago. Maybe we're not good friends, but we're friends.

After I was "released" from my duties as head writer of *Days*, I was persuaded to take on the head writing chores of *Love of Life*, a soap on its last legs produced in New York. I shouldn't have accepted the job, but the Columbia executives had sweetened our deal. And they were holding out the carrot of an on-air guarantee to create and produce that late-night series they had been asking us for—if only I'd straighten out the failing soap. So I tried.

I concocted a story paying homage to Theodore Dreiser's novel, *An American Tragedy*. (Or was it the movie I paid homage to called *A Walk in the Sun,* starring Elizabeth Taylor and Montgomery Clift?)

Whatever, the show, which was the longest running soap ever, came to an end. Walter Kronkite marked its passing on his nightly newscast. Who knows, I may have hastened its demise. But with

Love of Life out of the way, I was free to pursue what turned out to be the best damned time I ever had in this business. Ellis and I embarked on our late-night show, *L.A.T.E.R.* — an acronym for *The Life and Times of Eddie Roberts*.

Chapter 19

"The Life And Times Of Eddie Roberts" -- And Others

I don't know why Ellis and I had such a good time writing and producing our late night comedy serial. Maybe it was because we were Executive Producers for the first time. It's a great feeling to be in charge—to have control . . . POWER! But it wasn't only that. Everything seemed to work. We were both at our peak. Ideas flowed back and forth. We made each other laugh. It was a perfect collaboration. Columbia produced the show with Metromedia, and the studio executives were expansive, enthusiastic and cooperative. For the most part. Of course, the budget was basic minimum. It was a daily taped show with no money at all for post-production. What was taped on the set went on the air. Period. But we were given a 13-week, 65-episode, on-air guarantee—and we were in heaven.

I remembered Norman Lear's adage: Be as outrageous as possible. And we were. The setting was a small liberal arts college in the San Fernando Valley, Cranepool U. (One of the sets was the Cranepool pool). The action centered around "Everyman" Eddie Roberts, who was an assistant professor of Anthropology, and fighting for tenure against all odds. His wife, Dolores, was determined to be the first woman to make it into major league baseball. They had an adorable eight-year-old daughter, perky but not precocious, and an eclectic assortment of friends and colleagues.

There was Chiquita, Eddie's chief rival for the coveted tenured professorship, who was not only a minority and a woman, but also

"The Life And Times Of Eddie Roberts"--And Others

physically challenged, in a wheelchair, and gay. There was Cynthia a rich, spoiled student with a mad crush on Eddie, who in the first episode locks herself in the bathroom threatening to kill herself. Her father was a racist state Senator, and chairman of the Board of Trustees of the college. Turner was a black radical leftover from the sixties, posing as a mild-mannered Sears salesman, who takes up residence in Eddie's basement—where he secretly plots the overthrow of the government. Then there was Mr. Billy, played by Billy Barty, the smallest P.I. ever to appear on TV, who was investigating the mysterious disappearance of the dean's wife. We also had a Chinese industrial spy posing as the coach of a visiting ping pong team from the mainland. And that was just for starters.

In need of extra cash to make ends meet, Eddie becomes a paid volunteer to test a radical experiment in male birth control, which renders him impotent. Dolores, doing her share to provide extra income, becomes a chicken advertising an expanding fast food franchise, Kluckerama, owned by an unscrupulous black entrepreneur, General Flanders, who sees Communist plots everywhere.

We took on fringe therapy groups, pornography, sexual exploitation, racism, intermarriage, and undocumented immigrants. We ran the gamut from A (abortion) to Z (zygapophysis). Remember, Eddie was an anthropologist. We were waaaaay ahead of our time and the studio and syndication executives loved everything we did—until we got on the air.

Metromedia scheduled us at various times throughout the country, but in southern California they gave us the 11 p.m. time-slot. In fact, they were so enthusiastic about the show they told us they were "warming up" that time period by showing reruns of M*A*S*H at 11 p.m. Only when we began our run in that time period, the M*A*S*H fans wanted to see M*A*S*H—not some new and radically different serial. Metromedia would have done a lot better warming up the time slot by showing *Bowling for Dollars*.

Even though our ratings were respectable, they were lower than the M*A*S*H reruns. So Metromedia went back to the old schedule and put us on later. And later. And still later. And each time they changed the time, the ratings got lower. When they scheduled the show at 1 a.m. (at least in southern California), we were about halfway through our 65-episode guarantee. And the ratings were pretty bad. So they informed us they were taking us off the air all together.

I was mad. They had to pay for all 65 episodes. It was absolutely stupid to replace us with the 18th run of *Sea Hunt* or *Lassie*. Ellis was philosophical, but never having been a network executive, I wasn't. He had to stick around that afternoon and produce the show, but I jumped in my car and headed for Metromedia, where I made an impassioned plea to Bob Whosis, the program chief, to keep us on the air no matter what the time period was. I cared about the show—and the actors and the writers and the crew. VCRs were just becoming popular. At least we could tell our few fans to tape the show.

I must have put on a pretty good performance, because they kept us on the air. I think we wound up at 2 a.m. but, by God, they aired every one of the 65 shows we made, and that's the truth!

When we finished taping the last episode, Ellis gathered us together on the floor of Stage 25 on the Warner lot, and thanked everyone for a glorious experience. Cast and crew, there wasn't a dry eye in the house. Afterwards, we went across the street to the Smoke House and got smashed.

We had worked on the show for almost a year with some special people, and it had been a memorable experience. I know it's corny, but there was a warm, family feeling among the cast and crew—maybe because some of the cast and crew were family; Ell's brother, Marc Daniels, gave us a real boost by directing the pilot. Once we were up and running, we were able to give Tracy a shot at directing—something she had always wanted to do. But we held our collective breath. It wasn't that we were worried about her ability to grasp the technical aspects, since she had observed scores of directors in the medium, and had boned up specifically with a tape specialist. We certainly were aware of her talent in working with actors. We were simply worried that she'd be late. That her dog might chew up her storyboard with all the shots on it. That she'd lose her only pair of glasses. That the guard would direct her to the wrong stage. None of the above happened. Tracy came in an hour early, was totally in control and fully prepared, and the episode came off splendidly. So she directed a few more.

Ellyn came home from Berkeley for the holidays, fell in love with the show, and asked if she could write an episode on spec. Sure, we said, and gave her an outline. She eventually wrote two scripts, and, with a little rewriting by her parents, they were aired. Ah the joys of nepotism.

My ex-brother-in-law Jerry Adelman, who had lasted two years longer than I had on *Mary Hartman,* joined us as a staff writer, and was responsible for some very funny scripts, especially the ones with Billy Barty playing a private eye. Michael Robert David, who had worked with me on *Days,* came aboard as a staff writer, too, and was very innovative. But I think I'm most proud of discovering a brand-new talent, a young woman just out of college who had never written professionally before. Her name was Diane Frolov, and she was extremely shy, but she wrote a fantastic tryout script, became a star member of our writing team, and has gone on to become a major force in television—writing and producing *Northern Exposure* and *Dangerous Minds,* mostly in collaboration with her husband, Andrew Schneider.

Our lead character, Eddie Roberts, was played by Renny Temple, a member of an improv group, War Babies, that originated in New York, and was brought out to the Coast by Dick Clark. Renny was so talented and well trained that we cast many of his fellow improv artists in other parts—including his wonderful wife-to-be Caren Kaye, Marsha Myers and Archie Hahn, who was also in *MH2.*

Udana Power played Eddie's wife, Dolores, with vulnerability and strength. By the end of the show's run, she was about to be given a tryout by a fictional major-league expansion team in Denver coached by her father, Ducky, played by our good friend, the talented Martin E. Brooks.

Maria O'Brien was Chiquita, our assertive, physically challenged minority rival for Eddie's job; and wonderful Joan

Hotchkiss played Lydia, a far-out, new-age therapist. There were many other terrific actors in our cast, too numerous to mention.

Perhaps if Metromedia had had more guts and kept us in our original time period, we might have found an audience. I was haunted by the feeling that no one saw the show. But that wasn't entirely true. I had at least one fan. A persistent one. She was eleven years old, and she had somehow found my unlisted number and called me daily—nightly actually—from Chicago to discuss the finer points of plot and character. She was bright and she liked the show, but eventually I had to ask if her parents knew she was making all those long distance calls. I didn't want the poor kid to get into trouble.

Every once in awhile, I would come across someone who not only saw the show, but admired it. During the triennial Writer's Guild strike of '88, I joined a young woman marching in a picket line around the Century Plaza Hotel, where a convocation of broadcasters was taking place. We fell into easy conversation as we marched around with our picket signs. She told me she had just created a new sitcom that was slated for the CBS schedule which, of course, was being held up by the strike. The series was called *Murphy Brown*—she was Diane English, and she was one of the handful of people who had seen *L.A.T.E.R.* Not only that, but she had written a review of it for *Vogue*. A good review. I'll always love that woman. And her shows, too.

Ellis and I ended our production deal with Corday/Columbia shortly after *L.A.T.E.R.* went off the air—with our heads held high and unemployed. It was a perfect time to visit son John, Carmen, and their growing family in the foothills of the Pyrenees in France.

Chapter 20

All My Children—Not The Soap

We had visited John several times since he and Carmen and Etienne (whom he had adopted), trekked off to France. It was always a trip—both in the physical and vernacular sense, because nothing they did in those days was conventional. They weren't even conventional rebels like the *emigres* who had fled to Paris in the '20s and '30s, those literary and artistic icons of my youth who hung out on the Left Bank, boozing and having affairs and still turning out memorable works of art.

John and Carmen and their friends were more ascetic, living in more or less primitive conditions in the unchic countryside, hundreds of miles from Paris, in small enclaves of international ex-hippies who were into vegetarianism, child raising, carpentry, folk art, music, and survival. John and Carmen dreamed of creating a sound and light studio that would combine Carmen's artistic projection of colors dripped onto a disc and magnified on a screen with John's spontaneous music, improvisationally played on a myriad of folk instruments: Tibetan temple gongs; hand-carved bamboo flutes, sitars, modern brass and stringed instruments—whatever he could get his hands on. At times the sound could be haunting and beautiful. At other times cacophonous and unappealing—at least to me. And to Ellis, too, who was more worried about where this would all lead, and how John and Carmen could support their growing family.

I knew where Ellis was coming from. He grew up in the Depression and his family had a tough time. He had served in the Army for five years and then worked extremely hard, in a competitive industry, before achieving financial security. No wonder he was a little impatient and concerned. The thing is, I'm not exactly sure where I was coming from. Ambivalence, I guess. On one hand, I admired John and Carmen's unconventionality—their willingness to try out new ideas and their courage to live an alternative life with the barest creature comforts and little money. On the other hand, I didn't see where they were headed, either, and I missed them terribly, especially the children who had increased threefold.

Jacobo was born in 1977 in Rouvenac, a tiny village in the Aude district. We visited him when he was a few months old, a robust, happy baby sleeping in a woven basket—much the way I remember Bible pictures of Moses in his basket in the bulrushes. The Rouvenac digs were pretty basic—a cold, dark, stone rowhouse bordering the only street in the tiny town. Living in a somewhat better house close-by were their friends, Celia and David Inayat. David's uncle was Pir Vilayat Kahn, the political and spiritual leader of one of the Sufi sects in India. I mention them only because Celia fascinated me. She was English to the core, with an aristocratic Mayfair background, and reminded me of Hemingway's Lady Brett. Yet there she was, living the same singularly alternate lifestyle as John and Carmen. Ah, youth.

We tried to visit them every other year, flying into Paris and sometimes staying at outrageously luxurious hotels like the Georges V; eating in five-star restaurants, doing the museums, sightseeing and stopping off at quaint chateaux before wending our way south to the Breughal-like environs of John and Carmen. Wherever we were in France, I would try to speak the language, even though my facility with all the romance languages is about on a par with Sid Caesar's. I, who took a course in French drama at Western College in which I supposedly read Racine, Corneille, and Moliere in the original, had a hard time making myself understood in a French restaurant. Not that it matters. The French don't want you struggling with their language. Either speak it fluently, like

Jackie Onassis did, or not at all. Period. So it was "period" for me, although Ellis always claimed that when I was in France (or any other non-English speaking country), I spoke broken English in a loud voice as a compromise. This is not true.

When our granddaughter, Paola, was about to be born in 1979, we flew over once again. We rented a Peugeot station wagon for the trip to Renné Le Chateau, where John and Carmen were living at the time, so we had plenty of room for the tricycle and miniature car with pedals we bought in Paris for our grandsons. After getting lost several times *en route*, we finally found Le Chateau at the top of a steep grassy hill with, of course, no road leading up to it. But it was a charming cottage with a beautiful view of rolling hills and fields, and John and Carmen (large with child) helped us lug our things, including the toys, up the hill. Ellis usually insisted on sleeping in whatever local accommodations were available, as long as there was indoor plumbing, but this time he accepted Carmen's invitation to take their bed. She, John, and the children were used to sleeping on mats on the floor.

It was always magic visiting them—the air, the healthy food, the candlelight talks, getting to know the children. This time was no different, especially since the boys were so ecstatic over their gifts. So ecstatic, in fact, that they began to fight over whose turn it was with the more popular of the two vehicles, the little auto. As the argument escalated, Carmen descended on both the tricycle and the auto, scooped them up, marched to the edge of a promontory, and heaved them into the rocky canyon below. Returning, she announced, "My children should not play with plastic toys. I do not approve of plastics!"

Plastics, that old devil-word summing up the hollowness of the phony/capitalist adult world to Dustin Hoffman in *The Graduate*, seemed to convey the same evil to our daughter-in-law. She was still the fiery socialist, opinionated, and in this instance, darn rude—since we had lugged those plastic toys all the way from Paris.

I've always walked a little on eggs with Carmen, but I admired her then and now. She's a wonderful mother, and a talented artist, and she's become more reasonable and less doctrinaire as time goes by.

A word about Carmen and John's house in Marses, about a hundred kilometers south of Carcassonne in the foothills of the Pyrenees, where they moved after Paola was born. They built it from the ruins of a stone barn with the help of their partner and friend, Michael Fles (who was the son of one of brother Ray's ex-girl friends). They turned the barn into a handsome two-story home, with tongue and cheek flooring, a fireplace, homemade furniture—and no indoor plumbing or heat. After moving in, they continued to develop their sound and light studio, but mostly they existed on their vegetable garden, odd jobs, bussing in Carcassonne during the tourist season, and joining in the *vendage*—when the entire family would help the local farmers harvest their grapes. They also had two horses, and a goat for milk. And help from Ellis and me, and the French government, which subsidized families with more than one child. (So much for Governor Pete Wilson and his miserly ways with immigrants.)

From time to time, John and Carmen would take their sound and light show on the road to other parts of France, and to Germany, Spain, and neighboring European countries. When they were invited to tour the kibbutzim of Israel, Ellis and I decided to meet them there. Once we made our plans, I was amazed at how much I wanted to immerse myself in Jewishness!

I fervently wish we could all get along—white, black, brown—all shades, all ethnicities, all cultures. I know . . . I know how important diversity is, the richness of all races, creeds, national origins. I know all that, but look at all the misery, and violence, and hatred, and horror these differences cause. Ellis, the most moral, ethical man I've ever known, claimed he was an atheist partly because he felt religion had caused more evil than good. Sometimes I wish religion hadn't been invented at all, or that we were all mixed up—all a shade of puce, maybe. While I'm fantasizing, maybe it would be better if we were one sex. Aren't there some single-sex, microscopic, cellular animals or insects that propagate? Would that bring peace? Probably not.

All My Children—Not The Soap

Having stated the above, I was absolutely thrilled to be going to Israel. Deep down in my Little Fallsian childhood, I buried my feelings of anger and resentment at being an outsider. Even though I kept telling myself how proud I was to be a Jew, why was I secretly pleased when people said, "You don't look Jewish?" Why was I so careful not to use my hands when I spoke, and always so careful with my diction? Ptui!

Suddenly, joyously, after the interminable trip from Los Angeles to Israel, I found myself among My People! Surrounded! In the majority! I couldn't speak a word of Hebrew, but I reveled in the native tongue. I loved the handsome soldiers (the female ones, too), the religious Jews in their tallises and black-brimmed, funny hats. Everyone was Jewish—not just the doctors and shopkeepers, but the bulldozer operators, the traffic cops, the garbage collectors, the flight attendants, the pilots—everyone!

The first day, we ventured out from the modern high-rise hotel in Jerusalem with our three grandkids to do some shopping for new clothes. While we were in a store buying shorts and T-shirts, there was a loud explosion in the street. No one in the store panicked, at least not the natives. The clerk simply asked us to move to the rear of the store, and soon we heard police sirens, which the kids found exciting. After less than a half-hour, we were completing our purchases, and by the time we left the store, everyone was going about his/her business as though nothing unusual happened. I suppose nothing unusual <u>had</u> happened, simply a small act of terrorism that injured a few bus passengers—luckily this time no one had been killed.

It seemed almost bucolic in the various countryside kibbutzim, where John and Carmen were invited. They set up art and music workshops for the children of the settlements during the day, and put on their sound and light show for everyone at night. I loved it. It was like being in a year-round summer camp. But, other than free accommodations and bountiful meals, John and Carmen didn't receive any fees—which didn't bother them, since they felt ahead of the game if they broke even on their road trips. I had to agree it was idyllic in Israel; meeting so many wonderfully dedicated and interesting people, touring the ancient historical sites, floating in the Dead Sea, romping at the seashore. I also had to agree with Ellis, and wonder when Carmen and John were going to Plan for The Future and Face Reality like all us other grown-ups. I'm still coping with my ambiguity on that subject, long after John and Carmen have settled into more conformist ways.

We left for home a couple of weeks later, with a promise from John that he and his family would visit us, and that he'd consider moving back to the States. After we left, the five of them took off for a tour of Egypt; traveling by local buses, which meant sharing space with farmers on their way to market with their goats and chickens. Shades of *Mary Hartman.*

It took several months, but John kept his promise to visit, after persuading Carmen he was reasonably sure that they wouldn't be corrupted if they checked out the States. They arrived at LAX one mild November in the wee hours of the morning, looking like a refugee family. John and the kids were in homespun clothes, donated by the Good Sisters of Limoux. Carmen was in her exotic long-skirted colorful getup. They settled in our rented Malibu house.

What a stretch—from the scrubby fields of the Aude district in southern France to the star-studded beaches of Southern California. But not really. Because the house we rented for several years was one of the least pretentious on Carbon Beach. It was built by Jim O'Reilly, a test pilot for McDonnel-Douglas, in the late '50s, and was simple and basic—a two-story frame structure with four small bedrooms and a great view. I loved it. Ellis tolerated it. I used it as an office and we spent almost every weekend there, but we still called Sherman Oaks our home. Friends routinely told us we were crazy to keep spending all that money on rent. Why, they asked, didn't we buy a beach house? Were they crazy? Buy a beach house in Malibu, that disaster area? During the twelve or so years we rented, we witnessed floods, mud slides, fires, huge tides that washed away the beach causing thirty-foot sink holes, and a couple of earthquakes—which don't count I suppose, because they happen all over southern California. Yet after each disaster, the faithful residents drain the water out of their homes, wash off the mud, replant

All My Children—Not The Soap

the greenery, rebuild, and re-enjoy the ocean, the beach, the mountains, the dazzling sunsets, the ambiance and beauty of that gem by the sea, Malibu. The truth about why we didn't buy a beach house was that even a modest one was outrageously expensive and we couldn't afford it, if we wanted to keep our real home in Sherman Oaks.

So each year we continued to rent our modest beach house nestled among the impressive homes of celebrities such as Doris Day, Mary Tyler Moore, Grant Tinker, Johnny Carson, Ann-Margret, John McEnroe, Tatum O'Neal and other everyday moguls, none of whom we knew, except to nod to when they jogged by. (Mary Tyler Moore always seemed to be moving backward while striding purposefully forward). We did become friendly with a good-looking, young couple shortly after they moved next door. I recognized Suzanne Childs, the refreshingly bright and glamorous weekend news anchor at the local CBS-TV station, but not her husband, Michael Crichton, who hadn't quite made the super-mogul status he enjoys today, although he was a successful writer and director. It was pre-<u>Jurasic Park</u>, and I think he was going through a period of writer's block (haven't we all!) and trying various ways to combat it. He and Suzanne would go off to some guru in the desert and observe "silent days" when they came back, which made it difficult to borrow a cup of sugar or a jumper cable. When he wasn't submerged in some womb-like tank undergoing another kind of therapy, Michael was friendly and we enjoyed their company when Suzanne invited us over for dinner, or when we reciprocated.

I remember going out with them for sushi one night. We went in my car, a Honda hatchback. Michael, who is very tall, could barely fold himself into the back seat, but he was gentleman enough to persist. I also remember teasing him until I got him to swim in the ocean with me. It has always been amazing to me that people who live at the beach in Malibu so rarely go into the ocean. I don't blame them, Ellis included, because I'm scared of the ocean, too. Scared stiff, as a matter of fact, of sharks and riptides and big surf, but also exhilarated by it, the colder the better. Anyway, it was nice to have a big, strong guy like Michael there with me, if only for a few times.

Even after their marriage floundered, we continued our relationship with Suzanne, a woman for all seasons. She is a broadcast journalist, actress, lawyer, prosecutor, and writer. Foremost, to me, she is my very special, close friend.

But what of John and Carmen? The truth is, the visit didn't work out. John and Carmen weren't ready to abandon either their hand-hewn home in Marses, or their dream of establishing a studio for alternative music and art. They stayed for several months, trying to make a go of things. Etienne, who was six, went to the Malibu Elementary School, while John worked as a construction laborer on faculty houses at Pepperdine University, and tried to figure out what kind of future he and Carmen could carve out if they moved back permanently. Meanwhile Carmen, who disapproved of what she could see of the culture and mores of Southern California, did approve of the beach, and made beautiful collages from the shells and pebbles and driftwood she collected while she took care of little Jacobo and Paola.

They went back to France without making any final decisions. It was hard to see them go, not knowing if I'd ever get to see them on a regular basis. It was especially difficult to say goodbye to the children, whom I got to know, and who were so very special and loving.

I felt especially bad about the non-relationship, the disconnection, really, between John and his brother and sister. It wasn't John's fault. Ellyn was away at Berkeley, and Steve and Anna, who had a two-year-old son named Kevin by this time, were in a world of their own.

Steven received his Ph.D. in Atmospheric Sciences from UCLA. He worked for a year or so at a think-tank in the San Fernando Valley before settling at the Jet Propulsion Lab at Cal-Tech in Pasadena. He works with a team of scientists, doing things like tracking the rotation of the earth in teeny tiny measurements, tracking the temperatures of the oceans and the long term effects they have on the environment, the weather and God knows what else. Once in awhile he tries to explain what he's doing, but I just don't get it. I don't have a scientific gene in my body. He must have gotten his expertise from Ell, who got a perfect math score when he took the SATs in Queens so many years ago. I simply don't understand what Steve does at JPL, but then I don't understand Steve.

I know a man is supposed to cleave unto his wife, and Anna continued to have a difficult time relating to Ellis and me—and John and Ellyn, too, but that shouldn't have kept Steve from seeing us every once in a while on his own initiative. You know, "Hi, how are you? I'd like to drop by if you're going to be home." The only time I saw him, Anna, or Kevin, was after prolonged negotiations—pleading, actually—and then they might or might not show up. Even on holidays and birthdays. It got more and more difficult, until finally Ellis gave up, and refused to either visit them, or try to coax them to visit us. When and if they wanted to see us—he'd be there. I should have done the same thing, but I couldn't. I tried and tried to find a way to break through the mysterious barrier that kept us apart, from communicating beyond the essentials. It seemed so ridiculous that Steve, who had been so close and loving and considerate—so much fun and imaginative and curious, distanced himself from us. Was it because of my illnesses, and his fear of getting too close only to lose me? Was it because he imagined I disapproved of Anna? Or was that what she thought, and was he caught between the two of us? It was maddening and frustrating not to be able to talk it out, come to terms with whatever it was, and work it out. Here it was the Age of Therapy, and neither Steve nor Anna would consider consulting a therapist to find out what was alienating them—not only from Ellis and me, but also from John and his family, and Ellyn.

It's hardly a consolation, but many of our friends, contemporaries who had children when we did, had problems with them. Drugs, alcohol, suicide—all kinds of dreadful things. Much worse than a lack of communication. So I guess we should have counted our blessings, but it was hard. I do manage to see Kevin now and then. He's bright, articulate and funny. He's been writing and drawing a Gary Trudeau-type satirical strip since he was about nine. Who knows? Maybe he can be a bridge to his parents someday and break the barrier. In fact, I think I detect signs of change.

Meanwhile, Ellyn progressed through Berkeley, majoring in Anthropology, and imagining herself in love with an English instructor, whose fiancé was doing graduate work three thousand miles away in Boston. One night she called us beside herself with excitement.

"Mom," she said, "I've got some fantastic news!"

I held my breath.

"Robert's asked me to marry him!"

I exhaled, reedily.

"Isn't it wonderful?" she bubbled. "It's the most incredible thing that's ever happened to me!"

"But honey," I gasped, "honey, wait a minute. You're only nineteen. You have two more years of college You're much too young to get married. Besides, I had no idea you were serious about Robert. Do you love him?"

"Not really," said she, "and I have no intention of getting married."

"I don't understand," I said. "If you don't love him, if marriage is out of the question, why are you calling?"

"Because it's the first time anyone's asked me to marry him," said she still excited, "and I wanted to share it with you."

God, I love my daughter. My unique and wonderful daughter. She continues to be the light of my life, still the best idea I ever had.

Her undergraduate days were not her happiest, though. She couldn't find her niche, her group, maybe her identity. For a while she shared an off-campus apartment with another student, and, in those pre-politically correct days, they called themselves JAPS: Lois was a Japanese American Princess and Ellyn was a Jewish American Princess—although not really. She shunned the Greek letter societies. She didn't possess more than one cashmere sweater, and she wasn't spoiled . . . much. As a matter of fact, she worked part-time one semester and full-time one summer as a cocktail waitress at the Rusty Pelican, zipping around tables in the briefest uniform imaginable. I think it was the best time she had as an undergraduate. She graduated with honors and a Phi Beta Kappa key, which she refused to send away for; but I did although I promptly lost it—which is okay because she wouldn't have worn it anyway. She applied to several law schools, and was accepted by some good ones, but opted once more for Berkeley and its prestigious school of law, Boalt Hall.

Ray and Tracy were as close to all of us as ever—celebrating graduations, birthdays, ups and downs, good times and not so good. Ray was writing a syndicated soap and a two-part Irwin Allen TV movie, and was in his eighth or ninth long relationship. This time it was with Mickie II, a Peabody Award recipient and local talk-show host. We all loved Mickey I, and expected Ray to capitulate and marry her, but no dice. Now it was a question of when Mickie II (whom we also liked a lot), would get him to the altar, but I wasn't holding my breath. A good thing, too, because she never got him there.

Then there was Tracy, defying nature, still dazzlingly beautiful, running her successful actor's studio, and involved with a much younger man.

When Ellis and I returned from Israel, we went back to work.

Chapter 21

Home Again

Through the years Ellis and I—together and alone—came up with scores of ideas for comedy and drama series and TV movies. A lot of them were shot down before they got off the drawing board, but many of them made it to script, for which we were paid (thank God and the Writers Guild), although only a few made it to production and even fewer made it to the home screen. But there probably hasn't been a hit, failed series, movie or soap that we haven't pitched an almost identical idea for, and which almost . . . almost got a "green light" before the one that did. That's because there are only so many original ideas, and they were used up around the time of Aesop. Of course, that's never stopped any of us from trying to put a new twist on an old idea, or the networks from picking and choosing likely candidates and then discarding most of them after paying huge sums of money for them.

When I think of the awful waste of talent, time, and money spent on thousands of unused properties gathering dust on network shelves (are they computer discs now?), I could cry. Mostly my tears are for my projects that have been discarded. They have mounted up after more than thirty years in this business. Every once in awhile, when I'm looking for something else in my files, I read one of them and Damn, I think, that was good. Of course, some weren't so good, and others were pretty bad. But on the whole, probably the best stuff I've written is gathering dust on one of those shelves.

When we got back from Israel Ellis and I wrote a movie for CBS that was typical of one of our failed efforts, but which we both liked. It was called *MAN AND SUPERWOMAN,* but it wasn't about a woman in a cape who flies, it was about the difficulties faced by a woman trying to juggle a job, a kid, and a marriage. Maybe it wasn't Hallmark Hall of Fame quality, but it was a heck of a lot better than the usual woman-in-jeopardy or disease-of-the-week fare that does make it to screen.

One of my problems was that network and industry execs typecast talent. If you're an actor, say, George Clooney, who plays the heartthrob of ER, they don't want to cast you as a ruthless killer in a movie. In the same way, if you've been successful as a soap writer, they're reluctant to give you a shot at a cop show, or a movie, or a sitcom. Even though Ellis had lots of experience on cop/action shows, and I wrote some movies and comedies, they pegged me as a soap-writer and kept shoving soaps at both of us.

But, hey, the money was great, so when Jackie Smith, head of ABC daytime, asked us to create and develop a new soap—we plunged into a series we called *Jenny's People,* an urban soap about the downsizing of the steel industry in Pittsburgh, and how it affected the rich owners of one of the plants, and the large, close-knit blue-collar family employed there. I still don't know why it never got on the schedule. Jackie, who could be a stickler and drive writers crazy (even old pals like Ellis and me), also had good taste, and she told us it was the best thing we'd written. But the soap it was supposed to replace had a sudden upsurge in the ratings, and there were other scheduling problems, and *Jenny's People* languished on the shelf.

So we took a staff job as executive story consultants on the prime time soap, *Knot's Landing,* in its second year of a remarkable fourteen-year run. It was a spinoff of *Dallas,* which had been created by David Jacobs with input from Michael Filerman, and both David and Mike were the Executive Producers. In those early years, *Knot's* was more an anthology show than a soap. Many episodes were self-contained stories about one of the neighbors who lived in the cul-de-sac. I remember two of them in particular—

Ellis wrote one and I wrote the other.

In the one that Ellis wrote, a distinguished elderly gentleman, suffering from the beginning stages of Alzheimer's, sees Abby Cunningham (Donna Mills), and confuses her with a long lost love of his youth. Abby, the bitch of the series, plays along with his fantasy so she can trick him out of his fortune—only to get immersed in the fantasy herself, even after learning he's penniless. Donna was terrific in the episode, but the most memorable thing was that Lew Ayres (the actor who starred in *All Quiet on the Western Front* in 1927!), played the elderly gentleman.

In my favorite episode of the ones I wrote, the remarkable Julie Harris, who played Lilimae Clements, returns to Knots Landing and her daughter Valene Ewing (Joan Van Ark), is forced to provide a home for her. Lilimae, who appeared briefly during the first year of the series, was supposedly back home, down South; but she never left Southern California, and turned up as a bag lady in MacArthur Park in downtown L.A.

The memorable part of that episode happened during the first rehearsal of the script. It was only the second year of the series, but the actors had already become bored, and they horsed around at rehearsals like grade school kids forced to spend recess in the classroom because it was raining. This was especially true at the initial reading of the script, when all the regulars gathered in David's office and read their parts using Russian accents (or Italian, or French, or whatever), and generally trashed what had been written. Until Julie Harris showed up. Consummate professional that she is, she read the script as it was written—and with respect. Chastened, the other actors followed suit.

For the most part it was a good year on the show. I liked the actors—especially Michele Lee, Ted Shackleford, Joan Van Ark, and Donna Mills, who had been a chum ever since we worked together on *Love is a Many Splendored Thing*. I think I bugged her because I could still beat her on the tennis court, even though she was much younger and taking private lessons from big time coaches, and appearing in celebrity charity matches.

At the end of the year, Ellis and I moved on. He optioned a

novel he was anxious to adapt to the screen, and I was offered a writer/producer deal at Embassy Productions, owned by Norman Lear (who had no idea I was working for him again), and run by Michael Weisberg.

I scored the first week at Embassy by landing a pilot deal with NBC for an hour prime time serial based on Peter Davis' nonfiction book, *Hometown*. It was a wonderful book, a sociological study of Hamilton, Ohio, a city of about 50,000, located an hour-and-a-half from Cincinnati, and even closer to my old alma mater, Western College. The author, who won an Academy Award for his heart-wrenching film about Vietnam, *Hearts and Minds,* turned the small city inside out, writing about the industries, the unions, schools, churches, courts, cops, leaders, followers—all the citizens high and low and in-between. I found it fascinating. It was the kind of material I wanted to write about. I invented fictional families with interwoven pasts and a prodigal son, a writer, who returns to record it all.

It didn't get on the air. It's one of the dust-gathering scripts I read now and then, and sigh over.

Michael Weisberg, the head of Embassy, said I wasn't cooperative with the young network executive assigned to the pilot. (Why couldn't I have gotten an executive like Ellis had been at CBS?) Michael said I intimidated the woman after she insisted on changes that I felt would compromise the project. Well, sure I did. She wanted the usual sex, and intrigue, and affairs, and sex, and villainy, and melodrama, and sex. I wanted to do something closer to reality, something like the stories of the real people Peter Davis had written about.

So I exited Embassy and free-floated in "Freelanceville" until Joanne Brough at Lorimar called and asked if I'd be interested in becoming the Supervising Producer of *Falcon Crest*.

"Sure," I said, "when do I start?"

Falcon Crest was the third in Lorimar's triple crown of successful prime-time serials, maybe not as highly rated as *Dallas* or *Knots Landing,* but close. It was hard to believe that Earl Hamner, the same man who had given us a show as lovely and wholesome as *The Waltons,* created it. Because *Falcon Crest* was pretty raunchy, and almost as camp as rival *Dynasty.* Actually, I don't think Earl had that kind of show in mind when he created it, because one day he showed me the original pilot which had been scrapped for a much racier version before the show went on the air.

I was hired to replace the original Supervising Producer, who was out of favor with the Lorimar executives for some reason or other, but the weekend before I was to report to work, the two Story Editors, who worked as a team, quit. The word was they quit because they were gay, and the Supervising Producer was homophobic and giving them a bad time. At any rate, when they quit the Lorimar executives panicked—if all three writers (that included the Supervising Producer) left there wouldn't be any writers on staff who knew the show. Only me. So they rehired the Supervising Producer—and then there were two. Supervising Producers, that is.

And that wasn't too great an idea.

Not that the remaining Supervising Producer wasn't the epitome of cooperation and helpfulness to me. But somehow I feel he just might have had something to do with what eventually happened during my tenure, because, after all, this was his job and his territory, and I don't think he really wanted to share it.

Jane Wyman was the star of the show, the powerful, imperious, manipulative Angela Channing, matriarch and reigning queen of the wine country in the fictitious Tuscany Valley substituting for the Napa Valley in northern California. She played a similar role on the set, a true-life Norma Desmond who knew all the crew members by name—the gaffers, best boys, iatsies of all crafts and stripes, whom she truly liked and who adored her. She was remarkable. Always prompt, rehearsed, professional, line perfect and convincing. One served at her pleasure both on the screen and on the set. If she became displeased with people in either venue, they were goners.

My colleague, the other Supervising Producer, was a good friend of hers. I was open for a pleasant camaraderie, too. I got along fine with Earl Hamner and the other stars. Robert Foxworth, who played Chase Gioberti, was an extremely thoughtful and intelligent actor. Susan Sullivan, a talented actress, played his wife,

Maggie. Then there was sexy ingenue Ana Alicia and the two young male leads, bad boy Lorenzo Lamas and good kid Billy Moses.

For a long time that production year, things seemed to be going well. I enjoyed writing and editing scripts, attending production meetings, editing and casting sessions, and visiting the set. But gradually strange tales drifted back to Earl, the Executive Producer, of weird things I said on the set; observations and offhand remarks that were at best, frivolous, at worst, rude. But all of them were untrue, and Earl only told me because he was amused. I don't think he believed them, either. Whoever was whispering in Earl's ear (and I have a pretty good idea who it was), was making it up, engaging in a backstage intrigue for sinister reasons, like getting me chucked off the show.

And whoever it was must have had Jane's ear, too, because relations between us were becoming cooler and cooler. Toward the end of the year, I was in her dressing room discussing a script when she said something slightly derogatory about the actor who played her late husband. He happened to be an excellent actor, and a friend of mine, and I defended him in a non-confrontational way. That was the last time Jane and I talked one-on-one.

At the end of the year, Earl offered me the job of Co-Executive Producer for the coming season. I was excited about it. Then I got a call from Joanne Brough, the Lorimar executive in charge of the show, inviting me to have lunch with Earl and her at Antonio's, a chic restaurant on Beverly Glen near Mulholland Drive.

I thought we were celebrating my promotion, so I ordered a martini instead of wine before lunch. We were schmoozing the usual show biz schmooz when the drinks arrived and we ordered. I chose the outrageously priced lobster. After all, this was a celebration and I wasn't paying. Then Earl, the kindest and gentlest of men, began a sentence that took a long time to finish. The syntax was pretty complicated, too. But the upshot wasn't. He thought I was a wonderful writer and a good person, but he was reneging on his offer to make me the Co-Executive Producer next season. Seems he was going to distance himself from the show, not be around all that much, and he needed a "show runner" with more experience than I had. And again he said lovely things about my capabilities, only I wasn't quite "seasoned enough as a producer."

I was off the show. It wasn't until later that I found out the real reason. It was because Jane Wyman told him that if I became the executive producer she would not work with me. The backstage Machiaveli had struck again.

Back at the luncheon, Joanne Brough, the most gracious of executives, tried her darndest to make Earl's announcement as painless as possible, but a pall hung over the conversation. By this time, I had finished two martinis. Lunch was about to be served. I excused myself to go to the women's room to freshen up. It was around the corner from our table.

I entered the nicely appointed lounge, and tried to figure out how I felt. Was I furious? Stunned? Mad as hell? I guess so. But not really. Nothing like the *Mary Hartman* episode, but then I hadn't had anything to do with the creation of *Falcon Crest,* and other than enjoying the work and the pay, I wasn't emotionally involved. Or was it simply getting easier to accept these professional ups and downs? Probably a little of both. I did think it was kind of dumb to invite me out to what I thought was a celebration lunch and tell me I was fired. Yeah, I guess I was put out. Pissed, actually. And I was damned if I'd go back and sit through lunch making civilized chitchat.

So I left the restaurant without being seen, got in my car, and drove home, feeling a little childish and silly.

"Take that, you guys," I thought, and couldn't help giggling. I know it was the martinis, but it <u>was</u> pretty funny to keep them waiting and wondering what the hell I was doing in the ladies' room. We lived just a short distance away, down the hill into Sherman Oaks, and when I got home I told Ellis what I'd done. He thought I'd acted unprofessionally. He was right. I'm still glad I did it.

Late that day, I went back to my office, and Earl poked his head in. We looked at each other, started to laugh, and then had a nice talk. But I wasn't going to be back the next season. A week or so later I finished my last script, gathered up my things, and turned out

the lights in my office.
"Goodnight, Jane."
"Goodnight, Ann."
"Goodnight, John Boy."

But it wasn't the end of my relationship with Lorimar. Joanne Brough championed my cause at the production company, and Lee Rich, the CEO, offered me an excellent development deal. I moved to the Lorimar executive office building on the MGM lot in Culver City, and spent the next three years as a highly paid writer/producer churning out pilots and TV movies.

I was sailing along from job to job, but at this point Ell was more or less becalmed. Writing and producing for television is a hurry-up-and-wait kind of job. When you're working on a series there is hardly time for anything—family, holidays, hobbies. But when you're between jobs there's too much time, and you worry that you're never going to work again. We were in pretty good shape financially. He didn't have to say this time, as he often had, "We'll be okay until the first of the year (or whenever), but then we have to go into our savings." It used to be pretty scary when our savings and job prospects were limited.

Besides, Ellis had earned some time off. He loved classical music. He was an avid reader—history, good contemporary fiction, and mysteries (Dick Francis was a favorite). He enjoyed fixing things, and he loved golf. Hated it and loved it. The only problem was that now that he had time to play golf, his legs weren't cooperating. Maybe it was arthritis or poor circulation, but his legs hurt a lot. This didn't stop him, of course. He'd take Dr. Dave's pill-of-the-week, and play with his buddies on many of the beautiful public courses in the area. He had this deliberate but inconsistent sort of game; squatting down before each tee, holding up his driver to get the lay of the fairway, the wind current, and God knows what else; and then driving the ball over two hundred yards—every once in awhile hooking, or slicing, or duffing it. His precise procedure in addressing the ball used to drive Tony Barr up the wall, but Philip Barry, Mike Morris and Konrad Kellen weren't bothered at all. Maybe because they all had their golfing idiosyncrasies, too.

Meanwhile, Ellyn had fallen in love the way she does most things—really, truly, everlastingly, 100 percent. And who could blame her? William Rufus Lindsay (who has never been called that except when his large family wants to tease him), is every mother's dream. Of course, I didn't know that at first, I just knew she was involved with a fellow law student named Bill, who was a year behind her since he had taken time off after graduating from Dartmouth before entering Boalt.

We were supposed to meet Ellyn and Bill together when they came down to Los Angeles to clerk in different law firms for the summer. But Ellyn got held up the afternoon of the meeting, and poor Bill had to face us alone . . . The Parents! I opened the door and there he was, tall, dark, handsome, and scared to death. Which was funny since Ellis and I having heard so much about him—how brilliant he was, how he was elected editor-in-chief of the law review for the coming year—were a little scared of him. It was a bit awkward the first hour or so until Ellyn arrived, and even after that it took time for us to relax with one another. In fact, it wasn't until several hours later, when Bill and I were playing Scrabble, that I felt relaxed enough to shade the rules just a smidgen, and change a move I'd already made by putting down the word 'marbled' earning seven letters, fifty points and the game! (Sometimes I wish I weren't so competitive.)

Bill, who has become a very important part of my life, wasn't easy to get to know. From the Midwest, although he was born in Canada, he must have found it difficult to relate to us, too. We do tend to be effusive and emotional and vocal—and I suppose, opinionated. Bill doesn't let it all hang out. He's deep—complex. There's an awful lot going on there. And worth the effort to find out what. He can be funny and warm and amusing, too. But you have to work at it.

Ellyn and Bill got engaged almost as quickly as Ellis and I had so many years before. When she graduated from law school, she took a job as clerk to State Supreme Court Justice Stanley Mosk so she could stay with Bill in Berkeley while he finished his last year. At first (or maybe the whole time before they were married), they kept the fact that they were living together a secret from Bill's father, who lived in Columbus and possessed more conservative views than us "liberal Hollywood types." I suspect he knew all along, and simply didn't let on. I mean, what else could he think when he'd call early in the morning or late at night and Ellyn answered?According to her he'd boom out, "Is Bill Lindsay there?" And never question what the hell she was doing in his tiny apartment at such odd hours. The apartment was in a semi-dilapidated house just off Telegraph Avenue that was so small the bathroom was bigger than the living-room. I don't think they even noticed.

Life was good. I had a lot of projects in the works at Lorimar. Things could only get better.

Chapter 22

The Best Of Times . . .
The Worst Of Times

Ellyn had been planning for a fairy tale wedding all her life. She and her best friend, Mara, spent endless hours holed up in her bedroom when they were kids drawing bridal gowns and wedding processions. They married Barbie and Ken so often they outdid Liz Taylor. Now that she was getting married herself, could the real thing seem like *déja vu*? Not a chance. If Ellyn had been excited because a man she wasn't in love with had asked her to marry, now that she had been asked by her True Love, she lived in a haze of excitement bordering on ecstasy. How she continued to clerk for Justice Mosk, study for, and finally take her bar exams, I'll never know. She and Bill set the date for the last day of May 1985, a week after his graduation from law school. As mother-of-the-bride, it was up to me to plan everything. So why did I panic? Isn't that the part written for the father-of-the-bride?

I know I've mentioned having missing or defective genes of one kind or another—science genes, awareness of intrigue (gossip) genes, etc. Here was a new category—planning-for-a-formal-wedding genes. Thank God for Ellis. He was a super take-charge person. He loved detail work. He always took care of our finances: the bills, investments, taxes, vacations, travel plans, house improvements, service repairs, leaking roofs, plumbing—those kinds of things. Now he stepped in and found Viktor, the wedding planner at the Bel-Air Hotel, and the rest was easy. Almost. Because it certainly wasn't up to him to shop for a wedding gown with Ellyn.

Ellyn gave herself one weekend to find the wedding gown of her dreams, and it happened to be the weekend when she was expecting to hear if she passed the bar. Not a good time to shop. Not only that, I wasn't feeling up to par. Things were pretty tense at Lorimar. I wrote several pilots, which had been well received at the networks, but none made it into production. Plus, I was in the starting phases of a TV movie about a New Age evangelist, and in the middle of developing a comedy soap. I figured I wasn't feeling great because of stress—too much on my plate, even though I liked everything on it. Especially the stress of shopping for a wedding gown with Ellyn.

We made the rounds of the wedding boutiques in Beverly Hills, and Ellyn looked beautiful in everything she tried on. But Ellyn wasn't going to be satisfied until she tried on Everything in Every Store in Southern California! We took a break, and did tea at Neiman-Marcus (no relation), and Ellyn went off to call Bill in Berkeley to find out if she had been notified about the bar results. She seemed to take a long time. When she finally returned her face was a sickly shade of green. I held my breath. She tried to be casual and noncommittal. She wasn't.

"Nothing came in the mail," she said.

I rushed in where any fool would tread.

"You know how the mails are on Saturday," I said. "I'm sure you'll hear Monday."

Utter gloom from usually sunny Ellyn.

"I called four friends who took the bar the same time I did. Three of them were notified they passed. The fourth said he heard they notify those who didn't later."

Why did it seem so hot in the Garden Grove Tearoom? I rallied to the cause. I said everything I could think of to cheer her up. She was going to pass, the notification was in the mail, and even if by some fluke she didn't, there were lots and lots of brilliant lawyers who had to take the exam two or even three times.

We had one more bridal shop on our agenda. It was in Northridge, in the valley, and that's where Ellyn found It. The perfect wedding gown. It highlighted her terrific figure. She looked absolutely breathtaking. Would I lie? And, oh yes, that Monday, the letter arrived in Berkeley notifying her that she had, indeed, passed the bar.

The wedding was a smash. Bill's family arrived from several states and Canada. It wasn't exactly the Cohens and the Kellys but close. There was a nice symbiosis between us. They are a big, warm, fun, loving family, and we all seemed to enjoy each other, in spite of the fact that Bill's father Jack, a dyed-in-the-wool conservative Republican, considered me a "flaming liberal."

The weather was perfect—up until a few days before the ceremony, when it not only turned cold, but rained. And rained. And got colder. We had planned this elaborate outdoor extravaganza in the garden of the Bel-Air Hotel, next to the pool with the majestic swans, and the temperature was hovering in the fifties. (That equates to sub-zero weather any other place on the globe). It was as though Cole Porter was trying to prove his point—California was cold and damp. I couldn't believe it would rain on Ellyn's wedding.

The sun came out on May 31st. The temperature rose a few degrees, and the guests were only mildly numbed by the cold as they assembled in their summer finery for the late afternoon ceremony—except for my sister-in-law Emily, who had the sense to bring along her fur coat.

John came all the way from France with seven-year-old Jacobo, whose turn it was to travel. It would have been too expensive for Carmen and all three kids to come, and since Paola had recently traveled to Mexico with Carmen to visit her grandparents, and Etienne had been on a trip to Greece, Jacobo got the chance to attend his Aunt's wedding.

I was concerned about whether Steve and Anna and Kevin would show up from Santa Monica, since getting them to any family function was so tenuous, but they made it, as did several score of our favorite relatives and friends from all over.

In fact they were all there except, of course, notoriously late Tracy. I knew she'd be there. She _had_ to be there. She _would_ be there, wouldn't she? But she wasn't. Oh dear God, where was she?

The Best Of Times... The Worst Of Times

Everything was set. Rabbi Jerry Fisher (a Reform rabbi kept busy by these increasing intermarriages) was already in place alongside Father John Pearson (a classmate of Bill's). The trio of musicians was poised to begin the processional, but still no Tracy. I was just about to give the signal to begin when she breathlessly arrived. She had an airtight excuse. The back left wheel of her car had fallen off. Or was that the time her dog got lost, or her house caught fire—or was it the gardener who had fallen in the pool just before she left and she had to give him mouth-to-mouth while dialing 911? I can't remember and it doesn't matter. She was there.

And so the ceremony began. Bill's stepmother, Shirley, and I were escorted to our front-row seats. Bill and Jack (who was his Best Man), took their places. The bridesmaids proceeded down the aisle (Mara was her Maid of Honor), and then came Ellyn, looking absolutely radiant, escorted by Ellis, happy and proud and teary-eyed.

When we played the video of the wedding ceremony we couldn't understand why Ellyn and Bill were only taped from the rear while they pledged their troth. Ellis called the photographer, who explained he had footage showing their faces, but our daughter had cried through the entire ceremony, and he didn't think we wanted to see that. But that's exactly what we wanted to see. The re-edited version shows the two of them gazing into each other's eyes—Bill stalwart and devoted, Ellyn with tears streaming down her face.

The party afterwards was great. After much champagne Ellis and Jack did an impromptu Greek dance, arms around each other's waist, stamping their feet, even throwing a couple of plates! The FOEs and FOBs (friends of Ellyn and Bill) ate and drank and were very merry. Ray gave the wedding toast, which turned out to be a half-hour of standup comedy. No one could get him away from the mike (shades of Uncle Moe at my wedding—which Ray missed because he was in England with the Eighth Air Force). They tell me that about twenty-seven minutes into his monologue I began making drastic cut-off gestures by slashing at my throat, but I don't remember that. My agent Bob Einsenbach's young girlfriend passed out in the ladies room, and poor Muriel Goldman, who had flown in from New York, was dispatched to revive her. John joined the musicians to jam with a borrowed clarinet. Jacobo spent a lot of time atop Bill's fraternity brothers' shoulders as they danced. The festivities went on until midnight. It was memorable.

After a honeymoon in Hawaii, Ellyn and Bill moved to Washington, where they rented an apartment that had a living room larger than the bathroom, but only because the bathroom was too small to turn around in. Bill clerked for Federal Judge McGowan for a year before becoming clerk to Supreme Court Chief Justice Renquist. I recognize it was a huge honor for Bill, and I know the Justice and his late wife were lovely people, but . . . well . . . let's face it, I hate most of his decisions (Renquist's, not Bill's). Ellyn joined the Department of Justice as a research lawyer, which she hated. Then she became an Assistant U.S. Attorney in Alexandria, Virginia, which she loved.

Meanwhile, I continued at Lorimar in development hell. I kept making deals at the networks for pilots, movies, and daytime serials, but they never got into production. I began to be a little paranoid. Was I being deserted by Lorimar? Why weren't they pushing my projects? Why didn't my new William Morris agent, Hal Ross, get behind me, and match agency talent with my series pilots and MOWs, and package and sell the projects to the networks as he had promised? I'd left Bob Eisenbach, with whom I'd been for twenty-five years (making me feel disloyal and rotten), because of the possibilities William Morris offered.

I wrote good stuff, which was enthusiastically received by the network executives. What was keeping them from that final step—production? Was it the youth onslaught? Was I getting nudged aside to make room for the next generation? I couldn't accept that, even though I was aware I wasn't one of the boys (which now included girls). *Quel* irony. Had I succeeded in television in spite of gender discrimination, only to come smack up against age discrimination? Or was it something else? Maybe I wasn't aggressive enough. Pushy, actually, the way many of my much younger fellow writer/producers were. Instead of being amused at their machinations, and the way they sucked up to Lorimar and network execs,

The Best Of Times... The Worst Of Times

maybe I should have joined them. Not my style. Besides, I was still wheeling and dealing with all kinds of promising projects.

I wrote a pilot based on a wonderfully funny book, *For Better or Worse,* by Caryl Rivers and her husband, Alan Lupo. She was Catholic, a community college instructor, and an aspiring writer who hated details, was sloppy but big-hearted. He was Jewish, a reporter for an alternative newspaper, obsessively neat, big-hearted, funny. CBS loved it. It wasn't picked up. But Bob O'Connor, VP for comedy development was so impressed he gave me another pilot deal, and I wrote *Divorce Express,* adapted from Paula Danziger's book of the same title. CBS loved it. It wasn't picked up. I got yet another pilot deal, and this time I didn't adapt a book but wrote an original called *Scranton!,* a spoof of the prime-time soaps *Dallas* and *Dynasty.* CBS loved it, but they had just signed Carol Burnett for another comedy soap satire set in the raisin Capitol of California called something like *Bakersfield.* Go figure.

By this time my young mentor, Bob O'Connor, had left the network for what is known in the trade as "Indie Prod." He had his own company with eminent and equally youthful Len Hill, and invited me to create a sitcom, which he would produce. He had an arena that interested him—LA as the new national melting pot. I came up with the setting and characters, and we decided to pitch it to his replacement, Greg Mayday, the new head of comedy development at CBS. I made some notes on the project at the time because I was thinking of writing a book about my experiences in the industry, and calling it *Coming of Old Age in Hollywood.* The notes give a view of what it's like to pitch an idea for a new series to a network executive:

Notes On Pitch Sessions At CBS:

9/5/85—9a.m.
Arrived at Hugo's on Santa Monica Blvd. to go over pitch with Bob before 10 o'clock meeting with Greg Mayday. Place used to be a butcher shop. Now trendy; power people doing power breakfasts. I'm

227

early. Hate being early; feel exposed sitting at a table alone. Bob arrives. Is he getting pudgy? He's wearing a name brand sweater and has a cold. I never know what to wear for network meetings. Professional duds—suits like execs wear? Jeans and the sloppy look because I'm a writer? I settled for something in between—K Hep slacks and an expensive sweater. Bob talks about his cold; I talk about mine. He talks about scuba diving at night. Is he kidding? What about sharks. I mean I love to swim in the ocean but sharks eat at night. Betty Thomas (Sgt. on Hill Street Blues) is at next table. She nods, waves. We nod, wave. Hey, she might be good for lead in series we're pitching. It's time to leave for meeting and we haven't discussed how we're going to pitch idea. I'm not worried. After all, Bob must have heard thousands of pitches when he was head of comedy development.

10 a.m.

Arrive at CBS lot on Fairfax off Beverly in my 380 SL and get waved through guard gate without even giving my name. Nice perk. Is it the Mercedes or does he know me? Took me a long time to buy a German car. I'll never forgive what happened. Used to be very defiant about driving my old Honda in Hollywood. Something I had in common with Paul Newman. He drove a beat-up old VW. Later I found out he had a souped-up BMW engine in the old VW. So much for commonality. Find a parking space and climb stairs to reception where Ellen Franklin, the new Lorimar VP comedy development is waiting. Isn't anyone over 30? Give her a quick fill-in on what we're pitching as Len Hill joins us. Len's maybe 40, but I didn't recognize him. Actually I knew his former partner, Phil Mandelker, much better. Phil was first acquaintance I knew who died

The Best Of Times... The Worst Of Times

from AIDS complications; he had the best memorial service I ever attended: funny, irreverent, moving. Anyway, I said "Len, for a moment I didn't recognize you." He went semi-ballistic. Was he looking that much older? he wondered. Is he kidding? I could be his mother! I mean biologically speaking. Not counting the fact that a five-year-old gave birth in Brazil or Peru or somewhere down there. Bob finally arrived and we went up to the third floor.

10:10 a.m.
We're ushered into Greg's office, same one Bob had. Chair seems too big for Greg whose last name, Mayday, is the same as a distress signal at sea; any significance in this? Two other CBS staffers were there: Carol. . . can't remember her last name (oh God, am I getting Alzheimer's?), the Director of comedy development, and another very young woman, the manager of CD whose name no one remembers and is just there to take notes.

10:15 a.m.
Takes us five minutes simply to get settled and accept coffee or bottled water. Now comes the obligatory chitchat: a plumbing bill for $6800 dollars; the price of houses on the west side; houses in the Hancock Park section; Len talking about his new house; Greg's in the market but can't afford that section. Len says he saw a real buy, a smaller house only $610,000! (I remember, silently, about the first house Ellis and I bought for $13,250). Len says this great buy is a relic with high ceilings, large grounds, and it was built in 1927. "That's when I was built," I pipe in and get a laugh. But the truth is, I'm even an earlier model. But what do they know? Everyone over 50 is lumped together.

10:25 a.m.
Finally Greg asks what we're here to talk about, and

I let Bob talk. I'm rotten at pitches; not glib and funny and able to put the buyers at ease. Besides, Bob used to be sitting in Greg's oversized chair and knows the drill. And he's terrific. At least I think so. He talks about the feeling and the spirit at the centennial celebration back in '76 at the Statue of liberty and I'm kind of mesmerized and carried along as he describes the melting pot and Ellis Island and how that was such a meaningful time in our history, but how that melting pot is now here in Los Angeles. And he finally gets down to specifics and talks about our character ("think of Cher, her kind of independence and flair and color"); and then he talks about the two arenas the show would have: the workplace—the child welfare agency, and our main character's home life where she's raising kids from two marriages and one liaison. And then suddenly Bob cues me and I'm on to discuss the characters in *Share and Share Alike,* which is our tentative name since we couldn't think of anything else and we kept talking about the Cher character so we just sort of fell into calling it that, *Share and Share Alike.* I finish and Greg asks a few desultory questions and then we're out of there.

11 a.m.
Out in the parking lot we talk about how the meeting went. Hard to tell, Len and Bob and Ellen think. (I thought Bob was great; I was so-so.) Len says in future we should be more specific and detailed, and tells about a pitch session he went to with a young (did he have to say that?) *Saturday Night Live* writer. Seems this writer was describing a character who was indecisive but very anxious to please. Instead of saying that, said Len, this brilliant young *SNL* writer illustrated it by describing how she called her Mother and asked her what she should bring to her birthday party.

> MOM
> Jello mold.
>
> DAUGHTER
> What flavor?
>
> MOM
> I don't know. Strawberry or cherry.
>
> So the daughter shows up Saturday night with . . . ta da! ... both strawberry <u>and</u> cherry. I'm neither amused or impressed, but nod my head, hypocrite that I am and say, "great illustration, Len."
> P.S. We didn't get a pilot deal for Share and Share Alike, and I abandoned my idea for a book on coming of old age in Hollywood.

I had two other ongoing projects at Lorimar, in which there seemed to be a lot of interest. One was the TV movie about the wild and wonderful New Age minister, Terry Cole Whitaker, who was wowing Southern California converts in person, on tape, and on local TV. What a sensational character she was, funny, inspiring, motivating, all-loving, all-inclusive (gays adored her and she them), a self-invented original. She started as a bored housewife, entered and won the Mrs. America contest in the early '70s, and discovered she had a gift for empowering people to be all that they could be without joining the Armed Forces. And she did it with humor, and interpreting the Bible in her own unique way, describing her version of God as a benign, fun-loving kind of guy. While she was lifting peoples' spirits, and bringing them to God, she went through five marriages—one of them with a real sharpie who took her for all she was worth—and ended up with a sweet young man twenty years her junior.

Leslie Moonves arrived at Lorimar to head the long-form division just as Oliver Heskith and I made the deal for the movie with CBS.

I was also working on the daytime comedy serial Jackie Smith had twisted my arm to develop for ABC. I didn't want to work in daytime again, but once I got into *Fitzgerald and Finelli*, I fell in love with the project. The title characters were Suzanne Fitzgerald, a Boston Brahmin (loosely based on my long ago *Life* magazine colleague Marietta Fitzgerald Tree), who desserts her fiance at the altar, and escapes to New York to become a bleeding heart public defender forced to share a Greenwhich Village apartment with Francine Finelli, an upwardly mobile young woman from a blue-collar family in Brooklyn, who wants to carve a niche for herself in the world of communications by starting as a production assistant on a tabloid TV talk show. The reason they're stuck together in the same Village apartment is that both of them are on limited budgets, and each has been bilked out of two months rent by the former tenant, a fraudulent, holistic dentist who has fled to California to become a dance therapist.

Jackie Smith loved the project and promoted it heavily. She even announced its tentative scheduling on the network at an ABC affiliates' meeting. I was interviewed by trade papers. There was a front-page story, and picture of me in the Calendar section of the *LA Times* about its imminent arrival.

So I waited. And waited. Something was bound to break soon. But it was frustrating, and I wasn't feeling all that great physically, either. I came home one night about five months after Ellyn's wedding feeling rotten. Usually one of Ell's special martinis helped. That night it didn't. Ell and I had dinner, but I wasn't hungry.

I went into the bathroom feeling queasy, and weird, and—hemorrhaged. Not much, but I knew something serious was happening. This time, for some strange reason, I didn't panic. I told Ellis and called Mitch Karlin, the wonderful surgeon who had always been there for me. He said he'd meet me at the hospital. I packed a few things and Ellis drove me to the Bevery Hills Hospital. I didn't come home for seven weeks. It's a wonder I came home at all.

Chapter 23

On The Banks Of The River Jordan

Everybody who's anybody—along with lots of other people in southern California—goes to Cedars/Sinai or St. John's Hospital when they're seriously ill. I've had turns at both institutions, but this time Dr. Karlin, who is on staff at Cedars, wanted me at the smaller Beverly Hills Hospital, where he was Chief of Surgery.

It's closed now, but the building is still there on the corner of Beverly Drive and Pico Boulevard. I think it's rented out to movie studios for hospital shows, but I'm not interested in checking it out. All I know is, I try not to look at it when I pass by, because I don't want to be reminded of the time I spent there.

Two weeks after the first surgery to try to straighten out the mess inside me, I was moved to a huge room from which I could look east to downtown Los Angeles and beyond to the San Gabriel Mountains. On a clear day, I could see the snowy peaks of San Gorgonio and San Jacinto. Mostly the weather did as poorly as I was doing, and all I could see was the hazy neon sign lighting up Factor's Deli. Since I had no desire to eat, and, in fact, wasn't allowed to eat anything for three months, I avoided looking at Factor's, and gazed apathetically at the Christmas decorations blinking cheerily atop the Holiday Inn across the street.

What had happened to me anyway? Was I cashing it in? Crossing the Big Divide? Joining my ancestors? I was in my early sixties, about the same age as my mother when she died. When she died, I was the same age as my daughter Ellyn was now. Was this some kind of karma? Had the cancer resurfaced after all these years?

After pumping me full of blood that first night, I underwent abdominal surgery, and I guess it was pretty awful in there. After so many operations, scar tissue had formed strangulating adhesions involving most of the upper intestinal tract, as well as what was left of the lower. And the whole lot was gangrenous. Mitch Karlin's impossible mission was to untangle the mess, cut away the diseased sections, and hope there was enough left to reconnect things. He wasn't sure if he'd accomplished the mission or not.

God bless Demerol. It removes fear. It even makes you sound courageous and amusing after that pre-op shot, when you're riding down the elevator on a gurney to the operating room. Ellis had hold of my hand. Ray and Tracy were there, too. (Shades of the birth of Steve). I squeezed Ell's hand, and told him not to worry. I made jokes about how a writer will do anything not to have to write. I remember how stricken they all looked, but I wasn't worried. I wasn't anything. It wasn't up to me anymore. Out of my hands. I was rolled away from them, through the doors into the OR. All I had to do was count backwards. Then nothing.

Except that I woke up. Not feeling much of anything, not even pain. You never do that first day. It's the second day, and the third, and the fourth, and the fifth.

Whenever surgeons go to work on your intestinal tract, the most persistent post-op question is, "Are you passing any gas? A little wind, maybe?" To fart is a blessing. Not to, to be "closed" is trouble with a capital "T." I never opened after the first operation. I had that ghastly tube that went up my nose, down my throat, and into my stomach. And we waited. Two weeks went by without any progress. Ellis was with me night and day. We didn't say much. I didn't feel like it because of that damn tube, and he didn't bother with platitudes, knowing that his being there was what mattered. Ray and Tracy stood guard every day, too, and my good friend Suzanne Childs kept close tabs.

A few days before Thanksgiving, Ellyn flew in from

Washington. I thought I'd be home by the time she arrived, and able to go to Marc and Emily's family Thanksgiving dinner. But I still hadn't "opened," and I was feeling miserable, and all I wanted was to be left alone. I didn't even want to see Ellis, who kept looking for signs of improvement. I didn't feel like chatting with my darling daughter, either. I hated the cheery get-well cards arriving every day, with their flowery sentiments or hopelessly tacky doctor jokes. Cranky, oafish, irascible, I begged everyone to go to the Daniels' dinner just to get rid of them. They all sensed my need because they all went—except, of course, Tracy, who always does exactly what she wants to do—and she wanted to be with me.

It's kind of wonderful how Tracy and I have grown closer and closer together as we get . . . sorry, Tracy . . . older.

Anyway, Tracy and I sat in the gloom of late afternoon that Thanksgiving, and I realized I wasn't going to get better unless something drastic was done. I think I knew I'd have to undergo another surgery, a sort of do-or-die procedure that Mitch was holding off on. I talked it over with Tracy, who was terrific. She didn't play big sister, and try to kiss it and make it all better, or even—what was harder for me to deal with—invoke prayer and positive ions, or incantations, or other sincere exorcisms, spiritual or otherwise. She just handed me the phone, and told me to call Mitch and get him to tell me what he was going to do and when.

What it was, was removing practically all of my upper intestinal tract—with the distinct possibility that I wouldn't survive the surgery, or, if I did, that I'd have to be fed through a port-o-cath for the rest of my life. Then again, maybe he didn't tell me all that. Maybe Mitch wasn't exactly sure what he was going to do, but at least he was going to do something.

So, the day after Thanksgiving, I was riding the elevator down to the OR again, clutching Ell's hand again, feeling better than he or the other members of the family gathered in the waiting room, because I was on blessed Demerol again.

They tell me that Mitch emerged from the operating room several hours into the surgery to announce that I was hanging on, and when pushed said I had maybe a 20% chance of making it. He explained what he was doing, and showed the family Polaroid pictures of my guts, in living color, heaped on the table. As I understand it, no one looked. The pictures are in a medical book Mitch contributed to, although so far I haven't received any royalties.

Obviously there is no way to make this suspenseful. I survived, even though along the way I had an out-of-body experience. Actually, they're not all they're cracked up to be. At least mine wasn't.

I woke up in the intensive care unit, a brightly-lit room, totally white. There was a squad of people surrounding me yelling at each other, just like an episode of *ER*. I distinctly remember someone yelling, "I can't get a blood pressure reading!" And even "We're losing her!" It wasn't at all scary because by this time I was floating somewhere just beneath the ceiling looking down on my body, my arms spread out Jesus-like, with tubes sticking out of every vein and orifice. That's all I remember about being outside my body.

But God, I do remember being in intensive care. It seemed like an eternity, but I think it was more like a week. I was alone in a small, all-white room that had a huge clock on the wall facing me. It had a sweeping second hand that lurched from second to second, and I counted with it: one, two, three—up to sixty for a minute, then I started over again. Sixty more times, and another minute. In fifteen more minutes I could get another pain shot, oh blessed, blessed drugs!

Well, it's okay. I got though it. I improved enough to be moved, finally, back to my big room overlooking Factor's Deli and Mount San Jacinto, on a clear day. I still had tubes sticking out all over me. I counted them once, fourteen. One of them, the nasal/gastro whatsis sucked out awful looking green stuff that was collected in a jar. Yuck.

Mitch, who claims he's not religious, says that at one point during the surgery, he was at a total loss; didn't know what more to do, how to go on, and that God took over. Now why would God do that for me? Or Mitch? What about that honor student on the bus in LA who was gunned down in a stupid drive-by shooting? What about kids in cancer wards? Hurricanes? Terrorism? Massacres?

I'll never understand it. I'm never going to discover a scientific cure for anything. I'm not going to create an artistic masterpiece. I'm even too old to make the women's Olympic softball team and drive in the winning run for the USA. So why was I spared? And what am I supposed to do to pay back? Should I just cool it and be grateful, and quit wondering why I get to see the sun set, and my grandkids, and other wonderful things? Maybe so . . . probably so.

I came home from the hospital a day before Christmas, still tethered to the port-o-cath by an umbilical-like tube that went directly into a main artery. The strange thing is that I gained fifteen pounds on what is called TPN; total parental nutrition, a combination of nutrients, including lipids and vitamins and I-don't-know-what, concocted and supervised by Dr. Ray Weston, Tracy's internist who became my friend and medical miracle worker. Slowly, I got stronger and better and began thinking about going back to work. I even began to have an appetite, although I still wasn't allowed to eat anything by mouth.

I wonder if anyone is aware of how many TV commercials advertise food? Glorious pizzas, luscious hamburgers dripping goo, egg McSomethings, junk foods, cheese, ice cream, and crunchy cereals with honey and nuts. Cheap franchise restaurants, featuring lobster and steak and pasta were tantalizing. It got to the point where I wanted to squeeze the Pillsbury Doughboy to death! Then one day, about three months after I entered the hospital, I was allowed to try a piece of toast. White toast with a hint of butter on it. I have never, ever, eaten anything so excruciatingly delicious. There are no words to describe it. The texture, the subtlety of flavor—an experience never to be forgotten.

So, gradually, I was weaned off the TPN and began eating on my own. This meant that I was "functioning," which is a euphemism for going to the bathroom, which is itself a euphemism, which I did a lot.

I started back to work for a couple of hours each day—with drainage tubes concealed in my clothing, and clamps still holding my oft-opened abdomen together until they self-dissolved.

Lorimar was terrific. They never stopped paying me my generous salary. But the handwriting was on the wall. My three-year contract was coming up for renewal, and I hadn't managed to get a single pilot or TV movie on a network schedule. I was close several times, but no cigars—not even a cigarillo.

I made some notes about my final days at Lorimar for the book I never wrote about growing old in Hollywood:

Don't Cry for Me, Lorimara:

4/5/86— 3:15 p.m.
Driving south on 405 in heavy traffic and smog after a pitch session at NBC with twelve-year-old executive who wouldn't know a good movie idea if it bit him in the butt. Told him the vehicle for Walter Mathau and Ann-Margret; he's a staff writer on a sitcom, she's his real estate agent wife; they're both fed up after he's replaced by a younger writer and she loses a big commission on a beachfront mansion when it collapses into the sea as she's about to make the deal. On impulse they buy a mobile home and have mad, crazy adventures on the open road. Kid exec. yawned. Can't do comedy movies on TV; network's looking for women-in-jeopardy. I yawned. Why am I doing this, knocking myself out? Why not go home and put my feet up?

Lorimar's asked for an extra week to make up its corporate mind about picking up my option for another year. Another year with a 20,000 dollar bump. Not bad, but who am I kidding? Why not retire with dignity instead of letting them drop me? Do the things I love: live at the beach; read books; visit the kids and grand kids (if I could just get John and family out of the Pyrenees); learn French; study Greek mythology.

Shit, that jerk just cut me off! Take it easy; don't kill yourself getting even, not after what you've been through.

3:45 p.m.
Arrive at MGM lot. Guard expects me to park in structure; the Hell I will. I park in front of producers' building in an unmarked spot; they still haven't painted my name on a space. Charlie Hauk, Miller/Boyett, Bill Blinn have spaces. Where's mine? Not a good sign (i.e. no sign). They probably decided a long time ago not to pick up my option.
3:51 p.m.
Take an elevator to second floor still not ready for stairs after the surgeries although I'm getting much stronger. Only thing is I worry about getting stuck in the elevator. Is this a late neurosis? Better check it out with the therapist. Wait a minute, I don't have a therapist.
Walk by Moonves' office to see if there's any word on revisions on Terry Cole Whitaker movie I gave him last week. Empty.
Into my office, greeted by my cheery, great assistant Karen (Cosmo) Cooley. What a wonderful person: quick, efficient, pleasant, fun. Perfect except for an obsession with Perry King. She'll get over it.
She tells me there's only one call: meeting with David Goldsmith (Lorimar's VP dramatic development) at 5 p.m. to discuss. . . things. Don't like sound of . . . "things." Karen hands me material that David wants me to look at. Idea for late night serial. Hmm. If I weren't going to be picked up, he wouldn't send me material. Wait a minute, that's a double negative. They *must* be picking me up because they're sending me material. On the other hand, is this bribery? I can stay if I do the series? Suppose I hate the material and don't want to do it? Am I out, finished, washed up?
4:05 p.m.
In my inner rather opulent office looking at "the

material." Try to be open-minded but hate it. Hate the title, "Desire Under The Magnolias"; hate the sleazy characters; hate the dumb storyline, slapstick situations, sexy innuendos, schlocky jokes, lasciviousness. Nothing redeeming about it. How much do I want to keep working here?

4:45 p.m.

Shoot breeze with Karen and Nick Castle the young triple threat writer, producer, director who shares the office suite. He's got go ahead on theatrical film about a boy who can fly. Guy's going places, deservedly. Leave for David's office.

5:00 p.m.

David is talking to the creator of the "material." Can't and don't want to remember his name. Decide to be candid about the "material." Tell it like it is. I search for something nice to say about it first. Stumble around tripping over syntax; finally tell the truth. "Material," I tell them, is series of badly written, vulgar dirty jokes; *SNL* at it's grossest. I don't want to work on it. The pronouncement goes over like a lead balloon. I try to soften my critique by offering a few suggestions like starting over again with new characters, a different premise. Get similar response to my overall reaction. What's heavier than lead? The creator of material leaves. David looks at me and laughs, tells me I'm probably right, which doesn't make it easier for him to tell me that they're not picking up my option. I ask him what would have happened if I loved the "material" and wanted to work on it. He says they probably would have extended my option and they still will if I want to do it. I don't. He understands. We're friends. I like him; he does lots of volunteer charity work; probably won't last long in this industry. Too altruistic. He tells me there's no rush about leaving and he'd like

to work with me again. We hug; I leave and have my usual no reaction reaction.
4/6/86 — 10:30 a.m.
Making rounds at Lorimar discussing projects still under consideration with various execs even though I'm leaving at end of month. Run into CEO David Seltzer who took over from Lee Rich. He looks a little sheepish, asks if I have any time later in the day. Is he kidding? Time is all I have. I tell him no time later, time now. We go into his sumptuous office. He tells me he's sorry things haven't worked out; he has highest regard for my talent and ability; everyone in management thinks I'm quality goods. I get a few things off my chest: my feeling that the company didn't support my projects enough; never attached a star to one of my pilots; or gave me a book they optioned. He apologizes, tells me, unfortunately, I'm getting to be a hard sell at networks. Plus Lorimar is changing its setup; overhead is way out of line. Says, "we need younger writers who are hungry and will work for coins instead of bucks." We part friends, but don't hug.
11:00 a.m.
Back to my office where Cosmo gives me my messages: Nordstroms; Ellis; tennis club; Mercedes' mechanic; Josie Emerich. Josie Emerich?! She's new head of ABC daytime (Jackie Smith's jumped to NBC). Wow. Could she be resurrecting *Fitzgerald and Finelli*, comedy soap I created for Jackie?
11:05 a.m.
Put in call to Josie in New York. No, it's not about *Fitz and Fin*. Wants to meet with me about head writing their #1 soap, *General Hospital*. Huge disappointment but try not to show it; set up meeting with her later in the week at ABC offices in Century City.

So much for my notes. When I got home that night, I told Ell about Josie's call. He was totally against my head-writing another soap. I hadn't fully recuperated, and was still walking around with a drainage tube hidden under my clothing. He reminded me of the many times I vowed never to go back to the all-consuming grind of head writing daytime soaps: that we weren't in need of the money; that John and Carmen were thinking about an extended visit from France with our three grandchildren, and if they came they'd be staying with us; and a lot more logical, sensible reasons to call Josie and cancel the meeting.

But I knew in what was left of my gut that the alternative—sitting home uninvolved and unemployed—would be worse for my health and my psyche. Besides, I said to Ell, "It wouldn't hurt just to talk to Josie." I had this plan in the back of my mind to get Ellis to work with me. All the time I was sick and recuperating, he hadn't even tried to get work. When I went back to Lorimar, he went back to freelancing and was having the same difficulty I was having selling anything. The only difference was I was getting paid because I was still under contract.

So it came to pass that I met with Josie on a dreary, drippy day in Century City, exuding cheery confidence (which I didn't feel because my tummy was making strange noises, and I was worried that the plastic bag strapped to my calf under my pants leg was showing).

Josie is an older version of Rosie O'Donnell—without Rosie's personality, humor, or warmth. Maybe all they have in common is their Irish ancestry and their generous figures. Then again, maybe Josie isn't even Irish. Suffice to say, there are some people one has an immediate rapport with—Josie wasn't one of them. It was the same kind of relationship I had with David Jacobs. There was an awkwardness between us and a failure to communicate. I never had fun with Josie. It was all bottom line. Maybe it was because she was new at the job, and felt I was being forced on her. That was because the legendary Gloria Monty, who, as executive producer, had taken *General Hospital* to new heights, left the show and was replaced by my old pal, Wes Kenney—who had asked for me. And that was because Pat Falken Smith, the same head writer I'd followed on *Days of our Lives*, left the show, too, for unknown reasons. (Maybe ... probably ... litiginous Pat was up to her old tricks suing someone on the show, or the network, or both.)

At any rate, the meeting with Josie was successful, and I was offered a lucrative contract. Ellis came aboard, too, as a story consultant and outline writer. I left Lorimar for "Gower Gulch," the Columbia studios in Hollywood where GH was taped, hardly losing a day of work. At that time, Ellis was a governor of the Academy of Television Arts and Sciences, so we went to the EMMY Awards shortly before we started work. Ironically, we were seated almost next to David Goldsmith and Les Moonves. It felt good telling them about my new (and higher paying—although I didn't tell them that) job. So there, you guys.

I was counting my blessings again. Not only hadn't I crossed that river to Jordan, I was making more money than ever. Ell and I were working together again, plus John and family were at long last coming home. I love happy endings. Then again, just like in soaps, this wasn't the end.

Chapter 24

Life With It's Joys And It's Sorrows

Ellis and I spent a couple of weeks at the beach house before going to work on *General Hospital*. It was a time to recharge my batteries, to rest and relax before plunging into the happenings in Port Charles, the fictional upstate New York metropolis where the soap took place. Actually, it would have been better if I'd gone directly to work without taking this time off, because instead of resting or recharging, I worried.

The weekend before the idyll was up, I visited some tennis buddies at the Malibu Racquet Club whom I hadn't seen since I'd been sick. I sat at the head of the stairs in the airy, pleasant clubhouse with Harriet Wolpin, a delightfully bright and knowledgeable woman who was a gifted sculptor, but a so-so player (I'm so-so, minus), and I almost freaked out.

"My God, Harriet," I said, "I must be crazy. I took this bitch of a job and I'm not even fully recovered. . . plus John and Carmen and their three little kids are arriving from France, and staying with us for months!" Harriet didn't say anything particularly profound, but she somehow gave me the feeling that I'd be able to cope. This worldly woman, who has since gone to her untimely reward, put things in perspective.

"A job is a job is a job," said she. And she was right. I was reminded again of Ell's famous admonition to me in Rome when I was about to head write *LIAMST*: "What is the worst thing that can happen? You'll get fired."

Life With It's Joys And It's Sorrows

Of course, I did get fired, but that didn't happen for a couple of years.

In the meantime, John and family arrived, and moved in with us in Sherman Oaks. This was an exploratory trip. John and Carmen had worked hard to establish an Art and Music studio in Europe, but it couldn't sustain them financially. They had to see if it could work here in the States, or if (as Ellis and I fervently hoped), they should pursue other avenues. John eventually finished his course work for a degree from Cal-State Northridge, and went into teaching. Carmen has pursued a number of interesting projects. She opened her own preschool, which she ran for several years. She even went into the long-distance telephone business, hoping to become what was once an anathema to her—a capitalist! Along the way she has always kept her hand in Art—from silk screening to potting.

For this extensive visit, however, they were examining their options, including the possibility of returning to their pioneer life in the foothills of the Pyrenees.

Their children: Etienne, 10; Jacobo, 8; and Paola, 6 were an absolute delight. Having lived with no electricity, indoor plumbing, junk food or other 20th century essentials, they were unique and unspoiled. The only TV they ever watched was during a brief period when Etienne traded an old bicycle for an older TV set which John rigged up with batteries. It worked for a while, and their favorite show was *Starsky and Hutch*. (In French, of course). The fact that I knew Starsky, i.e., Paul Michael Glaser (who had been in the first soap I'd written) enhanced my standing with them enormously. They ate whatever was put in front of them—healthy, hearty, vegetarian food—until they discovered a delicacy called french fries on the Santa Monica pier (which, of course, they had never seen in France), and that became their food of choice on outings. They were typical kids, not angels. Etienne was the big brother, bossing and teasing Jacobo until Jacobo would yell, *"Basta, Etienne! Basta!"* Paola, who was quite shy and quiet, was fond of the expression *"comme ci, comme ca,"* which she conveniently used to answer just about any question she was asked. Jacobo turned out to be a terrific mimic and took to standup comedy, imitating performers and newscasters on TV.

When they came here, they were fluent in Spanish, which they spoke at home. Etienne and Jacobo were also fluent in French since they both went to school, and all of them spoke English, if hesitantly. They loved the idea of having a big family, especially Jacobo, who would ask, whenever he met a cousin or a great-aunt or uncle, "Is he/she a part of the family?" Ray was terrific with them, taking them on adventures all over the city and beyond. They took to him just as my kids had (and still do), which made me wonder yet again why he didn't settle down with one of his ladies and have a bunch of his own.

The living arrangements were tight. The three kids were in one bedroom, John and Carmen in another, Gabriela, our housekeeper, had her room, and Ellis and I had ours. Carmen, who grew up in a middle-class family with schoolteacher parents, certainly was no stranger to modern appliances. But she had prided herself on "making do" for so long with so little in Chiapas and France, that she had a wee bit of contempt for all the gadgets and paraphernalia we take so for granted.

"An electric squeezer for juice?" she'd query. "Is much better to squeeze by hand. More nutrients."

It didn't make sense, but Gabriela was tolerant. Actually, Carmen's Marxism had softened quite a lot. My other daughter-in law's caste system hadn't budged from its hard line. Anna still wouldn't have anything to do with Carmen. Maybe it wasn't the fact that Anna was from El Salvador and Carmen was from Mexico. Maybe it was because Carmen had had a child out of wedlock, who had been adopted by John as an infant, and was our darling grandson, Etienne. Who knows? Anna was not approachable on the subject. So much for my dream of having Steve's and John's families close. This didn't mean that Steve and John couldn't take up where they had left off some twenty years before, and reestablish the wonderful relationship they had growing up. That never happened, either. John was certainly open to it, but Steve, who could almost be easy and fun when he was alone with us, could also get tense and uptight at times, especially when Anna was with him. This made things awkward for all of us, especially the kids, who had to be confused by the strange vibes surrounding our rare encounters.

I remember a Sunday at the beach house with John and Carmen and their children waiting for Steve and Anna and their son, Kevin, whom I wheedled and cajoled into coming out for a visit. It had rained for several days, leaving rare and wonderful sand dunes on the usually flat beach. Perfect for kids to climb on, and jump from. When Steve and family finally arrived, the atmosphere was as tense as ever. Ebullient Carmen, who deliberately—or not—refused to acknowledge the tension, turned to Anna.

"So, Anna," said she, "what are you doing with your life?" Anna stiffened, drawing herself up to her full five feet, two inches.

"I am taking care of my family," said she, quite angry.

Was she intimating that Carmen wasn't taking care of her family? That it was none of Carmen's business? I couldn't figure out why she thought Carmen's question was hostile. So I suggested we all go out on the beach; and the kids ran out and began having a wonderful time together, climbing and jumping on the dunes and actually relating to each other. Great, I thought, at least the kids are making contact. After about an hour however, Anna found it necessary to cut the visit short. That was about the last time Anna or Kevin saw John or his family.

I still tried to get the families together, but it got harder and harder to get Steve and Anna to visit us—even when Ellis and I were alone. If we wanted to see our grandson, Kevin (who in spite of everything is a delight), we made arrangements to see him at their place. Even then it was difficult, since there were all kinds of excuses about why it wasn't the right time.

Ellis finally put his foot down. He would no longer ask them to visit us, or ask to visit them. If they wanted to see us, they were welcome. But no more wheedling, cajoling, nudging, pleading or begging. He was right, of course, but it was awfully hard for me, and I'm afraid I couldn't give up. (If only as in *Mary Hartman*, we could all simply have gone to the House of Pancakes and worked things out!)

Meanwhile, Ellis and I went to work on *General Hospital.* The first few months were fun and exciting. After spending three years at Lorimar spinning my wheels and never getting anything on the tube, it was a rush to see my material on the air every day. Ellis and Wes Kenney, the Executive Producer, and I came up with some wild and crazy long-term stories to carry on the new look and pace of the soap set by Gloria Monty, who had not only given the world Luke and Laura, but opened up the arena with fantastic mystery/adventure stories shot on location. This was a new dimension for soaps—which made the transition from radio to TV in the '50s, but continued their slow pace of personal dramas, talked out over endless cups of coffee in the small town kitchens of mid-America. Of course, through the years, the soaps became more sophisticated—moving from kitchens to bedrooms, to courtrooms and operating rooms; but they seldom wandered outside, for obvious technical reasons. Gloria Monty was one of the first and best to change all that. Only, like many innovators, she may have gone a bit too far. I mean, at one point she had some cockamamie plot involving an Ice Princess who was about to deep freeze the world. We tried to be every bit as outrageous. We paid homage to Ernie Lehman's *North by Northwest;* combining it with *The Manchurian Candidate* in a story that had Scorpio, Sean, Anna, and Duke chasing all over Mount Rushmore after a sweet-faced country singer who was programmed to blow up the national monument simultaneously with Lenin's tomb in Moscow's Red Square, starting World War III, when he heard a certain musical coda.

We also did a story about a beautiful, doomed scientist, Greta the geneticist, who was blackmailed into giving her research on cloning to the Bad Guys, in spite of which she ends up dangling over Niagara Falls clinging to a cliff! A far cry from the kinds of stories I did on *Love is a Many Splendored Thing*, when all Iris had to contend with was being blind, pregnant, and fatally ill.

Leslie Charleson, who played the plucky, doomed Iris on *LIAMST,* was (and is) plucky Dr. Monica Quartermaine in *General Hospital.* The Quartermaines, Monica's husband Alan (Stuart Damon), his mother and father (Anna Lee, David Lewis) were the richest, most powerful family in Port Charles, and provided opportunity for intrigue and humor. Because soaps eat up so much material, we always borrowed (paid homage—stole?) from the best literary material. My co-headwriter on *General Hospital,* Norma Monty (Gloria's sister), came up with a delightful version of Agatha Christie's *Ten Little Indians,* involving an extended Quartermaine family after an eccentric uncle's inheritance which involved greed, lust, secret panels, disappearances, and murder-most-vile. It was a lot of fun, and exceedingly well played. But then, I've always been impressed with the terrific work soap actors do day-in and day-out, memorizing pages and pages of dialogue three and four times a week, adding their own personalities and charisma to roles, so that they form a kind of symbiosis with their fictional characters.

All the good soap actors make what they do look so easy and natural, that even sophisticated viewers wonder if they're not simply improvising their roles. As for less sophisticated viewers, they are surprised to learn that the words are actually written down. Of course some actors have been known to say things about the words written down such as "I can't say this shit!" And some actors, forgetting lines, do make up their own. There are those who sometimes make grammatical errors, which are not written down or caught in editing. I used to hate getting letters from English teachers pointing these errors out, since they were attributed to the writers, not the actors.

All in all, it was a good gig, writing *General Hospital.* We did some memorable stories, along with the more sensational ones. One memorable one involved that fine actress Jackie Zeman, who plays Bobbie Spencer, R.N. When a desperate criminal (played by Nat Christian, a wonderful actor/filmmaker) holds the entire hospital hostage, Bobbie suffered a major accident, causing her to become paralyzed. During her rehabilitation, we introduced a quadriplegic actress, Nancy Becker Kennedy, and were able to dispel some myths about the abilities of the physically challenged.

Around this time I got a note from one of my favorite childhood friends, Chappie Tanzer Brown. I'd hardly seen her since moving away from Little Falls decades before, except for a brief visit when she was in Los Angeles on vacation with her husband. She wrote to tell me she was a devoted fan of *General Hospital,* and thought I was doing a spiffy job writing it. She mentioned that she was sick—but never missed the show. I called, and found out she was, in fact, dying of cancer. Her attitude was unbelievable. She accepted what was happening, and told me it was "pretty neat, actually, to know how much time you have. This way I can go through my things and decide what I want to give to whom. I can settle a lot of other things, too." I had experienced so many good times with Chappie—sleeping over at her house, camping, outfoxing mean old Miss Barbour—the Girl Scout leader, canoe trips, early-morning dips in the freezing Adirondack lake. Whenever I reminisced about Little Falls, Chappie was in my thoughts.

Since she was a big fan of General Hospital and liked the actors so much, I decided to make a backstage video of the show, and see if some of the actors would send their greetings. Neither Ellis nor I were adept with our new cumbersome camcorder, which was nothing like today's palm-sized, easy-to-operate models, but we brought it to work one day, anyway. Then we found out there was an ironclad rule that no cameras were allowed on the set. But—the actors found out what we were trying to do and were wonderful—as actors always are in situations like that. Everyone who was there that day: Finola Hughes, Tristan Rogers, Jackie Zeman, Maree Cheatham, Rachel Ames, Brad Maule, and others, were charming and funny and upbeat as they spoke directly to Chappie, wishing her well. Chappie was absolutely delighted with the badly framed, amateurishly photographed results. I understand she almost wore it out running it as often as she did.

Things were going along pretty well on the show, and at home, too. Our enlarged household settled down. The children enrolled at Sherman Oaks Elementary School. John and Carmen put on a couple of sound and light shows at Tracy's theater to small but enthusiastic audiences, and they appeared at a Venice Club for very little money, but things didn't look promising financially. John was thinking about finishing his academic work for a degree at a local university by cobbling together his Berkeley college credits from seventeen years before, but he discovered that some of them wouldn't transfer. Besides, they were homesick for their place in the Pyrenees, and I was afraid they'd go back and stay there. Whatever they decided, they had to go back, to either settle down or pack. So after about three months, we drove them to the airport for the return trip to France and I guess I lost it. I tried hard not to pressure John and Carmen about returning permanently, but when I said goodbye to the kids at the airport, I got emotional. I love those kids. I had come so close to not knowing them at all, and now that I had gotten to know them so well, I couldn't bear the thought of only seeing them occasionally for the rest of my life.

Now I wonder how much that scene at the airport influenced John and Carmen to sell some of their hectares, rent the stone house they built themselves, pack up, and change their lives forever by coming back to live in the USA. I think they know I wasn't being consciously manipulative, but it certainly had an effect on them. I was kind of impressed, myself, since I so rarely allow my emotions free rein.

After John and his family left, Ellis and I got into a pleasant routine of work, weekends at the beach—where I played tennis and Ellis golfed, and we'd have dinner with friends—and then work again. After a while, the fun began to drain out of the work part. Josie, the network daytime VP, was never satisfied with my stories, the ratings (even though they were perfectly respectable), or anything else for that matter. As I mentioned before, there are certain people one has a rapport with and others one doesn't. Josie was one of the latter. And so was my co-headwriter, Norma Monty, who was a holdover from the previous writing staff. A necessary holdover, since I didn't know the show when I took over and she was intimately aware of everything about it. Norma had been an English teacher in New Jersey before joining her sister on the show in various capacities, winding up on the writing staff. I'm not sure if she worked on other shows, but she was inventive, with a good story mind, and she certainly knew the *General Hospital* characters and their backgrounds. But she wasn't a writer. And she wasn't fun to work with, and besides that, she didn't like me. At least I don't think she did. I mean, there was a definite chill in the air every time we were together—which was frequently, since we were obviously supposed to work closely.

I like to work in a loose, open, fun-filled, sometimes boisterous, comrades-in-arms-type of atmosphere. Norma made this almost impossible. At our first meeting, when the new executive producer, Wes Kenney, took both of us to dinner at Lucy's, I was prepared to have a couple of martinis and become best friends. Norma was stiff and formal, and remained that way all the time I was on the show. I would come to the office in jeans and a T-shirt. Norma would be dressed exquisitely, her hair coifed, her nails manicured, her jewels real.

There were two outline writers who were holdovers, too; big Jim Reilly, a massive man with massive talents, and Gene Palumbo, equally talented and with a perennial, "George Hamilton" tan. Both were political, and since they could sense the tension between Norma and me, they didn't dare take sides—although they were alert to see if there'd be a winner. So, even though they made the job easy in some ways, their uneasy loyalty made it difficult in other ways. I hate show business politics. I hated it on *Falcon Crest*. I hated it at Lorimar, and I hated it on *General Hospital*. I felt like saying, "Come on, guys, we're all trying to get five hours of television on a week. We're all good at what we do, so let's cut the intrigue and the pettiness and the dissing and whatever. Can't we all just get along?"

There were compensations. It was fun working with Ellis again, who didn't seem to notice (probably on purpose) any difficulties. Then there was Wes, indefatigable and effervescent, who called me into his office one day to ask if I had noticed anything peculiar about one of our leading actresses' behavior. Of course I had. She was heavily on the sauce, and probably doing more than a few recreational drugs. How she managed to remember her lines and speak them trippingly (although a little thickly) on her tongue was a mystery.

"I've got a favor to ask you," said Wes. "A few of her friends are getting together in my office and they want you to come."

I didn't get it.

"It's an intervention," he said. "She'll be there, too. And the facilitator."

I still didn't get it. Was it some kind of initiation? Were we going to meditate or pray or . . . levitate?

No, it turned out to be a way of getting an individual who was unaware of his/her problem, or ignored the problem, or refused to do anything about it, into a rehabilitation program.

"But if a person refuses . . . ?" I began.

Wes was as uneasy about the situation as I was. He was persuaded to go along, because the process was successful for others in similar situations. The "friends" are there for support and to back up the facilitator, who persuades the alcoholic or drug abuser to go directly to a "facility" such as the Betty Ford Clinic.

"Directly?" I asked, "as in not passing GO or collecting their personal belongings?"

I was appalled. I refused to go. Besides, I wasn't a close friend, and I found the idea kind of Gestapo-like. Actually, Wes felt the same way, but he had already committed himself, so he had to go through with it.

As it turned out, this was one of the cases where it didn't work. I was told later that, after several hours, the actress (surrounded by a few close friends and the facilitator) refused to be carted off to rehab. The story had a happy ending, anyway, since she was made aware of her problem, and either cleaned up her act or was more discreet about her habit, because she's still going strong on the show.

It was 1988 and I had been head-writing *Hospital* for two years and it was getting to be less and less fun. Beside the chilly atmosphere between Norma and me, the writing offices on the Columbia lot where the show was taped were underground and windowless. I worked at the beach as much as possible, but there were obligatory meetings several times a week in our tomblike headquarters, and they added to the general pall.

So when the writers voted to go out on strike early in the year,

I actually felt a sense of relief. We writers went on strike every three years, every time our contract with the AMPTP (Association of Motion Picture and Television Producers) came up for renewal. For good reason, because the producers are a tight, stingy, unenlightened bunch of bottom-line scroungers—against whom we've had to fight for every basic benefit in our contract—minimums, pensions, residuals, credits, etc., etc. We're the only talent union to put our jobs where our mouths are. I can't remember when the directors or actors have gone out on strike. They wait for us to soften up management, since our negotiations always seem to come up first. By the time the WGA settles with the AMPTP it's easy pickings for the DGA and SAG.

In 1985, the WGA strike was a two-week laugher. By '88 we had built-up a head of steam, and were backed by a 96 percent strike vote if management refused to withdraw their "requests" for lowering residuals and other insulting rollbacks. When they refused, we hit the bricks.

I know going out on strike is no laughing matter, but every time I've been on strike (which works out to about nine times since I joined the union in '61), it has been pretty funny. At least it looks kind of funny. I know. I know. It's a serious business. It hurts writers who have mortgages, school tuitions, and grocery bills (as it did Ellis and me through several strikes), but if you've ever seen a writer's picket line, you'd know what I mean; young mothers with strollers, jocks in warm-up suits, out-of-shape old timers of both sexes, chic hyphenate-types. Trouble is, we just don't look like serious strikers. Personally, I always felt a little self-conscious and embarrassed—as if I was acting in a revival of Odets' *Waiting for Lefty*. On the positive side, you get a rare chance to shmooze and network on a picket line. Once every three years, at least up until '88, it meant a chance to get out of the office and into the streets with colleagues, trudging along outside the studios and networks, carrying signs and feeling a sense of solidarity and comradeship.

In '88, I was happy to get out of my windowless office in Gower Gulch where *Hospital* was taped, and breathe the smog and carbon monoxide of the LA streets. This sense of euphoria contin-

Life With It's Joys And It's Sorrows

ued for the first several weeks, even the first couple of months. The strike began to get old in the third month as spring segued into summer, and the heat and smog increased. Picketing lost its allure, and the work stoppage was not only causing misery among writers, it was affecting thousands of other out-of-work entertainment personnel.

As the impasse wore on, and the two sides refused to budge, Hollywood became a production ghost town. Tempers flared, dissonant voices were raised, and it became mordantly evident that something had to be done. It wasn't until some outside Big Guns (like lawyer Ken Ziffren and then agent Mike Ovitz) stepped into the breech, that the strike was finally settled early in August. It had lasted five months, and the work stoppage was such a devastating blow to the industry that writers haven't been out on strike for ten years. A lot of writers think this is a good thing, but almost an equal number think it's a sellout. By the time the next negotiations came up in '91, I was on the Board of Directors again, and voted with the majority to support an idea our executive director Brian Walton created with his counterpart in the AMPTP, Nick Counter, called the Contract Adjustment Committee—which is a way to resolve problems between writers and management without striking. What you do is talk them to death. But dead issues don't lead to results, and after another peaceful, non-traditional negotiation in 1995, it was time to dump the CAC (Contract Adjustment Committee) and go back to management with an aroused and alerted membership willing to fight instead of make love. (By 1997 the ambiance between the Guild and its nemesis, the AMPTP, was a little too peaceful as we headed into another contract negotiation. This time the majority of the membership didn't even know the Executive Director and the Board were engaged in a "fast track" negotiation with Counter and the AMPTP. I certainly didn't know it when I foolishly decided to run for the Board again after a five year hiatus. What I did know was there were a lot of things writers deserved and weren't getting: a fair share of the billions being made from films and tv scripts in foreign markets plus an equally deserved chunk of money that was being raked in by the producers in the burgeoning cable tv markets. Also there were a lot of issues screenwriters were angry about: endless unpaid rewrites, late payments, creative rights and a general lack of respect for the creative person most responsible for any film or tv product, the writer!)

The election for Board members and officers was pretty dicey the Summer of 1997. Unfortunately I was elected along with all the officers and most of the other candidates who, unlike me, strongly endorsed the contract. I felt it was weak and unsatisfactory. When the contract failed to be ratified by a mere sixteen votes, the majority of my colleagues on the WGAW board were enraged. What followed were bitter, heated, acrimonious meetings that lasted until midnight and beyond. Many times I wondered what the hell I was doing there since I felt the most beleaguered of our tiny minority cell – patronized, shouted at but giving back as much as I got. But then I'd remember all those terrific writers who fought the good fight before, writers like Ellis who helped strengthen the Guild, who went out on strike time after time to get the benefits that so many young writers take for granted, and I'd take a couple more aspirin and go back into the board room and into the fray. Well it was finally worked out. Not to my satisfaction, but wait until next time. Meanwhile I find that those majority board members whom I'd wanted to choke are not such a bad lot. In fact I like most of them. I can even understand how Ted Kennedy and Orrin Hatch can be such good friends off the Senate floor.

But getting back to those five months we were on strike in 1988, many screenwriters used the down time working on novels, plays, narrative poems – any kind of writing except writing for the screen. That didn't mean, however, that certain network executives and producers didn't expect their striking writers to work on scripts and story projections that could be rushed into production as soon as the strike was over, which, of course, was totally against strike rules. I think Josie Emerich, network VP of daytime at ABC, thought I'd come back to work with a two-year story projection all neatly worked out. She was disappointed, because I'd hardly thought about the show, which continued in production and on the air in spite of the strike, written by willing scabs—as were all the soaps.

But I did go back to my windowless office with a lot of enthusiasm. Five months is a long time to be out of work. As a strike concession, management agreed to extend all staff writers' contracts the five months we had been out on strike, a Guild demand I appreciated after what happened.

And what happened was that Josie and I had a dramatic showdown. Not at the OK Corral, but in a conference room in the Century City offices of ABC.

I can't remember exactly how it came about, but it certainly had to do with Josie's disapproval of practically every story I wanted to do on the soap. A lot of the stuff was hastily written, and not thoroughly thought out. But hey, there was a lot of slack to take up, a lot of material to cover, and we had to hit the deck running, and get the show on the road, and, if I could, I'd try to think up more cliche phrases to use in my defense. On the other hand, Josie must have had one helluva time during the five months the seasoned professional writers on the four or five soaps she oversaw were out on strike. So she was pretty tense. And I was pretty stubborn by the time she called for a face-to-face story conference. Only it was a face-to-faces story conference, since she insisted on the presence of the entire writing staff—including the writers' assistant and the continuity coordinator. With the scriptwriters, the outline writers, the story consultants, Wes, Ellis, Norma, Josie and her next-in-command, there must have been sixteen people sitting around the table. Which made it totally impossible to have a serious story meeting, since everyone knows you cannot do a story by committee.

So there we were, Josie and I, sitting directly across the conference table from each other with legions of writers, producers, consultants, and assistants on either side of us, and Josie refused to look at me. A weird situation. I started the presentation, trying to sell my story ideas to Josie, but I couldn't make eye contact with her. So I gave up.

"Josie," I said. "This is no way to run a ball club. I'll meet with Wes and Norma and you and we'll discuss the future of the show.

257

But I can't do it like this."

Well, maybe I didn't put it that simply—or nicely—but that was the idea. An idea that didn't work, because Josie was every bit as stubborn as I was, and things escalated from there. She picked apart my Anna/Duke/Scorpio story. She ridiculed my Bobby/Jake/Lucy surrogate-mother story. She tapped her pencil on the table as I outlined the Quartermaine projection. At one point, staring at something on the wall above my head, she accused me of not caring about the characters on the show. Then she turned to the story consultant, a retired novelist who had been on a retainer for about fifteen years, and whom I rarely consulted, and asked him for his ideas. That was too much for me, so I stood up and, in graphic language, told her what she could do with her characters and her show—and stomped out of the meeting. Needless to say, I was informed later that day that my services would no longer be required.

By this time, John and family were back from France and had settled in Sylmar, a working-class community in the northernmost reaches of the San Fernando Valley—tucked up against the San Gabriel Mountains. He decided to get his degree in music from Cal-State Northridge, while Carmen refined her talents in an Art Institute, and the kids enrolled in public school. Jacobo and Etienne joined Little League while Paola took ballet and tap lessons. Instant assimilation!

Meanwhile, Ellyn and Bill came back from Washington and found a house on a tree-shaded street south (very south) of Beverly Hills. Bill had finished his clerkship for Supreme Court Chief Justice Rehnquist and joined Gibson, Dunn, and Crutcher, a large downtown law firm. Ellyn transferred to the Justice Department's Central California District, where she continued as an Assistant U.S. Attorney prosecuting federal cases.

So it was a good time for Ellis and me to put our feet up, smell the roses, visit with extended family and friends, and forget about the rat race. But neither of us were ready to unplug our word processors. Besides, Ellis hadn't been fired. I had. He was doing a great job on the show, and even though he was partisan in his sup-

Life With It's Joys And It's Sorrows

port of me, they couldn't fire him for that. So he stayed on as an outline writer, and they brought in our old litigant pal, Pat Falken Smith, who couldn't have been nicer or more respectful, as the new head writer. Show business can be quite nutty but wonderful at times.

I settled into freelancing again, writing several pilots (which didn't get on the schedule), a nighttime soap paying homage to Frederic Durenmatt's *The Visit* (which didn't make it to air), and a sequel to a popular TV movie called *Who's Julia?*, produced by our good friend Phil Barry (which, alas, never saw the light of day, either). Even though I was making money, it was a frustrating time professionally.

Emotionally, my life was on a kind of roller coaster. Ellyn got pregnant, which made our special relationship even more special as I empathized with every queasy moment, every scare, every worry, every moment of wonder and joy. While we were anticipating the baby's arrival, Ell's brother Marc was diagnosed with terminal cancer. Sometimes Life does imitate Art (if you can consider a good TV show Art). Soapy maybe, corny probably, but way back in the sixties *Ben Casey* opened every week with senior doctor Sam Jaffe drawing male/female symbols on a blackboard and talking about the mysteries of life and death. That's what Ellis and I were preoccupied with.

Bill and Ellyn, enormous with child, spent the weekend with us in Malibu in the middle of March, and when they came back from a walk on the beach, she said she thought she might be starting labor. So we began timing "twinges," but they were weak and far apart, and they left that Sunday night not expecting the baby for another week or two. The next morning at five a.m. Bill called us from Cedars/Sinai with the happy news. Katharine Marjorie Lindsay was born on March 20, 1989. I rushed out, found a 24-hr Thrifty drugstore, bought a Polaroid camera, and raced to the hospital. Ellyn was feeling giddy and ecstatic, just as I felt after giving birth. Bill, who coached through the entire process, looked a little dazed, a little green, but happy and exhausted. My new granddaughter looked magnificent—even though her head was temporarily cone-shaped because Dr. To had to use forceps to tug her out.

Barely five weeks later, Marc died at St. John's Hospital in Santa Monica. Emily and their three children, Amy, Polly, and David were with him. So was Ellis. We all knew it was imminent, but that didn't stop us from hoping for some miracle, some escape from the inevitable. Marc was extremely brave and stoical, even philosophical. He wasn't religious, nor were Ellis or I, which makes death that much harder to accept. I was with Ellyn, Bill, and my new granddaughter when Ellis came back from the hospital that bleak afternoon. He was devastated. Marc was not only his big brother; he was his mentor, role model, hero, and friend. Marc kept the family together during the Depression when their father lost his job. Ellis followed him to the University of Michigan and then into the theater, first graduating from the Academy of Dramatic Arts when Marc was teaching there, and then becoming his assistant when Marc was a stage manager. It was through Marc's friendship with Tracy that Ellis met her—which led to that Christmas party where I met him.

Although he made a valiant effort not to show how deeply he was affected, Ellis never got over his feeling of loss when Marc died. In some way, either directly or metaphysically, I think it had a lot to do with what happened not too long afterward.

Chapter 25

Ellis

Usually Ellis was able to express his feelings easier than I could. He cried at movies. He was visibly affected by catastrophes in the news. He was tender and sensitive and loving with me, our children, his extended family and friends. But he wasn't able to open up about Marc.

Life went on, as life has a habit of doing. We were enjoying our new grandchild. We even volunteered to take care of Katie one weekend when she was in that impossible (though adorable) stage between crawling and walking, and found ourselves totally exhausted by the experience. As for working, I was fiddling around with various story ideas, and Ell was still writing an outline a week for *General Hospital,* which gave him enough time for golf. In fact, he began to give me pointers on the golf course since I had time, now, to join him. Under his tutelage, I was getting the hang of it. I enjoyed those long, lazy afternoons riding around in a golf cart, gazing at the distant mountains, smelling the flowers, and occasionally getting off a good shot between several awful ones. Ellis was relaxed about his game, and I tried to be, but there was one hole on a beautiful course halfway between Malibu and Thousand Oaks that drove me wild. The tee was on a rise, and you had to drive off this hill, over a rocky gorge to the green below. There was a forgiving woman's tee, which avoided this yawning gap, but I was damned if I'd use that. Unfortunately, the first time I drove off the tee I had a lucky shot that sailed over the gorge somehow and landed close to the green. It was my undoing, because I never got a drive like that again. I have no idea how many balls I drove into the snake-infested gorge after that, but Ellis simply handed me another ball, not even suggesting by a look that I do the obvious and use the gender friendly, sexist tee.

Before we knew it, the new decade rolled around, the nineties, the decade that would mark our fiftieth anniversary! Hard to believe. Were we really that old? Apparently so, because in June 1990, my college decided to give me an award. Not an honorary degree. Western College didn't exist anymore. All that was left was a lovely campus (taken over by Miami University), and a feisty alumnae association, run by an even feistier executive director, Jacqui Wallace—who was determined to keep it going as long as the last alumna drew breath. The award was for "distinguished service" which I hoped (same as Lauren Bacall about her '97 Oscar nomination), was for my body of work and not simply because I hadn't croaked. I wanted Ellis to come with me, but he had scheduled some minor surgery, which he didn't want to postpone.

Generally, Ellis' health was good. Years before, he'd had a scare, polyps in his throat, that luckily turned out to be benign. Otherwise, he'd had a hemorrhoid operation when he was in the Army (in a field hospital tent in the desert), minor hernia surgery, and a routine prostate procedure, graphically explained to me as a "rotor-rooter" widening of the gland; it sounded awful but wasn't dangerous. He was moderately overweight, on medication for high blood pressure, and had to watch his cholesterol—but then so does every other senior citizen. His legs bothered him a lot, and he took anti-inflammatory pills, which didn't help because they still ached miserably. He hated not being able to walk the golf course or the beach, but all in all with his great teeth, full head of hair, strong build, and youthful appearance, he looked the picture of health.

So when his urologist suggested it was time for another "rotor-rooter" prostate procedure, Ellis, who rarely put things off, scheduled it as soon as possible. Besides, since it was a couple of days before the alumnae weekend, it gave him an airtight excuse for not attending. I didn't blame him, but I didn't want to go if he was going to be in the hospital.

Ell could be stubborn at times, and he insisted. He argued that I wouldn't be leaving until a day and a half after the operation. That it was minor surgery, which he'd gone through before, and he assured me there was nothing to worry about. So I made plans for the flight to Cincinnati, looking forward to seeing my old roommate and soul sister Martha McKee Keehn, and spending a nostalgic weekend roaming our old campus haunts.

That Wednesday in June, the surgery went well and Ellis was out of recovery early and back in his room. I had stayed late and was back the next morning, planning to go to a network meeting at NBC after lunch to pitch a TV movie with Joanne Brough, who would produce it. Ellis had a good night, had already been out of bed, and was his irreverent, cheery self. He was looking forward to watching the golf tournament on TV, and I was feeling better about leaving for the alumnae weekend the next day. We were chatting animatedly about something or other, when he suddenly felt dizzy. And cold. I lowered the bed, put the covers around him and rang for the nurse. When she arrived, she took his blood pressure and said it had dropped quite a bit, but that it was nothing to worry about; it happened frequently after surgery. Ellis seemed to feel better in a short time, but I think the incident scared him. I didn't want to go to my appointment, but I didn't want Ellis to think I was worried by canceling it, either. I had another hour before I had to leave, and when Ell continued to feel okay, I took off for Burbank.

I met Joanne in the NBC cafeteria. When she asked how Ellis was, I burst into tears. Not at all like me. Was it a premonition? What was I doing there about to pitch a dumb idea about some Harvard MBAs on an urban outreach program? Joanne offered to call the meeting off, but since we were already there, I semi-pulled myself together, and we went through with the pitch— which got a luke-warm reception.

I got back to the hospital, and Ellis was in fine fettle. His doctor checked him over and said what had happened "was to be expected." Ellyn was there, regaling him with stories about fifteen-month-old Katie, and he was complaining about the food, always a good sign.

I still didn't want to go to the reunion in Ohio the next day. I packed and went to the hospital Friday morning. If there were any question at all about how Ellis felt or looked I wasn't going. When I got to his room, he was flirting with a middle-aged nurse. He looked good. He felt good. I left for Cincinnati.

The next night at the alumnae banquet, I received my award, an engraved medallion with my name spelled wrong. (It was fixed later and sent to me). I had a good time. It's nice to be appreciated and honored by your peers. And it was great fun to spend time with Martha and some of my old college chums. After the banquet, we sat around reminiscing, and then Martha, Helen Kaslo, and I went back to the dormitory room we were sharing, and I called Ellis.

It was three hours earlier in Los Angeles, and it sounded as though he were hosting a party in his hospital room. Indeed he was. Ray and Tracy were there, and our good friend Suzanne Childs. Ellis was telling stories; doing a Jean Gabon imitation in French from a revival of *La Femme du Boulanger* we had seen recently. He was still laughing about what had happened the day before. When I had left for the airport, he had told me to wave to him from George Burns Drive, which I did, tirelessly, only he forgot to appear at the huge plate glass window on the fifth floor to wave back. I also found out he had taken the group on a funny tour of the art hanging on the walls of the fifth floor surgery wing. But he was anxious to hear about my evening, and insisted on talking to Martha and Helen to get the lowdown on what had been said about me, and how my acceptance speech was received.

I came back the next day, Sunday, and went to the hospital from the airport. Ellis was watching the golf tournament, and I climbed on his bed to watch it with him. He was impatient to get home, but because of the "incident," his doctor wanted to keep him in the hospital an extra day. He spent Monday mostly out of bed, and we walked the hospital corridors, had lunch and dinner in his room, and cuddled on his bed watching more of the tournament.

Tuesday, June 19, he called at the crack of dawn. The doctor had already been there, checked him out, and he was ready to come home. "No rush, honey," he said, "take your time." When I got there an hour later, he was dressed, packed, and ready to go.

I drove home through Benedict Canyon, being careful not to go over the speed limit (which Ellis always accused me of—with good reason). We were both feeling particularly wonderful that morning, almost giddy. The weather had something to do with it. It was one of those fine, cool, sunny mornings. Not bleak, the way June usually is in southern California, not hot and smoggy, either. It felt crisp and full of expectation. Maybe we should take another cruise. Maybe Ell should quit his time-consuming, unexciting job on the soap, and we should think about writing a feature film. Then again, maybe we shouldn't work together. Maybe we shouldn't work at all. It was a wonderful feeling to have that option.

When we got home, Ellis went into his office and began making phone calls. I could hear him laughing and carrying on with his sister, Miriam, in Pittsburgh. I had to market. I wanted to get something special for lunch. I looked in on Ellis, still on the phone, and told him I was off to Westward Ho. He was laughing when he waved goodbye.

I was back in less than an hour, and Gabriela helped me carry the groceries from the car. I went to see if Ellis was ready for lunch. He was in the bedroom, and had put on a jacket—one from our show, emblazoned with *L.A.T.E.R.* on it. He looked pale and said he was cold. I was a little put out with him.

"You're just home from the hospital," I scolded. "You should be taking it easy. Better get in bed."

I started to take the quilt off the bed when Ell staggered a bit.

"Oh-oh," he said. He didn't seem alarmed, simply matter-of-fact. Then he said, "You'd better call the medics."

That seemed awfully dramatic to me. I didn't think he was serious. But now he looked extremely pale, and he lurched toward the bathroom. I tried to support him as he braced himself with both hands against the sink counter.

I knew something terrible was happening. He was rigid. His eyes were open. He was still standing there, braced against the counter, but he wasn't moving. He didn't even seem to be breathing.

I yelled for Gabriela. She came on the run and helped me lower him to the floor. We propped him against the tub, and she hurried out of the room. I scooped up the phone and dialed 911. I got through almost immediately. I was on auto pilot, no feelings, nothing. They said they'd be there right away. They said he should be lying down, not propped up. Gabriela hurried back into the room with candles! She wanted to light them, to say prayers. This was crazy, crazy. I sent her away to open the front door. I got Ellis on his back. Had the emergency operator told me to try artificial respiration? I tried it. Closed his nostrils, breathed into his mouth. Pressed under his rib cage. Nothing. Oh God. I tried again. . . and again. How long had it been? Why weren't they here? Nothing was happening. Nothing.

And then the sirens. Lots of them. Fire trucks, an ambulance. Medics crowding into the bathroom, moving me aside—all kinds of equipment, oxygen masks, medical gibberish. Did I hear "flat line?" But they continued to work on him. They asked me what medication he was on. They wouldn't bother if it were already too late, would they? After several minutes, they told me they were taking him to Encino Hospital. I managed to reach Ray at his house and told him. The medics said I could ride with them in the ambulance. I remember passing our neighbors who came out to see what had happened: the Paulsons, Sharon at the end of the block, Alice and Steve Elliott.

Ellis never regained consciousness. His heart had stopped for several minutes, and even though the emergency room cardiologist had miraculously managed to get it beating again, Ellis was gone. Wonderful, bright, funny, dear Ellis—my lover, my best friend was no longer there.

We kept a vigil at his bedside for four days. We hoped against hope. There are miracles. People in deep comas come out of them sometimes, don't they? A caring, sympathetic nurse in the intensive care unit told us to talk to him, that he might be able to hear us.

And we did. Especially Ellyn. And me, although I felt self-conscious and terribly, terribly guilty. I didn't believe he could hear me. I didn't believe he was there. I didn't even feel that it was his body lying in the bed, hooked up to all the beeping machinery, monitoring functions that had no purpose now. I talked to him, anyway, feeling stupid, and helpless, and distanced. Because I wasn't there, either. It was a scene I had written scores of times, only now I was acting in it—but I wasn't doing it well. I wasn't believable. I wasn't feeling it. The dialogue was forced and full of cliches.

"Ellis, come back to me. I need you. We all need you—the children and the grandkids, Ray, Tracy. You're our rock, our center. You can't leave now. There are too many things left to do. Things we haven't had time for until now."

Bad, bad, bad dialogue. Phony performance. Why? I really did need Ellis, and so did the kids, grandkids; the whole damn world needed his decency, his honesty and morality. One moment he was here with all his thoughts, memories, wisdom, a lifetime of experience, deeds, love—and then . . . nothing. Gone.

Where were my real feelings? Why couldn't I reach them when half of me had been ripped away? For forty-six years, more than three-fourths of my life, he had been a part of me. We were one, together, an entity. Ann 'n Ell, a team, a unit, us. I was twenty-two and he had just turned twenty-six when we took a vow to love and honor each other "until death do us part," but who says it stops there? I still loved and honored him. So why couldn't I let go? Why couldn't I feel?

The next few days were a haze. Decisions had to be made that only the children and I could make, even though Ray and Tracy were full of love and concern and support. Steve, John, Ellyn and I were the ones who had to make the awful choice.

Ellis was on life-support machinery. His doctors gave him no chance of surviving. Even if by some miracle he did come out of the coma, he would be totally incapacitated with no memory, no comprehension, not Ellis at all.

A specialist, a neurologist, was brought in and confirmed what the other doctors had said. No hope. I asked for a second neurological opinion. Another specialist examined him with the same result. It was three days after the heart attack when we sat together with a hospital counselor in a small, dreary, isolated lounge near the intensive care unit, and made our decision. Would it have been easier if we were Orthodox Jews? Or born again Christians? Or unlapsed Catholics, Buddhists, Janeists, or Native American Spirit Worshippers? Of the four of us, I think John is the most spiritually connected. At least, he thinks about such things, and seems to have a strong inner faith woven from many different religions. I'm not sure Ellyn spends much time thinking about religion, although she tries to maintain her Jewish heritage by observing some of the holidays. I don't know anything about Steve's religious beliefs, but I seriously doubt he has any, and as for me. . . I'm still waiting for enlightenment—without much hope.

We agreed, however, that Ellis would want us to remove the life-support system.

That night, as we had every night, we all gathered for dinner. Ray and Tracy were there, as were John and his family, and Ellyn and Bill. John's son Jacobo, who was eleven, knew Ellis was very sick, but he pressed John for more information, and when John told him the truth, that his grandfather was not expected to live, Jacobo was devastated. Ellis and he had a special relationship. Jacobo seemed especially tuned-in to Ellis. He sought his attention and companionship, and there was a kind of magical communication between them. They shared stories and jokes; played board games and chess. Jacobo would leave sticker notes on Ell's bulletin board to "the world's greatest grandpa." He couldn't bear the thought that he was losing him. His face crumpled in grief and shock. He got up from the table and ran outside. John went after him. I followed and looked outside. They were sitting on the curb in front of the house next door. John had his arm around him and he was crying inconsolably. I closed the door and went back to my bedroom, our bedroom. I sat in the dark and, for the first time, cried.

Ellis died the next morning, June 23, 1990.

Chapter 26

And Five Plus Three Is Eleven

I guess I'm superstitious. I've kept a lucky, small, flat stone in my change purse for twenty-five years. I don't know why it's lucky. I simply picked it up on the beach one day and designated it lucky. I haven't taken my wedding ring off since 1944. I've kept a silly poem that accompanied a gift Ellis gave me on my thirtieth birthday in my wallet for forty-five years:

> "From John, age four
> And Steve, near six
> To Mom who's twenty-seven.
> And cows wear shoes
> Bikes have ears
> And five plus three is eleven."

So it sort of follows that it was difficult for me to take Ell's clothes out of our closet right away—or even for a very long time.

I wanted Jacobo to have something special from his grandfather, so I gave him Ell's watch. I gave Steve's son, Kevin, who has turned into a gifted photographer, Ellis' prized Minolta. Etienne, our oldest grandson, has Ellis' wallet and his golf clubs. Paola and Katie have some personal mementos, and I'm saving the fancy chess set for our youngest grandchild, Benjamin Ellis Lindsay, who never got to meet his grandfather since he was born the year after Ellis died.

I know it was wasteful not to give his clothes away in a reasonable amount of time, but I liked seeing them on his side of the closet. I liked touching them, smelling them. They were a comfort. Ray, who loved Ellis, took some of his ties, handkerchiefs, stuff like that. John accepted some sweaters—Ell's other clothes were too big for him. They would have fit Steve, but the thought of wearing his Dad's clothes made him uncomfortable. So it wasn't until I remodeled that part of the house years later that I finally packed up everything and called the Vietnam vets. I don't think that organization is too style conscious. Besides, men's clothes don't change from one year to the next.

I never would have gotten through the days and weeks following Ell's death without depending on the kindness of family and friends. Tracy, emotionally challenged, always late, trauma prone, often distracted, seemingly disorganized—always comes through in times of real crisis. She was there for me then. Her strength and understanding, her healing powers and love were remarkable. Ray, my other lifetime buddy and supporter, couldn't have been more understanding and strong and full of love. I'm truly blessed with siblings like them. I know how rare and unique they are.

Ellyn and I clung together, trying to help one another. I was tremendously grateful that she had Bill to comfort her. John was caring and philosophical, but Steve was as hard to read as ever.

Then there was my friend Suzanne who made all the arrangements for Ellis' memorial service. I'm not exactly sure why, but I wanted it in a sacred place with a rabbi officiating. So my WASPY friend Suzanne auditioned rabbis, and found a synagogue for the service. Rabbi David Baron, from the Synagogue for The Performing Arts, presided and said a few words; but he had never met Ellis so it was mostly *pro forma*. I also wanted The Kaddish, the traditional prayer for the dead, recited. I guess that was a strange request, too, since Ellis hadn't even had a Bar Mitzvah, and even though he didn't think religion was the source of all evil, he felt it came pretty close.

The day before the service, I rushed out to the Sherman Oaks Galleria and bought a hideous dress, which I never wore again. The service was held on a Thursday. It was probably the hottest day of the year, but it was a good house, well over two hundred people were there. I think Ell would have been pleased. I know he would have counted the house. He was good at that from his days as an assistant stage manager. All the children spoke; even Steve, whom I feared wouldn't show up. Chris Knopf sort of MC.'d the program, giving a wonderful tribute himself. Ell's sister Miriam, Ray, Tracy, and Suzanne spoke, too. I sat through it dry-eyed. Numb, actually, until John played a movement from a Brahms concerto on his flute. Brahms was one of Ell's favorites.

There's something to be said about a (more or less) formal farewell. We hear a lot about "closure" these days. But it is important. Attention should be paid.

John's children delayed going to summer camp to attend the service, so two days later he asked if I'd like to drive up to the Sierras when he dropped them off. Ellis loved the woods, and I like them second best after the ocean, so I was glad to go, to get off by myself and try to sort things out. John and I only stayed a couple of days, but it was beautiful and serene high up in the mountains, and the next day I went off by myself and discovered Huntington Lake, less than ten miles away.

I parked the car and walked down a woodsy path to the shore, and sat in a secluded sun-drenched spot. I didn't sort much out. All I did was sit there staring into the water, feeling a terrible sense of emptiness. Tracy wasn't around to ask me what I was thinking about, so I didn't have to feel silly by telling her I wasn't thinking about anything. I just wanted to stare at the water as the sun danced on the gentle waves, making them sparkle. Huntington Lake is a lot like the pristine lakes in upper New York State's Adirondack Mountains where I spent so many summers at camp. It's unspoiled, with rugged campgrounds, a few cottages built on leased government property, a marina at each end (no jet skies allowed), and that's about it. I took pictures to show Bill and Ellyn, and they fell in love with it, too. We've gone there for at least a week every summer since.

Back home, Ray and his girlfriend Mary Ellen offered to stay with me for a few weeks although I assured them it wasn't necessary, that I was perfectly fine. But I didn't object when they quietly moved in. I <u>was</u> fine. Too fine as it turned out. I began having a series of auto accidents, fender-benders, several of them. And crying jags at the oddest moments. Three weeks after Ell's death, I went to the tennis club for the first time. I felt . . . fine. Normal. I was looking forward to playing. I ran into Beverly, a woman I knew quite peripherally. She expressed sympathy and asked how I was doing. I burst into tears and couldn't stop crying. I waved her away, got back in my car, drove down Pacific Coast Highway, and got into a three-car pile up. No one was hurt. Even the cars weren't damaged severely—although just putting a bump on somebody's fender costs thousands these days. I'm not even sure it was my fault. But this was about the fourth accident in a very short time.

Someone suggested grief counseling. I gave it a shot. I went to a group session of people who had lost spouses. All women except for one man. It was led by an intelligent, supportive, caring therapist. I listened for awhile. Boring. Some of them had been there for over a year. I didn't think it was going to work for me. I didn't think I was going to participate. Then it was my turn to say something— if I wanted to. They couldn't stop me. I don't know what I said. I just rambled on and on. And cried. The therapist nodded approvingly. The women were sweet. The man looked sleepy. I never went back.

Mostly, I'd go through periods where I didn't feel anything. Take the play I attended shortly after Ell's death. Our talented neighbor Alice Hirson, was in an original comedy at an Equity-waiver theater in Santa Monica, and invited me to a performance. Then she felt terribly upset, because she realized it was about a man who has a heart attack. A funny heart attack. I couldn't imagine why she was upset. I wasn't upset. I didn't make any connection at all between the character in the play and Ellis. Besides, she was very good in the play.

It was Irma Kalish who finally got me back on track. She was producing a sitcom called *The Hogan Family*. She and her husband

Rocky were at Ellis' memorial service, and came to the house that hot afternoon. Amidst all the tears and sympathy and remembrances of good times, Irma said, "Listen, if you feel like writing an episode, you've got an assignment." About a month later, I called.

"Did you mean it about an assignment?" I asked her.

"Whenever you're ready," said my friend.

I was ready. At least I thought I was. I met with Irma and her staff of young writer/producers and pitched several ideas. We settled on one that involved the teenage twins' dog-sitting a pedigreed pooch, and surreptitiously selling his stud services for big bucks. I thought it was hilarious. I had a good time writing it, and Irma couldn't have been kinder or gentler—which didn't stop her from totally rewriting it. She made a magnificent gesture. One I'll never forget. It was a jump-start that got me going again. After that, I kept going and going like the Energizer bunny—with just about the same sense of direction.

In fact, I accepted anything and everything that came my way; invitations to dinner, concerts, political lunches, offers to run for office at the Writer's Guild. I was elected to the Board of Directors again, and after the first year of a two-year term accepted (against my better judgement), a nomination to run for Secretary/Treasurer of the Guild—and won that election. I became a governor of the Academy of Television Arts and Sciences. I served on all kinds of committees, from Age Discrimination to Women Filmmakers to the Contract Adjustment Committee, made guest-speaking appearances at UCLA classes, the American Film Institute, and other seminars. I joined the prestigious Hollywood Women's Political Committee, and attended their retreat in Santa Barbara—along with Marilyn Bergman, Jane Fonda, Paula Weinstein and all kinds of other women industry moguls, whom I found interesting and charming, but I have no idea what we talked about. I simply don't remember; except that one of the guests was an Ex-Governor of Ohio, and I took a hike with him and thought he was handsome. I even invited a visiting Russian screen-writing couple, who were part of a delegation sponsored by the Writers Guild Foundation, to stay at my house for a week that summer—and had so many Russian delicacies for breakfast the first morning that we all got indigestion. I was running so hard I didn't give myself a chance to think, because thinking was brooding and brooding was N.G.

Then I got a dog.

Ellis vowed after our last two dogs Ginger and her son Max went wherever good dogs go when they die, never to get another one. He was tired of feeding them, walking them, replacing chewed up items, and especially cleaning up after them.

I needed a dog, and I went looking for one at the shelters in the Valley. I almost decided on a mixed-breed shepherd, but something told me to go to one more shelter—and there he was. A nine-week-old bundle of almost-pure golden retriever who had just been brought in, and was sitting forlornly in a cage in the makeshift storefront office of Pet Adoptions. First of all, I liked the whole idea of Pet Adoptions. I could tell the volunteers never turned a dog away since several old dogs were roaming the office who had no chance of being adopted, but were being taken care of by the staff.

I asked to see the little bundle in the cage, and he was placed on the floor and immediately pooped. It was total love at first sight. The transaction was completed in about ten minutes, and the bundle and I were on our way home.

All the dogs we ever had threw up until they got used to riding in the car. But this guy seemed fine, until we got a block from the house, when he threw up into the gearshift. I had to suction it out with a turkey baster.

What can I say about Ollie? He's a terrific dog, large and furry, big enough to get my arms around and hug. He's almost everything a dog should be: loyal, loving, protective. (At least he barks and growls at noises in the middle of the night—although he didn't do a damn thing the one time the house was broken into when I wasn't there.)

But he has his idiosyncrasies. He loves to fetch a ball, but refuses to give it back. He insists on greeting visitors by jumping up on them and kissing them on the face. It's surprising how many people don't enjoy that kind of greeting. I've tried the usual techniques to discourage him, but after eight years he's still doing it—except when my son-in-law Bill visits. Him, he respects. Recently, he's been responding to Bill's daughter Katie, my nine-year-old granddaughter, who commands him to "Sit, Ollie, sit!" And he does.

Aside from his effusive greetings, he's sweet-tempered, gentle, and a little goofy. I mean, Lassie he's not. If we were out in the woods and I fell down a ravine, forget about Ollie going for the sheriff. Wouldn't happen. But he's a great dog—even if he does look a little like a seal as Tracy, a passionate dog lover, insists. Eventually, I stopped racing around. This was not solely my decision. One of the realities of being a widow is that invitations taper off. Dinner parties seem to be for couples, male/female couples, and there's a scarcity of older gentleman dinner partners to go around. There were, of course, friends who tried to fix me up, but I wasn't ready for that. Then there were surprising moments, like the night I stopped by Tracy's house *en route* to the Writers Guild Awards Dinner (I was a board member at the time). I had a new formal for the affair, and stopped to show it to Tracy. An old friend of hers was there, an actor I knew slightly who had just returned from a long national tour. He gallantly escorted me back to my car where he kissed me goodbye. Only it wasn't a peck on the cheek. I was startled to find his tongue halfway down my throat. Yuck! As my granddaughters would say.

Work, that's what I needed to do. I went to New York on a couple of daytime consulting missions. I wrote a script for *The Golden Girls*. I developed yet another nighttime serial with my brother Ray for Fred Silverman—which wasn't picked up. I played a lot of tennis, but the one time I tried to play golf was a disaster. Not because of the way I played, but because I couldn't play at all. I was with Diana Douglas Darrid. It was the first time I had played since Ellis' death. We rolled up to the first tee, and Diana hit her usual solid shot up the middle. I made a halfway respectable drive and I suddenly got all weepy. Diana had no idea what was wrong. Neither did I, except I felt overwhelmingly sad. Actually, it wasn't hard to figure out. Ellis and I had had a lot of fun playing golf recently. Being there without him was just too painful. It was years before I could go out on a golf course.

Skiing was a different matter, however, because Ellis had given it up ten years before. I hadn't gone without him, but that winter I had a real urge to ski again. Trouble was, not many people my age ski. I did have a friend, albeit several years younger, who still did. She had lost her husband years before and re-married a man who hadn't skied before he met her. In fact, Ellis and I went to Vail with them when Sy (not his real name) took up the sport for the first time. He was a natural and before long was skiing better than any of us. We had been quite close to Carla (not her real name) and her first husband, but only casual friends with Carla and Sy. Nevertheless, they skied—and I knew they went with friends every year, so I called.

"Carla," said I, "are you going skiing this year?"

"Annie!" said she, sounding delighted, "It's so good to hear from you. How are you blah, blah, blah."

I told her about my keen desire to see if I could still ski. I knew that she and Sy were more expert at this point than I was, but I planned to ski with an instructor or a group, and wouldn't hold them back. There was, as we say, a long pause. A very long pause. It turned out my friend of thirty years who, as a matter of fact, was planning a ski trip even as we spoke, didn't think it would work out.

"We've been going with these people for a number of years and . . . well . . . it would be . . . kind of . . . awkward. You understand, don't you?"

No, I didn't understand. I will never understand. Even though I've seen "Carla" and "Sy" several times since, and all appears to be quite normal, it isn't normal. I've given it a lot of thought, and I think they must have been engaging in wild sexual orgies with their friends on these so-called ski trips and <u>that's</u> the reason it would have been "awkward." Otherwise, what other reason could there have been?

One morning, about a week after that, I was lolling in bed, reading the *LA Times* and drinking coffee, when the phone rang. It was Mike Filerman. He was in David Jacobs' Lorimar office in Burbank.

"Whatcha doing?" he asked.
"Working against a deadline," I lied.
"Oh," he said. He sounded disappointed.
"Only kidding," said I. "What's up?"
He asked me how soon I could meet with them. I was there within the hour.

Chapter 27

Chock Full O' Knots

Most people think that *Dallas* came first and that *Knots Landing* was a spin-off. Technically it was a spin-off, but David Jacobs, who created both nighttime serials (with input from Michael Filerman), came up with the idea for *Knots Landing* first. CBS, however, wanted to experiment with a glitzier, bigger canvassed show to try out the format. When the network struck gold (actually oil), with *Dallas, Knots Landing* was "green-lighted." David moved Gary, the black sheep of the Ewing family, and his shy, naive wife, Valene (a name I always associate with an oil product), to a neighborhood cul-de-sac in suburban Los Angeles, with ongoing characters who became their friends.

The name, Knots Landing, is more appropriate for a small town in New England than a community in Southern California, but what's in a name? *Knots* turned out to be the second longest running show on TV (*Gunsmoke* is *numero uno*). I was on staff the second year of the show in 1981, when I left to seek my fortune elsewhere. Now it was ten years later, and David and Michael were inviting me back. The offer couldn't have come at a better time.

I didn't need the money—at this point I was blessedly financially secure; I did need the job for every other reason—physical, psychological, and emotional. It was practically impossible to work as a writer in series television unless you were on staff. "Freelancing" was becoming more and more difficult. There used to be a talented pool of freelance writers who could write for several different shows in a typical season. Not anymore. There's still a talented pool of writers, but they're either on staff or unemployed, because series TV is almost exclusively written "in-house."

Why was it so important for me to keep working now that I was entering (had entered/was well into) my sunset years? The obvious reason was the huge hole in my life, now that Ellis was gone. Of course, I could have filled my days with projects I'd put off for years—like studying Greek mythology, learning to speak conversational Spanish, or doing Good Works, but the joys of working have always had a far greater appeal. I love waking up in the morning with a purpose; to be needed, feel worthwhile, make money! Maybe I'm still trying to prove to Mother that I'm as swift and keen as my siblings, but I'm sure it's much less Freudian. It's probably as simple as doing something that's fun and getting paid for it.

Mike and David explained what was needed. *Knots* had *Landed* in the toilet. They had hired a new, hot Executive Producer at the beginning of the year, who had tried to make the serial into something that it was never meant to be. The fans hated it. The ratings dropped like Newton's apple. With good reason. The characters suffered from malaise. The stories were thin. The rooting interest was gone. There was no "Omigosh-what-happens-next?" It was so bad that David and Mike had stopped production halfway through the season to retool. My assignment, if I chose to accept it, was to return *Knots* to the lusty, exciting, adventurous, funny, caring show it had been.

I accepted the assignment, got the title of Senior Producer (how come it wasn't Co-Executive Producer like the guy I was replacing?), and moved into a large office on the Sony lot, which used to be the MGM lot, which used to have that big old lion on the roof. I never met the Co-Executive Producer I replaced, but I understand he's charming and charismatic, and had no problem moving onto bigger and better jobs. (Which is sometimes known as failing upwards in this business.)

I had exactly one week to catch up on ten years of back story, watch all of the episodes that aired that year, figure out what had gone wrong, how to fix it, and where to go from there. I should have been in a state of panic, but I felt unnaturally calm. I was still pushing my real feelings away, glad to distract my thoughts from Ellis. Obviously, the worst possible thing in the world had already happened to me, and nothing as petty as guiding a multi-million-dollar show back on track could register. Besides, it wasn't that hard.

In the script for the sixteenth episode (the one that prompted the shutdown), one of the storylines dealt with car-pooling. I'm not kidding. It was a major plot. Several scenes were devoted to the fun and excitement of sharing rides to work, which might have been okay for a series of commercials advertising over-the-counter medication for diarrhea, but was not okay for a primetime serial. *Knots* had to get back to life-and-death stories—Page, stalked by a homicidal ex-lover; money and power intrigues—Sumner's empire threatened by intramural jealousies; sex, lust, romance, mystery—who's that strange woman scoping out Meg, the adopted daughter of Karen and Mack?

There were four writers on staff, all of whom were dumped with the Co-Executive Producer—although two of them, Jim Magnuson and Lisa Seidman were asked to stay on to "oversee the transition." I was told I could keep these writers or hire whomever I chose. I will forever be grateful that I had the good sense to keep Jim and Lisa on staff. Jim is just about the most pleasant, upbeat, positive writer I've ever known. He was on a year's leave of absence from the University of Texas where he taught creative writing. He's written a dozen plays and six novels, but I think this was the first television show he'd ever done. With a National Endowment for the Arts Fellowship, and a fellowship from Princeton, you'd think he'd be a little above-it-all, yet he wasn't at all pretentious. Not your typical Hollywood TV writer. Maybe that was one of his problems. He agonized over his scripts. He tried to infuse them with too much depth, and when he tried to lighten up, he'd just miss. He'd be off kilter. But he was a pleasure to have in story meetings, and David Jacobs, who loved his novels, was somewhat awed by him—which is always good for an Executive Producer to be.

Lisa Seidman, on the other hand, was a young but seasoned and polished pro. She cut her teeth on *Cagney and Lacey*, had been on staff and written several episodes of *Dallas* and *Falcon Crest*, and was fast, a whiz at dialogue and structure, hard working, a real talent. I lucked out with Jim and her. They made going to work fun again. I even enjoyed visiting the set and renewing old acquaintances, although it was a little eerie to see that some of the actors looked younger than they had ten years before. Remarkable what a nip and tuck here and there, now and then, can do.

They were a talented group those *Knots Landing* actors, and many of them are neat human beings, too. Take Donna Mills. Please. Only kidding, because Donna has been a good friend since our days together on *Love is a Many Splendored Thing*. I admired her determination back then when she left for Hollywood, in spite of the handfuls of money CBS threw at her to try to keep her on that show. She knew what she wanted, and that was to be a Hollywood star—and she succeeded through dint of hard work, concentration, talent, and the gift of looking and staying gorgeous. With her knowledge of lighting and cinematography she could have joined either union. Before the camera rolled, Donna would look at herself from every angle with a mirror, decide where the camera should be, and then she'd check the lighting. If it wasn't up to her expectations, she'd go back to her trailer until it was. Demanding though she is, success hasn't spoiled her. She's loyal to her friends. We still play tennis from time to time, attend each other's celebrations and misfortunes: weddings, birthdays, floods (when her retaining wall collapsed years ago and her new house was under water she stayed with us), and funerals. Not only hasn't she changed her number in twenty years, she still answers her own phone.

Michele Lee, like Karen, the character she played, is warm and intelligent. She also shows up at benefits she's invited to—no small thing in this uppity town. She's a gifted director who has helmed several TV shows including *Knots*. Joan Van Ark may be a wee bit neurotic, but then who among us isn't? She's also a perfectionist when it comes to her work. She cared about the show, and never put the material down, which can hardly be said about many actors who love to trash the shows they're doing. When she was given a chance to direct an episode of *Knots,* she was prepared, thorough and professional.

Then there's Bill Devane who can be a pain in the neck at times—actually most times. Take the time, for instance, when Michele Phillips called to complain about the lack of motivation in a scene she was doing. Michele rarely complained, so Lisa figured something must be terribly wrong and went down to the set. There was Michele, sitting on a couch, and next to her, arms folded nonchalantly across his chest, was Bill—who put her up to it, knowing we would have thought twice about changing things for him because he was constantly grousing. Maybe that's because Bill is a writer, himself. He's certainly bright, with a biting wit that can and does leave teeth marks on his victims. I felt slightly on the defensive with him.

Ted Shakelford is a doll. A really nice guy. So is Kevin Dobson. But I didn't spend much time on the set. Mostly, I was hunkered down with Lisa and Jim, plotting the seven remaining episodes for the season; and jousting with David and Michael to get them accepted, in the works, written, and on the air. We must have done a good job, because the ratings improved and the network committed to another full year.

Before the start of the new season, I went on a short vacation with my brother Ray and his friend Mary Ellen, who were now in a serious relationship. They invited me on a roundabout motor trip to San Francisco. "Motor trip" evokes days of yore as when Mother would take her buddies off on adventures in the open Buick Phaeton, back in the thirties. Few people take motor trips these days. Everyone's in too much of a hurry to get there—except Ray. He's still the best person I know to take a trip with because he never plans them. At least in any detail. Generally, he knows when he's leaving and where he wants to end up, but it's the in-between things that are so great.

So for this motor trip to San Francisco there was no driving straight through the hot, arid Central Valley. We meandered along obscure country roads north of Santa Barbara, leading to a quaint little town called Los Olivos, which used to be a railroad terminal and is now a not-so-bustling winery center. From there, we headed to the Coast again, and wound up in Pismo Beach for the night. I went to their room for a drink before dinner. The television set was on. It was April 29, 1992. Early that day, the Simi Valley jury had acquitted the police officers who had savagely beat Rodney King. Now it was night, and Los Angeles was in flames. We never made it to dinner. We stayed glued to the set, watching as the anger and outrage of South Central Los Angeles erupted into a full-scale riot that practically destroyed that community and spread to other parts of the city. The next day, we continued to San Francisco, but it wasn't a leisurely motor trip anymore. All the fun had gone out of it.

Everything is grist for the mill when you're trying to come up with fresh ideas for an old TV show, and I used the rebuilding efforts after the riot (which weren't very successful) as part of a long-term story for the Bill Devane character, corporate mogul Greg Sumner.

A few weeks into the new season, Jim Magnuson had to return to his teaching job at the University of Texas, and Don Marcus (no relation) joined Lisa and me on the writing staff. Don was one of the former writers on the show who was fired along with the Co-Executive Producer. Before Jim left, he and Lisa suggested I talk to Don about coming back. Meeting Don, it took about ten minutes for me to realize that my luck was still holding, because we had an immediate rapport that turned into a wonderful working relationship, and has blossomed into an enduring friendship.

So there we were—Don and Lisa, Executive Story Editors, and me, whose credit was changed for some quirky reason from Senior Producer to Supervising Producer. Plus, a surprise new Co-Executive Producer, Barbara Corday, who had been brought in to run the show since David and Michael wanted a less "hands-on" involvement. I was just the slightest bit irked at her credit. It was the same credit as the gentleman I had replaced. There I was doing the same job—only better—that he had done, with a lesser credit. Was I being petty? Of course. But, to paraphrase Liza in *Pygmalion*, "credits are as mother's milk to TV folk."

Whistling Girl

My irk wasn't at Barbara. I like and admire Barbara. She co-created that classy show *Cagney and Lacey*. She's smart, attractive and capable. She's a practicing feminist, a political activist devoted to the right causes, and she knows the business—the way it works, the key people, how to run a show. No, my irk was definitely with David and Michael who hadn't told me she was coming aboard, and who could have been more equitable when it came to distributing credits.

It was hard to complain when I was making so much money and having such a good time with Lisa and Don—who still love to tell anecdotes about some of the allegedly outrageous stands I took defending the stories we came up with. I might have been a trifle stubborn, but when you're responsible for turning out over twenty scripts, you don't want people yanking on story threads that can cause an entire plot to fall apart. So okay, I didn't encourage Barbara to sit-in on story sessions. That didn't mean I didn't take her notes and suggestions seriously. Of course, I didn't change anything, but I was in charge of the writing. She was in charge of production. We respected and admired each other. Why else would she have loaned me her full-length mink coat when I went to Clinton's inauguration in January '93?

I went to Washington with a delegation of writers and directors to lobby the new administration (and newly elected members of Congress), on pending creative rights legislation, and to boogie at the Inaugural festivities. At the time, I was Secretary/Treasurer of the Writers Guild. The Guild, along with the Director's Guild and the Society of Cinematographers, put on a glitzy pre-Inaugural ball at the Sewall-Belmont House on Constitution Avenue, where I danced with Ted Kennedy, Jack Lemon, and Henry Kissinger; but not with Robert Reich because he never asked me, even though I'm short, too.

The rest of the year at *Knots* was a little bumpy, what with the heated story sessions at David's office on the Warner lot. I thought David and Michael weren't supposed to be so "hands on," but they still insisted on picking at our carefully-woven story threads, causing major plot lines to unravel which, in turn, unraveled me. I thought I handled the situation with finesse, but not according to Lisa and Don, whose stories include one about me jumping out of my chair and stalking around the room arguing (not without profanity) to keep our storylines intact. Overall, I think I won more rounds than I lost, but this didn't endear me to either Michael or David, who must have been keeping score, because a few years later when Lisa and I were working with them on a *Knots* reunion mini-series, it was payback time. More about that later. In the meantime, I was able to assign some scripts to freelance-writer friends, although Don and Lisa and I wrote most of them ourselves. There wasn't time to think or brood, and that was good for me. And, as Mother used to say, "activity breeds activity," so when Tracy found a play she wanted to direct and produce at her theater, I backed it.

Tracy insisted on giving me the producing credit, but I didn't do much except put up the money. The play, Tina Howe's gastronomically satiric *The Art of Dining,* ran for almost six months. Tracy drove everyone absolutely crazy during rehearsals, but the show was a smash. She did a wonderful job directing and mounting it, and the reviews were excellent. There was also a feature story in the "Sunday Calendar" section of the *L.A. Times* about the two of us: "Sisters' Paths Cross in Kitchen; Hollywood Vets team Up After Disparate Careers." In the picture accompanying the article, Tracy looks vibrant and glamorous and I look tired. Tracy says I haven't learned how to smile for the camera yet. Is there still time?

Back on *Knots,* the ratings were holding up fairly well, but everyone knew this was the show's last year. David and Michael were burned out. You could hardly blame them after fourteen years. Besides, they wanted to work on new projects. The actors wanted to move on, too. Joan Van Ark left before the start of the season to star in a pilot for another network. (That created havoc with our story, but Lisa and I came up with an intriguing explanation that actually enhanced the story, and she wrote one helluva funeral script for poor-old Valene.)

I was still having a good time, and feeling a little cocky. I was being wined and dined by agents who wanted me to sign with them.

I even wrote an op-ed piece in the *L.A. Times* about age discrimination in the industry in which I floated the idea that maybe, just maybe, some of the blame rested with us older writers.

"We get defensive, negative, and extremely hostile toward young network executives, producers, and show runners," I wrote, "forgetting that we were doing the same things when we were young. When we were in charge," I wrote, "we hired our friends and contemporaries, and weren't magnanimously offering jobs to older screenwriters. We also grabbed scripts for ourselves, because we had the energy and enthusiasm and greed that we accuse our young colleagues of now."

I ended the piece by suggesting we should stop bashing each other and call a truce.

"We older writers won't tell anymore kiddie/executive jokes or put you down for achieving success at such an early age, if you'll consider our talent, experience and age as the assets they are instead of debits that keep you from hiring us."

This advice went over like a lead balloon with some of my oldest and dearest friends. And soon Mrs. Smart Ass was counting herself among the grey-listed. Live and learn.

Chapter 28

Life In The Slow Lane

Lisa Seidman, Don Marcus and I had such a good time working together that we met several times after *Knots* folded in order to come up with ideas of our own for TV series. Lisa devised a romantic comedy/mystery that could have been a *Knots* spin-off titled *Scoundrels*. Don came up with a period Western family series he called *Justin and the Pecos Kid*. Based on Ellyn's work as an Assistant US Attorney, I came up with *Feds*, the Federal equivalent of *Law and Order*. Any one of them would have made a good TV series, and, as a matter of fact, *Feds* showed up as a network series a year or two later, only it wasn't ours. It was veteran producer Dick Wolfe's, which proves once again that ideas are a dime a dozen. It's having the reputation and clout that count in getting a network or production company to commit the millions it takes to get a new series on the air.

Tracy gets furious when she hears about ideas of mine (or Ellis', or Ray's, or other writer friends') that turn up on the tube written or produced by someone else. She's convinced there is foul play. That stories have been stolen, pilots have been purloined, and series have been expropriated. Sometimes they are. Most times they aren't. Television is a limited medium. There are only so many plots, premises, ideas, and situations to go around. That goes for characters, too. It's the execution that counts. The way the characters or the situations are handled that makes for hits. How many series have been based on a character who is a fish out of water, for instance? Yet the young, urban, Jewish doctor who winds up in an Alaskan hamlet was written with such originality—as were the other quirky characters who surrounded him—that *Northern Exposure* turned out to be very special, and very successful.

Lisa, Don, and I pitched our ideas to a network executive at NBC but nothing happened. So Lisa and Don accepted other assignments, and I flew to New York to talk to ABC executives about head-writing one of their daytime soaps—which I really didn't want to do because it would have meant moving back there.

I arrived at Kennedy on election night '94, and was picked up by my old pal, Martha Keehn, who agreed to share my Manhattan hotel suite so we could catch up with each other and listen to the election returns. What a disaster that night was. The Republicans swept the House and Senate, some obscure New York legislator named Pataki upset Cuomo in the gubernatorial race, and I had one of my rare but extremely painful intestinal blockages that kept me up all night. I have a certain way of dealing with those painful episodes, which I can't share with anyone because part of the ritual is keeping it a secret. It doesn't involve animal sacrifice or devil worship. It's simply superstitious and childish, and therefore embarrassing. But it worked. Finally. I went to the meeting the next morning feeling no pain, but looking a little like death warmed over. Actually, my heart wasn't into pulling up stakes, leaving my kids and grandkids, friends, and comfortable house in sunny California for an apartment in dreary New York; and I think my gut was trying to tell me that. I guess I'm just an organ-related kind of person. So I came clean with the ABC execs, and we parted friends. Martha and I parted, too. It was the next-to-last time I saw her.

The last time was the following summer when she and Tom celebrated their fiftieth wedding anniversary at the Mohonk Mountain House in the Catskills. Her wonderful children, all six of them, threw a great weekend-long party for them. I brought along the silent five-minute movie I'd resurrected, shot fifty-one years before when Martha came to visit, shortly after Ellis and I were married. We went to Central Park to fool around with a camera Ell borrowed from his Signal Corps unit, and we ended up improvising a *film*

Life In The Slow Lane

noir. The story line was spare: Ellis, in uniform, slips a coded military secret to a suspicious-looking, cigarette-smoking Martha, observed by an enigmatic, and rather dopey-looking me. When Ellis and Martha realize they've been observed, they flee—chased by me. On the run, Martha shreds the document, dropping some pieces and eating the rest. Ellis, also on the lam, picks up the dropped pieces and disposes of them by stuffing them in his mouth, although in his hurry, some of the pieces scatter in the wind. I rush into the scene, stop long enough to scoop up the remaining pieces, and, cramming them into my mouth, continue the chase. We all end up trapped by a wall facing Central Park West, feel sick, and in unison, bend over the wall and throw up. The End. A truly artistic bit of film making which, if analyzed carefully, reveals layers of symbolism and imagery. At any rate, it was a hit with the anniversary guests who couldn't believe Martha and I ever looked that young.

Six months later, I got a dreadful call from Tom. Martha, who never seemed to get sick, was gravely ill. I telephoned her a couple of times in the hospital. She was her usual upbeat, wry self. I wanted to fly back to New York, but she asked me to wait until she was home and convalescing. She never made it home. She died in April 1996.

At her service in the Congregational church in Forest Hills, there were close to two hundred people. We were invited to speak and I said a few self-conscious words, including the fact that she was my best friend. Then I looked around the church, and realized that everyone there felt the same way. Martha, without ever trying, was terribly important to all of us. She was a truly special, loving, beautiful human being. So down to earth. So full of fun and wisdom and insight. So accomplished at so many things: from quilt making to writing poetry, from mothering kids and grandkids to doing good works in Third World countries, from opening her home to people from all over the world to volunteering at a local homeless shelter. She was a whiz at word games and crossword puzzles and at whipping up impromptu meals for drop-in guests numbering anywhere from one to twenty or more. She loved martinis and, in spite of all of us nagging her all of the time, she continued to enjoy smoking. She was an excellent literary editor, a pamphleteer, raconteur. And so lacking in pretension, so willing to laugh at stuffy convention yet respect peoples' differences. I miss her. I want to pick up the phone and talk to her about everything and nothing in particular. I want to go on that trip with her to wherever it was on the Gulf Coast of Mexico we were always planning. I want to reminisce with someone I had such fun with so long ago. Did we really write a musical in college called *Orange is My Mother's Henhouse*? One of the worst things about getting older is having to say goodbye to friends who can never be replaced. Even though I share her with so many other people, she really <u>was</u> my best friend.

Martha wasn't old when she died. She was almost two years younger than I and since I'm not old, she certainly couldn't have been old. Yet my agent, the one who wined and dined me when I was making the big bucks on *Knots,* thought I was way over the hill now that I was dribbling in a few dollars here and there by consulting on shows and writing an episode or two. In fact, I rarely heard from him. To tell the truth, I didn't care. If anything, I felt ambivalent. I didn't know whether I wanted to work or play. I drifted along, went with the flow—and the flow was to play. So I went to London and Paris over the Christmas holidays; skied in Vail; sojourned in Cabo San Lucas with Suzanne; cruised the Carribean with my sister-in-law Emily on a tall sailing ship.

If the phone rang with an offer for an exciting job in between trips, it would have been icing on the cake. It didn't ring and that was okay, too. I put my feet up. I was smelling the roses. And waiting.

Chapter 29

Ray Gets Married... And Other Excellent Adventures

I've always had a special relationship with my siblings. Few brothers and sisters have stayed as close and cared as deeply about one another as Tracy, Ray and I. My own children never established the kind of emotional bond among each other that we've sustained over the years. Besides loving one another, we actually like each other.

Are we incestuous? No. Is my relationship with Ray anything like the rumored relationship between Dottie and Bill Wordsworth in the eighteenth century? Uh-uh. Oh, there may have been moments. Ray and I played "doctor" when we were little. There was a slightly erotic moment when Tracy gave me an alcohol rub when I was convalescing from an operation once, but hardly anything to write about. Which may prove to be unfortunate, since I know this memoir would be a helluva lot more publishable if there were more dysfunctional family anecdotes in it. But I have to tell it like it is. We simply find each other's company endlessly stimulating, refreshing, and interesting. After all these years, we still have fun together. Of course we get annoyed with each other. Sometimes we yell at each other. Sometimes we call one up to complain about the other, but mostly we are not only there for each other, we enjoy being there.

Tracy is forever bringing me *tchatzkis*: teddy bears holding tennis rackets or baseball bats, miniature wooden cows, small embroidered pillows with quaint sayings. One of them says, in cross-stitched pink, "Chance made us sisters; hearts made us friends."

Ray and I have been buds from the beginning. At least since the incident when I was two years old, and Dad took me out in a rowboat but forgot to tell anyone, which sent everyone, including Ray (who was only four at the time), into a panic until we showed up. It took Tracy and me a bit longer, since she was into boys and making-out while I was still getting a thrill out of toasting marshmallows on overnight camp-outs and playing baseball. Since my late teens, we've been as close as those proverbial peas in a pod. Of course, Tracy to this day insists that I wouldn't like her if we weren't sisters. That's ridiculous. Does she really think it matters that she's chronically late? Or that her dogs poop on my neighbor's lawn and throw up on my white living-room rug, and scratch holes in my alarm screens? Could she think that her constant state of chaos could affect my feelings for her? That, because she's accident-prone and is apt to trip on her five inch heels, fall down a flight of stairs and call me from Cedars' Emergency Room, I love her less? Or that when Ellis and I were waiting for her to arrive for dinner one night, and heard sirens on Sepulveda Boulevard and then got a call from a stranger explaining that Tracy was okay but her Volvo had exploded in flames on the Mulholland overpass, we would throw up our hands and desert her? Tracy wouldn't be Tracy if she weren't in the midst of an emotional crisis, which I not only expect—but have become accustomed to. These days my heart hardly pounds for more than a half hour after she calls at two a.m. to report that she and Nat were followed home and held at gunpoint by two hoodlums in ski masks, high on drugs, who robbed them but luckily didn't shoot them. Underneath the chaos and the drama is Tracy, the survivor; Tracy, the loving and loyal; Tracy, my sensitive, wise, witty, strong, giving, wonderful friend who happens to be my sister.

Ray, only two years older than I, has always been my mentor and protector—as well as my best friend when we were growing up. I depended on him. Felt safe because of him. Looked up to him. For two years after our father died, I couldn't go to sleep unless Ray looked into my bedroom closet and recited a mantra commanding monsters and all other Scary Things to "stay away from Dot's door." Of course, he couldn't resist torturing me by refusing to perform this ritual every now and then, forcing me to weep and beg. But it was only once or twice and a small price to pay for feeling secure.

I thought Ray was the smartest person in the world. I thought he was going to write the best, the most important novel of the century. When he went off to war, his letters from Europe were literary gems that Mother, with little persuasion, read to eager congregants at Friday night services in Teaneck. I wish I knew where those letters were now.

I guess Ray, the confident, assured middle child, didn't have the need, or the drive, or the obsession with making it that I, the not-so-confident kid sister, picked up somewhere along the way. So, while I was aggressively plunging ahead in the television industry, Ray was ambling through a number of interesting (but not particularly challenging) jobs in publishing, real estate, public relations, and story editing; finally settling down in Santa Barbara to teach English at UCSB. Teaching gave him time to travel, to write now and then—not caring too much whether he was published, and to meet people. Especially women. He was always involved romantically with an interesting woman, going back to Dorothy L.—whom he claims he would have married when he came back from the war, except that she sent him a "Dear John" letter. I'm not sure he would have married her—even though she was funny, bright and attractive. When he was 22, Ray didn't think about marriage. In fact, Ray didn't think about marriage for the next several decades. He was the "love 'em, form a long relationship with 'em, and when marriage seemed imminent, leave 'em" type. Uncannily, the women he left remained friends with him. And us— i.e., Ellis, Tracy and me.

There was nifty, clipped-speaking Pearl from England during World War II; Judy, a Claudette Colbert look-alike—whom he met in Marseilles after the war when he was studying French on the G.I. Bill. Back home, there was Bea, who raised golden retrievers and would have switched to raising children, but Ray moved on to Sally, scioness of a wealthy South Jersey Shore family. That only lasted until he moved to the West Coast, where he met lovely Sandy, who liked all the things he did. Maybe Sandy was too perfect.

When he was teaching at the University in Santa Barbara, there was tall, aristocratic Gail, a colleague in the English Department. Maybe that affair would have ended in marriage, except Ray moved back to Los Angeles to join my writing staff on *Love is a Many Splendored Thing*. I refuse to take responsibility for that breakup. It's only ninety miles from LA to Santa Barbara, and besides, soon after he moved back, he got involved with Marilyn.

No, if I feel guilty about Ray, it's because I lured him away from teaching because he was an inspired and gifted teacher. His classes were jammed. His students loved him. He taught English Literature, but like all born teachers he ranged over all the other disciplines, too. Of course, the academic bureaucrats weren't that crazy about him. I mean, the department wasn't throwing tenured professorships at him, so my phone call had an added impact.

"Raymo," I said that January day in 1970, when I'd been head writer of the soap for several months, "Why don't you quit? You can make more money writing about blind, pregnant, fatally ill Iris in a month than you can make in a year lecturing about Chaucer and Shakespeare!"

So Ray moved back to LA and became a TV writer, and I guess I do suffer some pangs of guilt, because deep down I think he was a more gifted teacher than a soap-writer. It's not that he hasn't done perfectly fine, becoming a head-writer himself and going on to write TV movies and other shows. And it's not that he hasn't made more money than he would have teaching. It's simply my own subjective feeling that his soul would be more nourished in a more philosophically uplifting field than television.

Besides, it was difficult working with Ray because of our family history. He'll always be my big brother. I'll always look up to him, defer to him, believe he's smarter, better read, more knowledgeable than I am. Try writing with someone like that. Impossible. It was hard enough writing with Ellis, although taking second chair in the beginning of our partnership was only fair, since he was the established writer. As time went on, and I made progress on my own, I preferred writing alone—or being in charge of a staff, working with writers with whom I had no emotional attachments. My inhibitions disappear when I don't have to hide my light under a bushel, as Uncle Mort would have said. Working with Ellis and then Ray, I worried a lot about bruising their egos. Was I too outspoken in meetings with producers or network executives? Did I push too hard for my ideas instead of theirs or ours? I worried even more when I got better jobs and made more money than either of them. What a paradox. There I was feeling empowered by the women's movement and my own success, but trying to downplay it as though it weren't really happening or was a fluke—luck. Ellis, of course, had a great deal of success early on, and didn't seem to care that much when his deals began to taper off. Or at least he wanted me to believe that. He was genuinely delighted when things went well for me. Ray, too, was always gracious and supportive. But come on, didn't either Ell or Ray feel just a wee bit jealous? I would have. But then, I'm not as nice as the two men I've loved the most.

Meanwhile, Ray was pursuing one of his favorite things. Marilyn by this time was history. There was a brief fling with Betty in La Jolla, and then came Mickey I, a high school teacher in Beverly Hills. We were sure Ray finally found the woman with whom he wanted to spend the rest of his life. What a good friend she became, what a unique and interesting person. It lasted a long time, several years. There's a Roman numeral after her name because she was followed by Mickie II, an award-winning journalist from Atlanta, who moved to LA and was the co-hostess of a popular radio talk show.

Mickie II was spirited and challenging. Sparks flew. There were dramatic ups and downs, give and take, yelling and screaming—which, of course, lead to passionate reconciliations. Just like real married people. Only they weren't. Married, that is.

By this time, Tracy and I simply shrugged when people persisted in asking us when our brother was going to get married. Years before, when I was still asking myself that question, my old friend

Patsy Bricken got fed up.

"For God's sake," said she, "leave your brother alone. He's the happiest guy I know. He's doing exactly what he wants to do!"

Which was true. So I stopped wondering about it, as my circle of women friends who had been involved with Ray increased.

Then Mary Ellen Jennings arrived in town. Ray met her through Tracy, because Mary Ellen was the unofficial executive assistant, friend, and confidante of the fabled Stella Adler—whom Tracy knew because years before Stella played her mother-in-law in Odets' *Paradise Lost* on Broadway. Stella, one of the founding members of The Group Theater, was a leading Broadway actress, had a brief fling in films, and then became the doyen of drama coaching. As a coach and teacher, she ignited the careers of countless Broadway and Hollywood stars. Every year when the weather got really nasty, Stella would flee New York and come to the West Coast for several months to conduct seminars and master classes for the culturally-deprived Hollywood creative community. Through the years Tracy and Stella stayed in touch, and when Stella made her annual trek to Los Angeles, Tracy would entertain her and her entourage.

Hollywood treated Stella like visiting royalty. She demanded nothing less. Her knowledge of the theater, literature—all the arts was formidable. As was her bearing and appearance. Even into her nineties she was magnificent-looking, tall, with reddish blonde hair, sparkling green eyes, and a beautiful complexion. She was imperious and did not suffer fools lightly. She would think nothing of dismissing celebrity actors in the middle of a scene in one of her classes, demanding that they get off her stage. At parties (where she was the guest of honor), actors, directors, writers, and other movie people would literally kneel beside her chair as they listened reverently to her pronouncements, or asked her questions in hushed tones.

When Tracy entertained Stella, she always invited Ellis and me, but I never enjoyed attending these command performances. First of all, it was difficult making my way through the kneeling supplicants. Secondly, the one or two times I inadvertently happened to get close to Stella, I was totally tongue-tied. What kind of cocktail talk does one exchange with Harold Clurman's ex-wife, who was Marlon Brando's mentor?

One night Tracy deliberately sat Ellis and me on either side of Stella at the dinner table. What a revelation. Stella wasn't the imperious Grande Dame I had made her out to be. She was amusing, inquisitive, a great conversationalist, and totally charming. From that night on, I was one of her biggest fans—although I never knelt beside her chair. But then, that never was her idea. It was Hollywood's way of paying homage.

So I could totally understand why Mary Ellen thought of her as her lovable grandmother—witty, vastly knowledgeable, a treasure of Yiddish folklore and music, as well as a warm and giving friend. Mary Ellen, a pretty, fresh-faced actress, worked and studied in Hollywood before moving to New York to attend Stella's classes where she quickly became one of Stella's favorites. Soon, she was invited to accompany her to the theater, to dinner, and eventually to help her with her lectures and research. After that, she began helping with dinner parties, traveled abroad with Stella and practically became a member of her family.

In 1990, Mary Ellen came west with Stella, and met Ray when he accompanied Tracy to one of Stella's parties. As I understand it, it was a magic moment. They were enormously attracted to one another.

But wait a minute. How many times had this happened before? And what about the extenuating circumstances? I know my brother is enormously attractive, but Mary Ellen is a lot younger than he is. And she lived in New York. Besides, Ray was involved with another woman. Okay, okay, the pattern was simply reappearing. But Ray had met his match. This Irish lass was not about to let go until he married her.

It took five years, but she got her man. I still can't believe it, even though they were married in my back yard by the same traveling Rabbi who married Ellyn and Bill. John played the flute, Mary Ellen's lovely sisters read passages from the Bible, her nieces and my granddaughter were flower girls, and Tracy was late.

Chapter 30

Is Anatomy Destiny?

In the fall of 1995, Tracy was contacted by Cathy Siegel, the Executive Director of the American Cinema Foundation, and asked to produce an evening of "provocative, passionate, and politically incorrect" drama for the Foundation's theater series. Tracy came up with an excellent idea—scenes from the controversial plays of Clifford Odets. The only problem with that was that someone already had dibs on it.

So Tracy, busy with teaching classes and running her acting studio, turned to me (her not-so-busy sister), and asked if I had any ideas for the evening. I did. One of the "provocative, passionate, politically incorrect" themes that has always fascinated me, and has been used by playwrights from Aristophanes to Wasserstein, is what happens when women refuse to accept their traditional role. On one hand terrible things happen *(Lysistrata, A Doll's House)*, on the other hand funny things *(The Taming of the Shrew, Born Yesterday, The Heidi Chronicles, A Woman's Place)*.

What was that last title? It was the title of the only play I ever wrote, *A Woman's Place*. I dare to list it with those classics because, when Tracy began to put the evening together, Aristophanes, Shakespeare, and Ibsen fell out because she didn't have time to rehearse actors for classical roles. It was impossible to get the rights to Garson Kanin's *Born Yesterday*, which left scenes from wonderful Wendy Wasserstein's *The Heidi Chronicles* and *Isn't It Romantic,* as well as scenes from my very available *A Woman's Place.*

Is Anatomy Destiny?

Happily, the evening turned out to have all three "p's." It was passionate, provocative and politically incorrect. Tracy produced it and directed actors from her studio, and I wrote and delivered the narration, in which I asked if anatomy is destiny (as Freud proclaimed), or if women can aspire to being more than wives and mothers, sex objects, care givers, and support systems?

It was a rhetorical question which I answered, nonetheless.

"Of course women can aspire to more," I said. "These days women's rights are a given. Women can go as far as their talent takes them, in whatever field they choose. No problem, right? Wrong. Women have a lot more to deal with than establishing their right to work. They have to make difficult choices. Should they marry? Have children? When? After her career is established but before her biological clock runs out? When she's still young and just beginning that long climb up the corporate or professional ladder? Will that leave her on the Mommy track? And what about competition with male colleagues who don't have to worry if the housekeeper or the baby sitter can't make it? What if she's more successful than her husband? What about sexual harassment in the office? What about time—for the kids if she has them; for her husband if she has one; for herself? What about the quality of life?"

The evening wound up with a spirited discussion led by a panel that included two UCLA professors, psychologist/author Susan Forward, and my daughter Ellyn, who was articulate and who made me proud. Ellyn doesn't seem to have the problems, mostly psychological, that I had trying to fit everything in—marriage, children, career. Maybe it's because of that ambition gene, the one that I seem to have in abundance, but that she has in proper moderation. Many Assistant U.S. Attorneys go into politics, become judges, law school deans, etc. But Ellyn loves being a federal prosecutor, and is perfectly content to stay where she is, even though her mother nudges her every once in awhile when one of her colleagues is appointed to the bench.

The evening was repeated at Tracy's theater, and was equally successful. Working on my autobiographical play again made me think about a request Ellyn made of Ellis and me several years before. She asked us to tape an oral history of our lives.

"Just talk into a recorder," she said. "Talk about your family history, about when you were growing up, whatever. It ought to be easy for you guys. You love to reminisce; you're always telling stories about the old days."

"Sure," Ellis said.

Of course we never did. Now it was too late for Ell, but I kept thinking about it, only I was too self-conscious to talk into a tape recorder. But I could write about it, couldn't I? I wouldn't even have to do any research. After all, it would be the story of my life. All I had to do was sit and begin. Turn on the word processor. Start. Soon. Only all sorts of important things came up: dental appointments, entertaining friends from out-of-town, remodeling the bathroom. It was clear I was suffering from writers' block.

I told Lisa Seidman what was happening one day when we were having lunch. Lisa, who was teaching an extension course in screen writing at UCLA, thought I might get a jump start if I signed up for a course called The Art of the Personal Essay. She had heard the man teaching it was excellent. What could I lose?

So I found myself in a classroom at UCLA one spring Wednesday night, along with nine or ten young to middle-aged women, and one or two men, who wrote gem-like small pieces about meaningful moments in their lives. The class was conducted by Bernard Cooper, a prize-winning author of several collections of small, gem-like revealing moments in his life.

Most of my fellow students had taken this course with Bernard one or more times before, and were happy to polish and re-polish their essays, hoping to submit them to obscure literary quarterlies when they were ready. But they were in no rush, and seemed content to keep polishing and re-polishing their material. They didn't quite know what to make of me, a TV writer, one who made a lot of money writing—among other things—soap operas for God's sake!

The way the class worked was that three students would distribute copies of their material to be read during the week so that it could be critiqued the following week. Challenged, I forced myself to start, and when I submitted the first couple of chapters of this memoir my classmates were politely enthusiastic—but almost all of them felt I was racing through the events of my early life. Why didn't I stop and deal with my father's suicide? That should have taken two or three chapters at the least.

They were right. I didn't deal thoroughly with my father's suicide, or all the other agonies and ecstasies I've lived through. Because of luck or genes or maybe even perseverance, I've lived a long life, and it's tough to get it all down without writing the equivalent of the Manhattan phone book. I never could have finished even a cursory account of my life if I had slowed down to deal thoroughly with all the revealing moments. There isn't enough time. There is never enough time. Wasn't it only yesterday I was lying on my Flexible Flyer at the foot of that snowy hill in Eastern Park, Little Falls, New York State, USA, the Northern Hemisphere, Earth? And now it's two/thirds of a century later, and I still feel like that kid on the sled—with a touch of the March Hare thrown in because I feel "I'm late; I'm late."

I didn't miss the class when it was over. Bernard Cooper and I never established much of a rapport. I was enormously impressed with his students. They were talented. I just wish they'd stop polishing their gems and get on with it.

Meanwhile, having started my memoir, I went racing ahead with it, until I was interrupted by a call from David Jacobs—who asked if I'd be interested in writing a *Knots Landing* reunion movie; actually a four-hour, two-part mini-series that CBS asked Mike Filerman and him to produce.

"Yes," I said with alacrity. Only later did I realize what I should have said.

"Knots to you, David, and your friend Michael, too!"

Chapter 31

Together Again

Writing the *Knots Landing* mini-series should have been a piece of cake. Especially when Lisa Seidman agreed to write it with me. No one knew the show better than we did, not even David and Michael, who weren't as involved as we were the last year it was on the air. Lisa and I wrote the final two-hour episode in '93, so it followed, even as night follows day, that we would know where the characters had been and what might have happened to them in the interim. That's why it made so much sense for David and Michael to hire us to write the reunion movie.

Only they didn't hire us. At least not at first. They hired another writer, who either quit or was fired after several weeks of meetings—without leaving a script, a treatment, or so much as a shred of an idea. What a waste of time. Why hadn't they asked us? Was it because the network didn't want us? It couldn't have been. Leslie Moonves, the president of CBS, had personally thanked me for turning the show around and improving the ratings at the end of the '92 season. Was it ageism? It couldn't have been. Lisa, half the writing team, was in her vigorous thirties.

Make that her less-than-vigorous thirties, since we were keeping a secret which Lisa only recently gave me permission to reveal. Two months before our first story meeting with David and Michael, Lisa told me she was having pain in her upper arms. I didn't think anything about it, since I'm a tennis player and I'm always aching somewhere. Lisa is not a jock in any way, shape, or form, and when she noticed a lump in her neck, I was alarmed and she was scared stiff. Her doctor insisted on a biopsy. I would have had it done the same day, but Lisa had planned a trip back East, and put off the procedure until she got back.

I drove her to the hospital and back home the same day. Then she waited for the results. It could have been a simple infection. It wasn't. It was Hodgkin's Disease, a viral cancer of the lymph system. The lump that she had felt started in the lymph gland behind her aorta and traveled up to the lymph nodes in the neck area. What a shock. I knew exactly what Lisa was going through.

It brought back the terrible anxiety I felt when I finally learned the truth about myself. Cancer. What could be worse? In Lisa's case, a lot. It could have been non-Hodgkin's Disease, which is a more virulent form of cancer. With the type Lisa had, her oncologist told her there was a 90% survival rate. The treatment was miserable. She had to undergo radiation—twenty-one sessions, five days a week on her upper body; then a short hiatus and an equal number of sessions on her lower body.

So throughout our work on the miniseries, the meetings with David and Michael, writing the story lines, the treatment, the outline, and finally the script, Lisa was suffering from the effects of radiation: nausea, loss of appetite, terrible dryness in her throat, and fatigue. It's a wonder she was able to work at all, but she claims working was the only thing that kept her sane. I knew exactly what she meant.

We laugh about it now. How Lisa had to work at my house because her oversensitive olfactory nerve picked up weird smells from her house. How she had to make emergency trips to the ladies room when she was overcome by nausea. The C.A.R.E. package of saltines and baby jars of applesauce she carried with her. Her sudden urge to nap in the middle of a work session. My admiration for her grew day by day. She was one courageous, plucky, committed woman.

David and Michael didn't have a clue about what she was going through. But then David and Michael didn't seem to have a clue about the *Knots Landing* project, either. Both of them were less than enthusiastic about the mini-series. They acted as though it were a total bore. They couldn't have cared less whether it was made or not. Maybe that was because David was finishing a pilot he was writing for NBC, and Michael was in post-production on a TV movie he was producing for ABC. The meetings, which were held in David's attractive offices at NBC, followed a certain routine. David was usually holed up in his private office clicking away at his computer, trying to finish his overdue pilot. Michael was usually late. We waited in the conference room, where there were boutique coffees and teas and mounds of bagels and biscuits and all sorts of goodies—which caused poor Lisa to grow queasier by the minute.

When the meeting would finally get under way, David would talk about movies—knowledgeably, interestingly, and endlessly. He really loves movies, and he's entertaining about them, but we were there to talk about our movie and he was avoiding the subject. That was either because he truly didn't want to do the mini-series, or he was burned out and trying to distract us because he didn't have any ideas on what it should be about. Neither did Michael, whose main talent has always been to tear apart a story once it has been written. All we were given was this: 1) Don Murray (who played Michele Lee's husband, Sid Fairgate), comes back as a lookalike bad guy, even though he had been killed off after the first season. 2) David wanted to "pay homage" to the movie, *Shoot the Moon*, by doing some kind of mid-life crisis story involving Michele Lee and Kevin Dobson. Period. End of story ideas.

So Lisa and I went to work and came up with the stories. One of them was the spine of the movie, and was taken from a series of articles I had read about a large corporation that had been sued by workers who were laid off. The workers, represented by a courageous lawyer, were promised their jobs would be safe when the plant was sold. Then the new owner fired the workers and moved the factory to take advantage of cheaper labor. We had built in characters to fit the roles: Greg Sumner (Bill Devane), the greedy corporate CEO; Gary Ewing (Ted Shackelford), who made the promise to the workers before he sold the plant to Sumner; Mack MacKenzie (Kevin Dobson), the courageous lawyer; and Abby (Donna Mills), the villainess who plots against both sides.

We also came up with a story for Val Ewing (Joan Van Ark), who reappeared in our series finale after being presumed dead (when the actress left the show in its last year to star in a sitcom). In our story Val has written a bestseller about her experiences called *Hostage,* which has been sold to the movies, and she is working with a burned out, alcoholic screenwriter—who comes on to her and drowns in an accident for which Val is held responsible. There were other stories, too, including the "homage to *Shoot the Moon* in which Knots' favorite couple, Karen and Mack MacKenzie, break up over his mid-life crisis. And, as they say in the ads, much much more.

Lisa and I worked for months on the project, meeting with David and Michael occasionally, and without much input from them. I kept asking to meet with the network and the Warner long-form executives, but we were assured it wasn't necessary. At long last, a treatment was sent to CBS, which responded with a page of notes, after which we were told by David and Michael to write the screenplay.

We sent in our first draft at the end of April and waited to hear from them. A week went by. Nothing. Another week and still no word. It was now May, and the four-hour, two-part movie was supposed to be shot that summer. We knew there had to be at least one or two rewrites plus a polish, and time was running out. So I called David.

"Oh," said he, as though he was surprised to hear from me.

"So," I said. "What do you think? Did you read it?"

He had. He liked it, thought it needed some fixing, but promised we'd get together after he met with Michael and, now that he'd finished his pilot, he'd be able to work with us.

Great. So we waited. And waited. Finally, I called Michael and asked what was going on. He said he hadn't met with David yet, but he would, and then we'd get together for notes on the rewrite.

We never met. I called David one last time.

"Look," said he, "we're paying you and Lisa in full. Take the money and walk away. It happens to all of us sometimes."

This was strange, indeed. I was so surprised I didn't know what to say. After I hung up, I still couldn't believe it. Cutting us off after a first draft? On a story they and the network approved? Based on a series on which I was Supervising Producer and Lisa was Executive Story Editor? Weird.

The miniseries wasn't shot that summer. Instead, they hired another writer. Lisa and I figured they hated our story, the one they approved, and were going in a totally different direction. We never got to see the new script until production was completed several months later. Surprise! It was our story, our structure, our characters (with different names). The only major element that had been changed was the dialogue, which, frankly, wasn't as sharp as ours. (Besides, Donna Mills told me that the actors improvised most of the dialogue, which may or may not be true). The shooting script didn't even have our names on it, only the third writer's name.

Well, that's show business.

But there's a happy ending. The Writers Guild restored our "written by" credit—along with the third writer. Entertainment Weekly gave the show a rave review, highlighting the humor, the stories, and the character relationships. Most important of all, by the time the show was aired during May '97 sweeps, Lisa was pronounced 100% cured!

Epilogue

"What's It All About, Alfie?"

I don't think Alfie or anyone else knows what life's all about. It's one of those mysteries we're never going to solve. Like, for instance, is there a God? And what is that concept anyway? What's the plan? There must be something that makes it all work; some intelligence; some force other than the one Luke Skywalker had with him.

During one of the late Carl Sagan's lectures at Cornell, he projected a tiny blue dot on a black screen, and told the audience that was the way Earth looked from the Voyager satellite. He's the man who told us about the billions and billions of solar systems in the universe, and that Earth happens to be in one of the most insignificant. But what I'd like to know is—what is the universe? The theory is it started with a Big Bang an infinite number of years ago and kept expanding and expanding into those billions of stars, and now it's contracting. But what does that mean?

I tried to read Stephen Hawking's book about time, which was supposed to explain it all for lay people, and God knows I'm one of the lay-est of people, but I couldn't grasp it. I mean what's the universe contained in? And how does this relate to Faith, Hope, and Charity? How does it get around to the individual? What about those five kids who died in a fire Christmas Eve in South Central Los Angeles? What kind of Divine Plan would include that?

Getting down to more trivial and silly episodes, how come Mike Ovitz gets 90 million bucks when he leaves Disney after a year, when he didn't accomplish anything? How come the Carnegies, and the Rockefellers, and the Mellons, and the Millikens got away with ripping off the country for billions and then gave a fraction of their booty back in museums, foundations, and libraries with their names on 'em? But at least they gave something back. Charles Keating, who ruined lots of old folks, didn't give anything back.

Even Will Shakespeare didn't know what it's all about, although he knew an awful lot. In the end, though, he said, "Life's but a walking shadow; a poor player who struts and frets his hour upon the stage and then is heard no more." That's kind of scary when your life is reduced to an hour. Even a movie is two hours. Of course, that was a metaphor, and that hour we get to strut and fret works out to a lifetime of hours that can be wonderful and awful, wildly adventurous as well as deadly dull, sometimes miserable but sometimes exciting. It's like that creaky, perennial, Jimmy Stewart movie that our TV sets are programmed to air once a year whether we v-chip it out or not. *It's a Wonderful Life*—on the whole. Mostly.

Which reminds me of a short story my brother Ray wrote a long time ago. It was about a small town shopkeeper, a thinly disguised character study of Dad. At one point the shopkeeper turns to his clerk and says, "The movies teach us about life, Max." I don't know why that particular line sticks in my memory. Maybe because it's true.

Then again, maybe in the mysterious scheme of things, life *is* a movie. A lush, emotional, old-fashioned movie. And if someone asked me what I thought of My Life, the movie, I'd have to say "I laughed; I cried; I loved it."

But it ain't over yet, and I think I hear the phone ringing.

About The Author

After graduating from college, Ann Marcus got a job on the *New York Daily News* — the first copy "boy" with a D-cup. In a matter of weeks she was promoted to reporter and parlayed her first by-line story to a job on *LIFE* magazine where she worked with famed photographers such as Alfred Eisenstadt.

After marrying screenwriter Ellis Marcus she produced three children and a play, *A Woman's Place*, which was produced in L.A. and lead to a long and successful career in television.

In the 60's she wrote sit-coms: *Please Don't Eat The Daisies, Lassie, The Hathaways, Gentle Ben,* etc. She was also a staff writer on Peyton Place and *The Debbie Reynolds Show*.

In 1969 she became headwriter of the daytime drama, *Love Is A Many Splendored Thing* (nominated for an Emmy) followed By *Search For Tomorrow* for which she won the WGA award for outstanding daytime serial.

Tapped by Norman Lear, Ann co-created and headwrote the satirical soap, *Mary Hartman Mary Hartman* winning the Emmy in 1976. She also co-created *Fernwood 2-Nite, All That Glitters,* and *Julie Farr, MD*. Other soaps she has helmed were *Days Of Our Lives, Love Of Life,* and *General Hospital* receiving several Emmy nominations along the way.

Between stints head writing or creating soaps, Ann has written TVmovies including *Women At West Point, Letters From Three*

Lovers, and *Having Babies, II*. She has also been Supervising Producer of *Falcon Crest* and *Knots Landing*. Recently she co-wrote the four hour Knots miniseries, *Return To The Cul-De-Sac* which aired in May, '97.

Ann's favorite TV endeavor was the syndicated satirical soap she co-created and executive produced with her husband Ellis Marcus, *The Life And Times Of Eddie Roberts* or L.A.T.E.R.

Ann is currently on the Steering Committee of the Caucus and the Board of Directors of the Writers Guild.

Widowed, Ann lives in Sherman Oaks with her golden retriever Ollie and enjoys frequent visits from her three children, their spouses, and her six grandchildren.